SURFING
SOCIAL STUDIES

THE INTERNET BOOK

Edited by Joseph A. Braun, Jr. & C. Frederick Risinger

NCSS
Bulletin
96

National Council for the Social Studies

NCSS Founded 1921

Editorial staff on this publication: Michael Simpson, Terri Ackerman, Dinaw Mengestu, Eric L. Miller
Editorial services provided by Carol Bloom, Bloom Ink Publishing Professionals, West Lafayette, IN
Art Director: Gene Cowan   Design and Production: Alexis Borrero

LIBRARY OF CONGRESS CATALOGING INFORMATION
ISBN 0-87986-078-2
PCN 99-076220

TABLE OF CONTENTS

THE INTERNET

Joseph A. Braun, Jr.
Department of Curriculum and Instruction
Illinois State University
&
C. Frederick Risinger
College of Education
Indiana University

This introduction describes why various Internet technologies have such a significant potential for influencing the social studies curriculum and improving our methods of instruction. Beginning with a historical overview of the Internet's development, it also offers a rationale why social studies teachers can ill afford to ignore this amazing set of tools for engaging students and enriching the curriculum.

Isn't it ironic? Like many other previous technological breakthroughs, such as the automobile or television, the Internet seems to be a road down which we humans are enthusiastically traveling despite knowing that there will be huge unintended consequences. We do not always apprehend what we have in our midst until it is too late to do anything, and the technology has already caused unprecedented changes in our activity and interactions. The automobile gave us great mobility, but also pollution and more than 50,000 fatalities a year. The television provides us the opportunity to participate vicariously in globally significant events like the Pope visiting Cuba or Princess Diana's funeral; yet it also serves up mindless pap or worse, gratuitous violence.

How did the Internet Start?

Considering its origins, the existence of the Internet itself is a salient example of how a technology starts in one direction but takes twists and unanticipated turns in its path of development. The technology was originally designed by the Rand Corporation, for exclusive use by the U.S. Department of Defense to withstand a nuclear attack and provide a communications system through which a retaliatory strike could be launched against the attacking nation. The Internet is now the largest computer network in the world, consisting of thousands of smaller regional networks that are interconnected, hence the name Internet.

Paul Barand, a researcher at the RAND Corporation, first proposed that under a thermonuclear attack, it was possible to decentralize authority for maintaining national and local communication links as the government conducted and controlled nuclear warfare. In other words, he proposed a computer-managed conferencing (CMC) system in which communications were not located primarily in one physical place. Specifically, he proposed that the system break messages into units of equal size and route these units along a functioning path to their destination, at which time the system would reassemble the units into coherent wholes. This idea was brought to fruition in 1969 under the genesis of the Advanced Research Projects Agency Network (ARPANET), which was designed as a Department of Defense program.[1]

ARPANET was the first computer-managed conferencing system in operation. It initially functioned to transfer the content of computer data, not person-to-person messages, to one of the four nodes that comprised the original links. But, once ARPANET existed, it was easy to include electronic mail capabilities. By the early 1970s, the United States government had imposed wage and price freeze policies to address the inflationary economic crisis at that time, and the need arose for the government to send information relative to enforcing these policies to geographically distant local headquarters. As a result of this experience, computer conferencing quickly spread for other forms of discourse—social, commercial, and scientific.

As ARPANET became more successful, the government declassified it from the status of a research project, and the Defense Communications Agency began using it extensively. Mailing lists that were not related to work began to appear on ARPANET, including SF-LOVERS, which is about science fiction. Some administrators overseeing the system attempted to stamp out the personal mailing lists, but they spread nonetheless. ARPANET was working just as intended: messages were dispersed throughout computer networks and brought back together for the user. This forerunner of the Internet proved difficult to police, even for the Department of Defense. A communications system that has been specifically developed to survive a nuclear attack is a tough prospect for censors to control.

By the mid-1970s, various other CMCs were also appearing in corporations, such as Xerox, which developed an inexpensive and flexible local area network (LAN) protocol named Ethernet. This and other networking technologies, such as those developed at Digital and IBM, spawned a need for these varied LANs to be connected together so people could use them all.

More and more people, largely scientists in academic and research institutes who wanted to share information, felt thwarted because Defense Department permission to civilians to use ARPANET was not generally granted. Thus, an imitation of the ARPANET mailing lists was created between Duke University and the University of North Carolina at Chapel Hill in 1979, and called Usenet. Usenet spread like wildfire from campus to campus and eventually around the world, aided by sympathetic computer center managers who saw the enormous potential it offered in transmitting information.

On January 1, 1983, the original ARPANET was broken into two networks: one military and the other public. Concurrently, the National Science Foundation (NSF) funded five supercomputer centers and two dozen regional networks, all of which were intended to interconnect with a national NSFNET. A year later, this NSFNET became a major network on the Internet. In response to scholars in disciplines other than science who wanted access to a computer-managed conferencing system, IBM and NSF established BITNET, which spread rapidly throughout higher-education institutions. By 1988, both Internet and BITNET had about the same number of users: approximately half a million each worldwide.

By the end of the decade BITNET shrank and began to be overshadowed by the Internet. In 1989, Tim Berners-Lee at CERN, a European laboratory for particle physics, proposed a graphic way of roaming the Internet. His efforts were eventually put on the Internet so others could help develop the software. In 1993 a user-friendly, graphic interface called Mosaic emerged from National Center for Supercomputing Applications at the University of Illinois. It gave millions of people a tool they could use to browse, search, and retrieve text, sound, graphics, and video through the use of hypermedia, or hyperlinks. Hypermedia are electronic connections that link pieces of information that have been written in the same language, called HyperText Markup Language, or HTML. This language makes it possible for users to search and access documents on other computers linked to the Internet. Through browser software, the user retrieves documents from what has become known as the World Wide Web (WWW). The Internet is the worldwide network of computers, while the World Wide Web is the network's information retrieval service.

The young creators of Mosaic were soon lured to a new commercial venture called Netscape, where their ideas have continued to evolve as more powerful browsers have been developed that combine several tools for searching the Internet under one graphic interface.

Bill Gates and his giant Microsoft Corporation were at first slow to respond to the revolutionary influence of the Internet as a computing experience, but eventually they produced a web browser called Internet Explorer, which was locked in competition with Netscape for market dominance in WWW browsers during the late 1990s. After a 1998 appearance by Mr. Gates and several other computer-industry giants before a U.S. Senate Committee investigating Microsoft's alleged monopolistic practices, the Justice Department filed an anti-trust lawsuit against Microsoft. At the Senate hearing, it was enlightening to hear computer titans making comparisons of themselves with those whose business practices first spawned antimonopoly legislation, namely the steel and oil magnates of the late 19th century. At the dawn of the twenty-first century, those magnates who influence the brands of computers and software we use to cruise the Information Highway are historically no less significant than John D. Rockefeller and Andrew Carnegie were a hundred years ago.

Why Would Social Studies Teachers Want to Use the Internet?

From a simple network of some 23 computers on the ARPANET in 1973, to the tens of millions of current users worldwide, the Internet has inalterably changed human communication patterns, just as the printing press did several centuries ago. The difference between these two revolutionary technological developments in human communication is the time it took for each to become widespread and readily available. It took as much as two centuries for the true impact of the printing press to be felt because it took that long for large numbers of people to develop the ability to read. By contrast, much of the world's population is already literate and can quickly gain the skills needed to consume and even publish multimedia information over the Internet. With more than 130 million WWW pages in existence, and truly countless e-mail messages, many have already demonstrated this potential.

The Internet makes available an unparalleled, and seemingly unlimited, repository of resources and ideas for social studies teachers. It offers access to library catalogues and historical archives; viewings of exhibits in art and historical museums; material from the latest editions of popular magazines and newspapers; the availability without charge of news, weather, and up-to-the minute reports on finances and sports; audio and video recordings of social studies-related content; and communication with like-minded individuals about a topic of mutual interest. As a repository for student portfolios and similarly as exhibition space for student multimedia projects, the Internet is an ideal format.

With the Internet, teachers now have the ability to reach far beyond the traditional sources of social studies curriculum materials, and can easily incorporate into their lessons primary source documents they retrieve through the WWW, or the input of experts through newsgroups and e-mail. The Internet is a truly revolutionary development in the production and distribution of curriculum materials, which can only contribute toward engaging teaching.

Ultimately, the Internet is only a tool, and, like any tool, its use can be very enriching, or frustrating and even dangerous. Depending on what information you are seeking, sometimes the Internet seems like a river a mile wide but only an inch deep. In seeking other information, the Internet may seem a mile wide and a mile deep. And, unfortunately, in too many places, the Internet is soaked in pollution and garbage. Thus, it is imperative that social studies teachers have guidance in the selection and use of WWW sites, as well as the decision to participate in on-line discussions through e-mail or newsgroups for instructional purposes.[2] Without such guidance, the Internet can leave one awash in information of significant dubious quality or worth to the development of future citizens in a democracy.

The chapters that follow were prepared to provide such guidance. The authors have provided their valuable time and expertise in exploring how the Internet can become an essential element in a teacher's repertoire of tools for engaging students in the social studies curriculum. For many readers, this book will be different from a novel or textbook, where one customarily begins on page one and reads the chapters sequentially in order to have the story or text make sense. This book is different: the reader is invited to dip in anywhere, unless he or she is a novice to using the WWW, in which case the first two chapters will be essential. All the chapters have a unique theme and are intended to provide conceptual grounding for the instructional approaches and use of the WWW sites that are identified and highlighted. Some chapters focus on traditional disciplines in social studies, including history, geography, and economics. Others are more topical, such as those on global education, multicultural perspectives, arts-based education, or teacher education. A concluding chapter on assessment will assist classroom teachers seeking to integrate the Internet into their regular classroom practice.

It is impossible to underestimate the importance of helping students develop healthy relationships and make responsible choices in classrooms and when using the Internet. To that end, chapters on values, civics, and democracy are all sources for rethinking how we prepare students to assume responsible citizenship in a democracy in an era of unprecedented global communications.

The students and teachers with whom we work were a source of inspiration as they gave us their honest, cutting-edge reactions to the ideas and strategies as they were play-tested in their classrooms. We are sure that you will benefit from their ideas and strategies as well.

Notes

1. See Howard Rheingold, *The Virtual Community: Homesteading on the Electronic Frontier* (Reading, Mass.: Addison-Wesley, 1993).

2. One useful regular source of such guidance is the journal for members of National Council for the Social Studies, *Social Education*, which publishes regular features and an annual issue dealing with the use of technology in the social studies classroom. The most recent such issue included an Editor's Notebook with useful criteria for judging the value of Internet-based lessons, as well as several articles presenting lesson plans. See *Social Education* 63, no. 3 (April 1999).

CHAPTER 1

EFFECTIVE INTERNET SEARCHING

Barbara Brehm
Department of Curriculum and Instruction
Illinois State University

The World Wide Web (web) is becoming the information system of the twenty-first century. More than 130 million pages are indexed by the largest search engines (Cohen 1998). The Internet is the conduit for social studies teachers and students to access original sources and current information not easily available in print. With so many social studies resources available on-line (millions of photographs, documents, multimedia presentations, and audio recordings), the challenge shifts from finding to filtering information for our students' active learning. As Mackenzie (1998) described it, we must help students prepare to be "infotectives" (i.e., they must gain the skills and knowledge to make efficient use of available on-line information).

Unlike libraries, the Internet does not have a standard list of subjects or keywords. Students must learn a new set of literacy skills to locate information on the web. This chapter sets the stage for developing these skills by suggesting strategies to help students frame good search questions, select relevant keywords, and effectively use the tools available for on-line searching.

Types of Search Tools

The most commonly used Internet search tools are search directories, search engines, and metasearch engines. All three types search electronic databases of Internet information, but each search tool varies according to purpose and size. Other Internet search tools, on-line library catalogs, and specialized databases are not covered here because of space and limited usefulness in K–12 social studies education. To access a list of links to search tools in the Netscape web browser, click the *Net Search* icon. In the Internet Explorer web browser, click the *Search* button. Search tools listed at the top of the window are not necessarily the best tools, nor is the list complete. Also listed on these search pages are specific search tools not covered in this chapter, such as the Internet Yellow and White Pages.

SEARCH DIRECTORIES

A search directory is a database of Internet resources, such as websites submitted by their creators or selected by evaluators and organized into subject categories. A search directory provides a structured hierarchy of categories listed by general topics. Under each category are subcategories divided into increasingly more specific topics until links to appropriate websites are listed. The best known and largest search directory is Yahoo! (www.yahoo.com). Students often find Yahoo! user-friendly and useful when they have a very broad subject that they must narrow. This is a good search tool for beginners. Yahoo! also has a keyword searchable index, which helps students search from any point in the hierarchy. They can limit their searches by category, such as searching only education websites, or they can search the entire database.

Yahoo! is most useful when searching for information that fits neatly into an obvious subject or category, but it is sometimes difficult to guess how certain subjects have been categorized. An example is the Universal Service Plan (USP), which provides $2.25 billion annually to assist schools and public libraries in defraying the cost of wiring for the Internet. Will the USP be indexed under *education* or *government*? In such cases, using a subject directory prevents an overwhelming number of returns for a common topic. Because subject directories catalog only a small portion of the web, the number of returns, or hits, is smaller than returns from search engines.

Other recommended search directories include Magellan (www.magellan.excite.com), which maintains a Reviewed Sites Only database with site evaluations. Sites are rated on content, ease of use, and appeal, but are not always current. Argus Clearinghouse (www.clearinghouse.net) provides good search capabilities of academic subjects. Although authors are often experts in the subject matter covered by each directory, Argus is not always current (Cohen 1998).

Special search directories that feature categories of interest to kids are available for younger students. Yahooligans!, Jeeves Kids, and AOL for Kids Only have selective databases of websites that exclude certain categories parents might find objectionable. Searching for certain words, such as *sex*, returns no hits. Lycos Kids Guides offers fewer categories but searches the entire Lycos database. The first three sites shown are good choices for younger students.

Search Directories
Argus Clearinghouse: www.clearinghouse.net
Focuses on academic sites.
Magellan: www.magellan.excite.com
Critically reviewed sites.
Yahoo!: www.yahoo.com
Largest, most popular directory. Focuses on popular rather than academic sites.

Search Directories for Kids
AOL NetFind for Kids Only: www.aol.com/netfind/kids
Fun and interesting. Accepts Boolean operators.
Yahooligans!: www.yahooligans.com
Good for younger students. Interesting topics and good graphics.

Search Engines
Alta Vista: www.altavista.com
Largest search engine. In Advanced Search, *Refine* allows user to include or exclude words that appear frequently in a search. Limit by date.
Excite: www.excite.com
The feature "More like this" retrieves other similar sites and attempts to search for concepts related to your search term.
HotBot: www.hotbot.com
Super Search provides an easy user fill-in template form of available search options, including searching by continent, date, personal name, and domain.
Infoseek: www.infoseek.com
Post-search option in left column provides sites that closely match your search.
Lycos: www.lycos.com
Ranks sites by Top 5 percent. Can specify that sites returned must have word in title.
Northern Light: www.northernlight.com
Indexes 1,800 publications not found elsewhere on the web. Nominal charge for full text articles.

Metasearch Engines
Dogpile: www.dogpile.com
User chooses from many engines to search and search order. Sorted by search engine.

Inference Find: www.inference.com

Searches six search engines. Returns by subject in clusters only. Only URLs with no description.

MetaCrawler: www.metacrawler.com

Searches six search engines and returns ranked results by relevance.

Metafind: www.metafind.com

Searches six search engines. Results may be listed by search engine, keyword, or domain.

SEARCH ENGINES

A search engine has a database of Internet files collected by computer programs called *robots* or *spiders*. The search engine software enables users to query the database. It usually lists the results by relevancy. Most search engines are commercial endeavors supported by advertising, which often appears as scrolling banners or flashing "Click Me" buttons. Such ads can be very confusing to beginning users, who often do click, and are surprised to suddenly find themselves at a different commercial site. The Northern Light search engine is an exception. It makes full text articles available from journal databases and other resources not indexed elsewhere on the web. User payments of $1 to $4 for full text articles support Northern Light, rather than advertising.

Ask Jeeves and Ask Jeeves for Kids accept natural language queries. Users can type in an entire question, such as " What impact did the invention of the cotton gin have on slavery?" These two search engines determine keywords within the question and select further questions from a knowledge base, which narrows the number of returns. Ask Jeeves for Kids searches are protected by Surf-Watch software. This search engine consistently returns sites that can be integrated with social studies curriculum.

CREATING A SEARCH

The main purpose of the web is publishing, not information retrieval. Although a master list of keywords, such as Sears List of Subject Headings for libraries or the Thesaurus for ERIC, does not exist for the web, a web author may designate keywords within the HTML code through metatags.[1] The metatags then help the search engines index these terms. This system does not work very well because not all authors designate metatags and not all search engines search metatags when compiling their indexes. Some unscrupulous authors include many keywords in metatags to attract users to a page to sell ideas or products. This causes some pages to be returned in a search even when they do not contain the keywords in the contents of the page.

The following steps in creating a search are recommended for upper middle school, high school, and adult learners. A lesson plan and suggestions for teaching younger students are included later in this chapter. This sample search begins with a query: *What impact did the invention of the cotton gin have on slavery?*

> 1. *Choose Keywords.* Keywords or search terms determine the relevance and value of the sources students find. Refining the keywords before going on-line saves time. Have students brainstorm, skim print references, or use a thesaurus to generate a variety of keywords on a topic. Possible keywords for this search include cotton gin, Eli Whitney, slavery, Industrial Revolution, and invention.

Other suggestions for selecting keywords include:

- Use keywords that are as specific as possible for broad subjects.
- Use specific rather than generic terms.
- Use modifiers with nouns.
- Use singular terms because most search engines also search for plurals. If a plural is used, only plural, not singular, words will be returned.

▮ Use lowercase instead of uppercase because most search engines are case insensitive, unless capitals are used.

▮ Use uppercase for proper nouns.

2. *Choose the Search Engine(s) to Use.* Search engines vary in the number of sites that they index, how they refine a search, the protocols they index, and how they display the results. The number of sites a search engine indexes changes rapidly as does the search engine that indexes the most sites. As of June 1997, Alta Vista had indexed 30 million pages; by May 1998, it had indexed more than 140 million pages (Cohen 1998). Infoseek and Lycos had each indexed 30 million pages, as of May 1998 (Sullivan 1998). More pages are not necessarily better, however, due to the huge list of hits that the user must examine. Precision of the returns and useful information in the listing are often more important than numbers. Factors to consider when choosing a search engine include:

▮ Ease of use.

▮ Type of information indexed (web, *ftp*, or *Usenet*).

▮ Provision for refining the current search rather than starting a new one. This feature allows the user to add parameters without retyping the original search.

▮ Inclusion of an annotation and URL (website address) returned. This saves time by helping the user decide quickly whether or not to go to a site.

▮ Ease of access (some search engines are frequently busy)

▮ Speed of search engine.

▮ Search interface display. A screen crowded with advertising or containing too many pages competes for attention and may require the user to scroll to submit the query.

3. *Enter Advanced Search Techniques.* All search engines include a simple search for one keyword. Using this simple search often returns too many irrelevant matches. Most search engines provide advanced searches, which offer more options to help the user further refine the search. Use of an advanced search gives the user fewer but more relevant returns.

If more than one keyword is entered during a query, a search engine finds all pages that contain any of the words. Placing quotation marks around words to be searched, designating it as a phrase, results in fewer references but ones that contain both words. Searching for *cotton gin* without enclosing the words in quotation marks returns irrelevant hits that contain, for example, gin, the alcohol. Searching for "cotton gin" returns only hits related to the invention. Some search engines offer a "search as a phrase" option, which returns the same results as using quotation marks.

Joining words or phrases with "AND" requires all of the words or phrases to be present in the returns. Searching in an Alta Vista advanced search for "cotton gin" AND "Eli Whitney" resulted in 550 documents returned, reduced from 3,103 documents found using only "cotton gin." Adding invention to the search reduced the number of hits to 208—still a large number of sites, but browsing a list of the first ten annotations showed nine relevant titles. They included information about the history of the cotton gin and the Industrial Revolution, including a story, an essay, a student report, a museum exhibit, and several factual sites. Including slavery in the search returned many irrelevant hits to the search. It may be necessary for the user to try a variety of keywords in a search to find the best matches.

Using "OR" in a search results in returns that contain either the keyword or phrase or both. Searching for "Eli Whitney" OR "cotton gin" will broaden a search and result in more returns. A Venn diagram can be used to explain the difference between instances included when using AND and OR. A plus sign (+) can also be used for AND, and a minus sign (–) can be used for OR in many search engines.

AND and OR are examples of Boolean operators. Another Boolean operator is "NOT." NOT is used to exclude sites. Some sites returned in the cotton gin search were restaurants. To exclude those sites, enter the search as "*cotton gin*" NOT *restaurant*. A similar search is a proximity search in which the word "NEAR" is used to indicate that the two words or phrases must appear close to each other in the text.

Read the Help section of each search engine for specific search options. Try the different search engines listed for several searches, as the need arises. Compare them, and bookmark, or save the URL for, the advanced search screens for two or three favorites.

4. *Choose Relevant Returns.* Relevancy rankings are typically based on the number of search keywords on the page, where they are located in a document, and how close they are to each other. Scanning down a significant number of returns before activating any links is recommended, as the first returns are not necessarily the best. Search engines may show only the URL, the first lines of text, or page summaries. Summaries are generally more useful than titles, and first lines are often misleading.

5. *Refine or Expand the Search.* If too few hits are returned, use synonyms to broaden the search. Watch for alternate keywords that arise from the hits to broaden your search. If you have too many irrelevant returns, add modifiers and try your search again. Clicking the Refine button in the Advanced Search on Alta Vista gives a list of words that occur frequently and the percentage of hits in which they occur. Each identified word can be included or excluded to narrow and refine the search. This is especially useful when a word has several different meanings, such as *gin* in the sample search.

Because all search tools filter information, using two or more different search engines will provide a more complete search. Your choice of search engines depends on the type of information and complexity of the search. Many sources agree that Alta Vista is the best all-around search engine because it is large and fast, and has good advanced search options. Alta Vista had the most relevant sites (9 of 10) for the *"cotton gin"* sample search. The other search engines listed at the end of this chapter returned from 5 to 0 relevant sites for the same search. Two other search engines listed only one relevant site among the first ten hits. This reinforces the use of at least two search engines for the best coverage of a topic. The University of California at Berkeley Library provides a detailed comparison of search engines at www. lib.berkeley.edu/ TeachingLib/Guides/Internet. Search Engine Watch (www.searchenginewatch.com) also provides current information and comparisons of search engines.

METASEARCH ENGINES

Metasearch engines, or multithreaded search engines, do not compile their own databases but instead search the databases of several popular search engines. Depending on the metasearch tool used, they return an integrated listing of hits or hits listed by search engine. The best metasearch engines eliminate duplicate site listings and combine results from several engines. At first glance, this type of search tool seems to be "one-stop searching." For general searches or obscure information, they work well. They do not allow for as much customization of searches as some individual search engines do, so hits may not be as relevant. As the quality of metasearch engines continues to improve, they become increasingly better choices to begin a search. The metasearch engines discussed here allow the student to set the time he or she will wait for the search. The longer the user is willing to wait, the more hits the engines will return. Some also allow the user to select the specific search engines they will query.

Dogpile searches the largest number of popular search engines and directories. It returns hits listed by search engine. Under Custom search, the user may select the search tools and the search order. These settings are saved and activated each time the user returns to Dogpile. For example, the *"cotton gin" AND Eli Whitney AND invention* search used above resulted in exactly the same results as the individual search engine searches and saved time.

Inference Find searches six search engines and sorts words by clusters. The clusters for the *"cotton gin"* search included an integrated list with Eli Whitney, Social Sciences, Commercial sites, and Education sites as clusters. Because the Inference Find screen contains no advertising and because the returns are organized in clusters, it is highly recommended for educational use. A disadvantage of this metasearch engine is that the sites are listed only by title and do not include the URL or a description. Inference Finds' screen display is uncluttered and less overwhelming for beginners than is that of most other search tools.

Although Metafind searches only five search engines, it removes duplicates and returns an integrated search that may be sorted by search engine, keyword, or domain. MetaCrawler searches six search engines and integrates the results. The UC Berkeley site (www.lib.berkeley.edu/TeachingLib/Guides/Internet/MetaSearch.html) contains a comparison of some of the metasearch engines discussed here. Knowing whether to begin a search with a directory, a search engine, or a metasearch engine saves time and results in the maximum relevant returns. If your keyword is obscure, begin with a metasearch engine to retrieve as many good sites as possible. If search words are common, such as *television* or *computers*, begin with a sophisticated search engine, such as Alta Vista. Continue to add or exclude keywords using the Refine option, until the desired information is located. A search directory can also be used for broad subjects because it has a limited database and thus will yield fewer returns. The State University of New York at Albany Library site (www.albany.edu/library/internet/choose.html) contains a detailed table of suggestions for choosing a search tool.

Teaching Students How to Search

As direct Internet connections become more common in K–12 schools, the Internet will become another reference tool for students and teachers to use. Knowing how to search the Internet effectively can reduce frustration and increase time available for processing information located.

Learning to search for information on the Internet effectively is a gradual process. Although primary students cannot yet search the web, they can view appropriate sites identified by the teacher. By fourth grade or fifth grade, students are ready to begin guided web searching. By middle school, students should be introduced to several search tools and begin searching on their own.

To facilitate learning to use the Internet in the classroom, the teacher should have some device to display Internet sites for a whole class. Bookmarking a site and then bringing it up and displaying it during class, using an LCD panel or other projection device, is one possibility. The drawback to this approach is that it requires a real-time connection. Problems can result because of Internet traffic or technical failures at either the local or distant site. Using Web Whacker or similar software, which temporarily captures the site on a teacher's computer or school intranet, can be a viable alternative. The site can then be displayed in the classroom without accessing the Internet. Because of copyright regulations, however, the site can probably be used in a classroom only for a week before it must be deleted under "fair-use" guidelines. Even for classroom use, it is best to ask permission of the website author before "whacking" a site.

For primary and special needs students, teachers will do most of the searching to locate suitable sites. Stories written by other primary students or graphics and multimedia are good choices for introductory integrated Internet activities. The following are examples from primary teachers of thematic units. During a Johnny Appleseed thematic unit, a first-grade teacher planned to share a few stories and illustrations by second graders that she found on the web. She intended to read only a couple, but the students were so enthralled, they asked her to read all that were posted. The class then sent a thank-you note to the other classroom, including some of its questions. Class members then wrote their own illustrated stories, which could have been either posted to the web as an extension activity or exchanged with the second-grade class.

Another example is a preschool special needs class that was studying farm animals. The teacher found a site that used a duck as the guide through the web pages of farm animals. A special needs student easily learned to click the duck icon to view the farm animals and actually accessed pages that the teacher had not viewed before.

Teaching Students to Use WebQuest

Once students are comfortable navigating through a website and have an adequate reading level, they are ready to use WebQuests and learn beginning searching. WebQuests were developed by Bernie Dodge (1998) at San Diego State University. A WebQuest is an open-ended problem-based activity, in which some or all of the information necessary to solve a problem is acquired from the web. The majority of information on the Internet is written at a sixth-grade or higher reading level.

WebQuests allow the teacher to select curriculum-related sites with easy vocabulary and pictures so that the students can find information that they can easily understand. This also separates the task of learning to process Internet information from that of learning to locate information, making each concept easier to learn.

A WebQuest provides a framework in which active learning and knowledge construction can take place. Students demonstrate their understanding of the knowledge gained by creating a product such as a web page, a HyperStudio stack, or a video to which others can respond. The WebQuest Page (edweb.sdsu.edu/webquest/webquest.html) explains the parts of a WebQuest and links to sample WebQuests. Sixth-grade students designed and used WebQuest of Ancient Civilization tours with this author. The Student Writing Center, the software with which the students were accustomed, was used for the travel brochure. If students using the WebQuest are in structured time periods instead of flexible scheduling, the author suggests including a Bonus section, which allows more advanced students or groups to extend their knowledge, while other students complete the WebQuest.

The next step can be introducing a WebQuest with only some addresses available, so students complete the WebQuest by finding additional sites. Revolutionary War Personalities, for example, uses Inference Find as the search tool. Once students are familiar with gathering information from the web, they are ready to learn to search the web. When students are comfortable using one search tool, introduce a second search tool. Encourage them to use both search tools and to compare results.

After students become comfortable using search tools, they should learn to evaluate the sites that they find. Evaluation is covered in more depth elsewhere in this publication. Elementary or middle school students can easily use a form to guide them logically through the evaluation of a site to decide whether it will help them as a reference for a report or presentation. Widely used K–12 web evaluation forms, which also include web design issues, and were developed by Kathy Schrock, are available at www.school.discovery.com/schrockguide/eval.html.

By upper middle school or high school, students should be using several search engines. It will be necessary to point out the differences, as well as the advantages and disadvantages, of the three types of tools. Having students search and compare several search tools on a particular topic expands student horizons and helps them develop their higher-level thinking skills. The author finds that, even at the college level, students tend to find one search tool, often Yahoo!, and use it consistently without considering its advantages or disadvantages.

When students are ready, introduce advanced searching, using Boolean operators and advanced features, such as Refine, on Alta Vista. Older students or adults just learning to use the Internet should begin with simple search skills on one search engine and then proceed to more advanced skills and metasearch engines as they become more skilled.

The Internet contains vast reserves of information, which are valuable to education but are difficult to tame. Search tools, such as search directories, search engines, and metasearch engines, can provide access to this information. Some popular search tools are easy to use but are not always the best. Students must learn which tool to use for certain types of searches and how to use advanced search techniques to locate the most information in the shortest amount of time. Once teachers become experienced searchers themselves, they can guide students to acquire such advanced search skills gradually. Enjoy the search.

Endnotes

1 A metatag is a type of code used in an HTML document to describe or list keywords for a site. The metatag can be descriptive or contain keywords. The tags are designed to assist search engines in sorting and categorizing websites. Some search engines use the tags to index sites, but some have grown suspect of their use. Your site could be dropped if you lace your document with keywords.

References

Cohen, Laura. *Searching the Internet: Recommended Sites and Search Techniques*. Available on the web at www.albany.edu/library/internet/search.html (1998, April 25).

Dodge, Bernie. *The WebQuest Page*. Available on the web at edweb.sdsu.edu/webquest/webquest.html (1998, November 19).

Mackenzie, Jamie. "Grazing the Net: Raising a Generation of Free-Range Students." *Phi Delta Kappan* 80, No. 1 (September 1998): 26-35.

Sullivan, Danny, ed. *Search Engine Watch*. Available on-line at www.searchenginewatch.com (1998, November 19).

CHAPTER 2

THE WEBMASTER'S TALE

Tim Dugan
Princeton High School
Cincinnati, OH

So now that there is a wonderful interface, and you've been zipping about the World Wide Web to all these wonderful sites, you may be asking yourself, "How do I go about making a website for my classroom or school?" To understand this, you must first understand what is actually happening when you are "on-line." Basically, you have connected your computer, usually through a phone wire, to other computers. With the right signal, you may download a file, or series of files, which your web browser usually arranges in some format (based on however the Hyper Text Markup Language, or HTML, is written). When you see that lovely page, with its graphics aligned, colorful background, animation, and sound, each of those items was downloaded as a separate file and placed in a specific order for you to view. The original files themselves are stored on someone else's computer, called a server. The way your computer receives access to them is the process that makes the Internet work.

Domain Names

Your computer, while it is connected to the Internet, must carry a specific identification, which we will refer to as your Internet number (more technically, an IP number). Think of this as a telephone number. Each website has its own number, which you can call. Many schools use "proxy" (stand-in) numbers for most of their computers because it is cheaper to dynamically assign a number only to those computers that are on the Internet at any given time. But to run a server continually, you must have a unique number. The IP number is something like this: 206.21.204.19. (Each set in the series is a number between 0 and 255.) Because most humans like names better than numbers, a Domain Naming System assigns a name to each. My server, for example, can be addressed by its name (www.phs.princeton.k12.oh.us) or its number (206.21.204.19). If you type either in the location box in your browser, you will get to the same place. With this system, it became easy to assign (read *sell!*) people specific URLs, or addresses. The secret to most addresses is to read them backwards; the suffix, or last three letters, is most important. The six major categories of names created since the Internet began are the following:

.com	Commercial sites (making a profit)
.net	Network providers (offering Internet access)
.org	Nonprofit sites
.mil	Military sites
.gov	Government sites
.edu	Colleges/universities

Today, the Domain Naming System is diversifying. For example, international firms may be given specific names. Two-letter codes indicate which country the site is in, such as the United Kingdom (UK) or France (FR). Today, without the two-letter country code, we usually assume the site is in the United States.

Server Software

A website is any computer that is (1) connected to the Internet and (2) is running a specific type of software that allows it to serve up files to anyone who calls it. The process resembles how an answering machine responds when someone calls a telephone number, only in this case, the process is much more sophisticated, especially in the types of files involved. To develop a website, you must follow two rules. First, you must have your own "number." Usually this means that when you call up your Internet Service Provider (ISP), for example, through a modem, you connect to the Internet through a number that the ISP's computer/router sends your computer each time. This means that the number is different every time you log in. It is not very convenient if you are running a website. Almost every website has its own number. Second, you must run some type of server software. Currently, several shareware versions of server software are available, and several others can be purchased. For the Macintosh platform, you could use the MacHTTP shareware and then purchase an upgrade called WebStar available at www.starnine.com.

If you are already on the Internet, you can obtain the software from any shareware site (e.g., www.shareware.com). Look for the most recent version of the software. Download as you would any file. Double-click on the application (MacHTTP), and you are now a "webmaster" of a website. Go to any other computer and open a web browser, such as Netscape, and type in the IP number for the computer with the server software (http:// then the IP number). What should come up is the "default.html" page. This is the name of the page the server serves up when it starts (if another page has not been specified). You can change anything about this page except the name. This becomes your site's "home page." The only other page you may want to change initially is the error.html file. This is what people will be served if they give your site as the location/domain, but any wrong address for the page. It is considered good form to include on this page whom they should contact to report this problem. This is a good thing because if you revise a page address and then leave a bad link, people are kind enough to remind you. It keeps the site running well.

HTML

Once you have the site's home page up and running, it's time to learn a little about HTML. The Visual Quick Start series, which I use for a variety of topics, is clear and easy to understand. What you have to know is this:

HTML files are just text files with some simple codes added to them to make the browser (Netscape or Internet Explorer) show the information in a specific way. Because HTML is simple text, you can write an HTML file in any word-processing program. Just do two things. First, save the document as a "text" file, not within the actual program (e.g., ClarisWorks, Microsoft Word). This saves the file from any additional coding. Second, make sure the file is named (something.html). PC users should add only <.htm> because PC disks (even when used on the Macintosh) do not like four-letter suffixes. Either file (.htm or .html) will display properly in the browsers.

You must learn eight major HTML codes; then you are on your way. They are:

- <HTML> and </HTML> These always go at the very beginning and end of the page.
- <HEAD><TITLE></TITLE></HEAD> These come right after the first command and include the words that will appear in the title bar at the top of any HTML file.
- <BODY></BODY> Between these two commands goes the bulk of the text on the page.
- <A HREF="http://www.phs.princeton.k12.oh.us">Princeton Site</A> This includes a link that would appear like this: Princeton Site. When you click on the words, your browser would go to that site and retrieve the file.
- <IMG SRC="billy.gif"> This would display the picture billy.gif file at this point on your web page. Remember, images are separate files and must be stored in the same folder as the HTML document. Otherwise, you must code the actual address of the picture like this: <IMG SRC="http://www.phs.princeton.k12.oh.us/Public/images/billy.gif">

▮ <P> Begins a paragraph.

▮ <HR> Places a horizontal rule across the page.

▮
 Operates as a carriage return.

Beyond these basics, acquire a good HTML book. Most beginners use either templates (pages made in basic form by someone else and then copied) or a web page-making program, such as Adobe PageMill or Claris HomePage. You really don't need to spend much money on software, though. Because all HTML is just text, highlight any formatting you see on a web page that you like, such as a table, and then view the Source Code in your browser to see exactly how to do the HTML.

Hundreds of different file types appear on the Internet. Fortunately, most people stick to the basics at first. They usually write in basic HTML, then add certain file types. Graphics such as gif and jpeg are image files. For more advanced scripting, you can find various web sites to help. Video, streaming or animation, audio/sound, and other visual effects are all possible for advanced webmasters.

Keep in mind, though, many of your students' parents are still visiting your site with a 28.8 modem and, as such, are only downloading files at about 4K per second. If you have a page that is more than 40 to 50 K, most people will tire of the wait and move on. Keep your school site filled with updated information, and limit your graphic size.

Maintenance

Once you have begun your development of the website, several issues must be addressed. First, if you love doing it and have the extra time, you may consider donating your services. Keep in mind that the larger the site, the more work you must do. Keeping the website filled with attractive and up-to-date information is the key to attracting new visitors. Many sites are simply posted with nothing done to them after that point, making them "ghost sites." As you have probably found, many links on the web are outdated. This will be are frustrating to visitors to your site. You may consider asking students and/or parents to be involved in maintaining the site. Often they have special interests and skills that will make the website much more attractive.

K–12 Website Applications

Whether you are at an elementary, middle, junior, or senior high school, your website has many uses. Some suggestions are outlined below:

LESSONS FOR STUDENTS

When students are in the Internet Lab, or at your classroom minilab, post the bookmarks or even the lessons to keep them focused. Students should never be brought to the lab just to "browse." They should be brought to complete a well-thought-out lesson. At our site (www. phs.princeton.k12.oh.us/ Public/lessons.html), the lessons page is filled with teacher-prepared lessons. On another page (www.phs. princeton.k12.oh.us/Public/dugan/ra1.html) is my recommendation for the perfect lab lesson—a lesson for how to build lessons called WebQuests.

SYLLABUS FOR CLASSES

Teachers can post both their syllabuses and sample work for students. (In addition to a website, you can easily set up a File Transfer Protocol (FTP) site to allow people to download documents. See ftp://www.phs.princeton.k12.oh.us/Pub/).

FACULTY HOME PAGES

Individual faculty and staff can post their own page to give students and parents a little information on their background. Having a picture on that page helps, too! We use a shareware HyperCard stack called MakeAPage Stack, which generates a simple HTML page after teachers answer a few questions.

TRAINING FOR STAFF

Be aware that a website can also be the center for in-service training for teachers. At our school, after going on professional leave, a teacher must demonstrate that he or she has learned something. Developing a web page lesson is a good way to share this information with the rest of the staff. (See sample at www.phs. princeton.k12.oh.us/Public/dugan/mayerson. html). Generally, staff members have a three-step growth period for making lessons on the Internet. The novice Internet user will first develop a Bookmark List. Novice users may even type out the sites they recommend to students. The Practitioner Internet User will have bookmarks annotated with the sites described and even perhaps the task he or she requests from students on the page. The third level (Expert/Scholar) will develop something that looks like a WebQuest lesson. This is a fully interactive, active learning lesson that anyone can use without additional information.

FACULTY E-MAIL

Having a central page where students and parents can look up your e-mail address invites parent-student-teacher interaction.

DIRECTORY TO MAJOR SITES

Each department or grade level can develop a set of bookmarks that highlights its work or field. See samples here: www.phs.princeton.k12.oh.us/Public/deprtmts.html.

STUDENT PROJECTS

Parents and students love to see student work displayed. Putting student work out where the world can see it is probably the best use of the website. The following applications are, perhaps, unique to Princeton High School's situation but may be applicable to other schools as well:

Viking LawSayer
The "You and the Law" course at Princeton High School is developing a high school Law Review called the Viking LawSayer. On this site students post articles on recent court decisions that they study (www.phs.princeton.k12.oh.us/Public/lawsayer/law.html).

Collaboration/Interdisciplinary
When teachers want to share their work and create lessons (for collaboration or teaming or interdisciplinary work), the web is a great tool/medium. See www.phs.princeton.k12. oh.us/Public/lessons.html.

Weather Page
Many people think this is the number one use of the Internet! It is amazing how interested people are in the weather. I link to the weather report, radar, and weather for our local area. I also link to a local web camera that allows teachers without a window to see outside!

Parental Involvement
As I mentioned earlier, get students and parents involved. It should be their website, too. If there is a special interest (a sport, an activity) that they are willing to do the work for, that saves you time and energy.

School Calendar
On our website, counselors post important dates for testing, etc., which go to a calendar that is available for students. Be careful, though, because any time you have dates on the site, you must keep your site current! See www.phs.princeton.k12.oh.us/Public/depts/couns.html.

Class Field Trip Reports
Some math/history students visited a local Jewish cemetery and put together a database. See www.phs.princeton.k12.oh.us/Public/Lessons/Cemetery/cemetery1.html.

Alumni E-mail

We maintain, as the result of a student project at college, a full alumni e-mail site for our graduates. It promotes the school to former students, but is a time-consuming project because college students change their addresses upon graduation.

Virtual Desktops

Virtual desktops serve as a good starting point for our teachers and students, whether in a lab or at home. In an organized fashion, the desktops list references sites and local, national, and international news sites that Internet users frequently visit.

Library Access

Princeton's librarians have developed part of the website for access to research collections that we own or subscribe to (Encyclopedia Britannica, World Book, Proquest). See www.phs. princeton.k12.oh.us/Public/HW/LC.html.

Ongoing Future Development

I'm currently working on several projects related to the website that involve cameras, video, and conferencing. The first attempt was setting up a web camera attached to the Internet server (Using SiteCam software available at www.rearden.com). Visit my class at www.phs.princeton.k12.oh.us/Public/docs/push1.html. To get a streaming video of the class (although it is only a few frames per second), take the number one (1) out of the address. I am also currently test driving a few different cameras and software programs (Enhanced CUSeeMe, Apple's VideoPhone) to begin working on video-conferencing. This could be a major area for applications in the next few years. As schools get more bandwidth through cable modems and other technologies, we are going to be able to open up the classroom to others. For example, I recently allowed my students to interview a history professor in Pittsburg, Kansas, to talk about the atomic bomb. Although we had some difficulties, the students were fascinated with the idea of talking with an expert. I also envision a time when a camera installed in the library could make that a central location for information. Any teacher could simply click on his or her desktop, opening a link to the librarian. Any questions, Ask the Librarian – rather like a Max Headroom for the new millennium!

Because many students love to "chat" in chat rooms either through Internet Relay Chat (IRC channels) or through Internet services (America Online, Excite), teachers apply this love of "chatting" to students evaluating each other's writings. More students are participating in collaborative writing over the Internet.

The possibilities are endless, once you have the server set up. The server becomes not only a repository for all HTML files at your school, but can also be an FTP (File Transfer Protocol) server, a web camera site, and even serve up a listserv (for mass mailings).[1] You are limited only by your own creativity!

Endnotes

1 A listserv is an electronic mailing list which is maintained by software (LISTSERV®, LISTPROC®). The software automatically distributes an e-mail message from one member of a list to all other members on that list.

CHAPTER 3

THE CLASSROOM WEBSITE

Timothy A. Keiper
Western Washington University
&
Linda Bennett
University of Missouri—Columbia

In the last few years, teachers have created websites at an explosive rate. According to Web66, an Internet school registry maintained by the University of Minnesota, there were 250 school sites in 1995. More than 12,000 school sites were registered by 1999. Although we do not know how many of these school sites were actually created by teachers, the trend is obvious.

Does this explosion mean that creating a site is worth the time and effort? Should you create a site for your classroom because "everyone else is doing it," your administration says you should, or because you've always wanted to tell your mother that you have "published"? Why create a website? And if you did want to, where would you start? In this chapter you will find an explanation of the role a school's website can play in social studies classrooms, an introduction to the process involved in creating a website, and a number of exemplary sites for you to consider.

Defining the Purpose

Designers of quality websites agree that determining the purpose of the site is the first essential step. A review of existing school sites shows an emphasis placed on communication with parents—through on-line discussions, easily accessible staff e-mail addresses, and classroom newsletters. Other sites focus on course administration by giving site visitors on-line access to syllabi, resource lists, or other materials. Although we acknowledge many valid purposes for quality classroom or departmental websites, in this chapter we address two that we believe should be given special consideration: (1) publishing student work and (2) creating on-line projects.

Publishing Student Work

With the Internet, we have an opportunity to extend or remove the walls of the classroom. This metaphor commonly refers to the removal of barriers to information and resources, but it also applies to the display of student work. As learning increasingly becomes project based, a variety of avenues for presenting projects becomes more important. Websites offer an opportunity for students to present their work to an audience outside the school culture. Instead of writing, coloring, or producing for the classroom wall, students are publishing on-line and soliciting comments from the electronic community. Take, for example, the site from Sundown Elementary School in Katy, Texas, located at www.katy.isd.tenet.edu/se/se.html. Here, students display their work on topics such as "Cowboy Stories" by third graders; "Flat Stanley Travels the Earth" by kindergartners; and "Alfabeto Español," a HyperStudio project by bilingual students. At the Parker Junior High School website located at gsbkmc.uchicago.edu/parker, student-created web pages on a variety of projects show the potential for student work publication.

On-Line Projects

A primary function of teacher-generated on-line projects is to save class time. Although students need to practice their search skills on the Internet, this is not always the objective, and too often they will end up surfing off into the electronic horizon. Notice how the site designed by teachers Douglas Perry and Wendy Sauer at www.misd.wednet.edu/~Wendy_Sauer/AmMem.html helps focus students on the topic "The Great Depression." The site provides links that allow the students to gain immediate access to a plethora of information, facilitating focused research. It also contains the administrative information for students to successfully complete the assignment as well.

Online projects can also be helpful in guiding students through tasks that require higher-order thinking skills. The site produced for local ninth graders by education students at Western Washington University focuses students on research topics. The project titled "Georgia Pacific," found at perl.wce.wwu.edu/tk444/sp98, asks students to create solutions to a complex problem rather than simply find the correct answer. At this site, students are asked to follow a series of steps in the research process to answer the locally controversial question: "Should the operating permit for the Bellingham Georgia Pacific paper mill plant be renewed at the turn of the century?" Sites like this one designed for a specific classroom can be especially engaging for those independently minded students who might require something extra to motivate them.

After the designer of a website or a website team has clarified the site's purpose and goals, the first stage of design can begin. Start with a brainstorming session to create a storyboard. Storyboarding consists of creating a diagram that represents the site's organizational structure. The artistic and creative qualities of the website originate from this design. The extra effort and time you invest at this stage will make the website unique and will ensure consistent focus on the goals. The team should refer to the goals statement throughout the design of the project. During the storyboarding process, pay particular attention to the content. A flashy design may be inviting, but if the content isn't strong, the viewer will be disappointed and move to another site.

A website resembles a spider web in that the pages within the site are accessed from multiple entry points. Because a website is not linear, develop a plan that allows the visitor to navigate easily. This calls for careful consideration of all links within the site, as well as external links.

Develop a template for the website to make the pages consistent. This will save time and effort, while it creates fewer HTML errors in the website. A consistent design will make it easy for the visitor to navigate through the individual pages and easy for other designers to update and extend in the future. As you make the design template for the website, note the rationale behind the layout. Replicating the decisions made in creating the template is difficult, so take a few minutes during the design stage to save time and frustration later.

Use the latest version of Adobe Photoshop for effective design of graphics for the web. The graphics in Photoshop are easy to update and will be visually unique. Keep the images small and simple so the visitor requires little time to download them. You may be tempted to have big, flashy, billboard-sized images, but whenever possible, keep the graphic size to no more than 30K.

Consider that it is common for your visitors to use a 640 x 480 pixel screen to surf the web (Seigel 1997), so design a site that stays comfortably within the optimum size browser window. Have several users view the site from different computers, and incorporate their needs in polishing the overall design. Helpful resources for creating a website are listed at the end of the chapter.

Exemplary K-12 Websites

By reviewing elementary school sites, you may be inspired to create an exemplary website for your classroom. The visual appearance of a home page is key to inviting a visitor to browse a website. For example, the music, ticker tape, postcard greeting, graphics, and color of Mrs. Cave's third grade classroom home page (www.public.usit.net/llcave) has invited teachers, students, and families into her classroom. She has provided opportunities for students to take field trips, submit creations, and communicate.

Develop a community in your classroom by featuring the students and their work. Mrs. Silverman's second graders at Clinton Avenue Elementary School in Port Jefferson Station, New York, are proud of their work (hometown.aol.com/Clinton2nd). The class home page focuses on the students with a class photo and a list of each student's name. Each student has a home page with samples of his or her writing and artwork. The students should be proud of their published work and feel a part of the Internet community and the classroom community.

Westford History in Our Back Yard (WHIOBY) is an exceptional student web page project (www.vetc. vsc.edu/ws/archeology/arch.htm). Fifth and sixth grade students at Westford Elementary School in Westford, Vermont, did an archaeological dig in the school yard and posted their results on the web. The site includes photos from the dig, field notes from the excavation, and topographical maps.

Elementary school students have several social studies projects on the Birch Lane School Community Home Page (www.birchlane.davis.ca.us). The Birch Lane Mission Day, Reduce, Reuse, & Recycle, the Birch Lane Colonial Chronicles, and Virtual Tour of Historical Davis are four current examples of how students have used the website to display their work in history, culture, geography, and ecology.

Other exemplary elementary social studies sites include that of Montgomery County Schools (www.mcps.k12.md.us/curriculum/socialstd/index.html), which has field trips, curriculum materials, and children's literature. On Kauai Island in Hawaii, the Kilauea Elementary School home page (165.248. 238.26/kilauea/kilauea.html) includes stormwatchers, a virtual field trip around Kauai, and SIMCITY 2000 Kauai. The website of Mrs. Larsen's fourth grade class (osage.voorhees.k12.nj.us/FOURTH/LARSEN/ JKIDS/STORIES/STORIES.htm) features the "Great State of New Jersey."

Web pages associated with the social studies classroom at the middle and high school levels are not as common as those tied to elementary classrooms. The social studies page located at www.gwi.net/brhs/ socst.html is an example of a student-created listing of resources. Boothbay Region High School students created this page under the direction of instructor Diane Crocker and Frances Aley, LMS. Although this is a very small version of what can be found at large social studies listing services on the web, much of the value for students lies in the creation process itself.

Medicine Lodge High School in south central Kansas developed a website within its advanced technology program. To quote the site, the program advantages include "a 250-user Novell Netware network, 6 full-time Internet connections, this website, one honey of a technology lab, and a student to computer ratio of 2.25 to 1, just to name a few." This website www.cyberlodg.com/mlhs/index.htm is proof that this school's technology is not collecting dust.

Administrative information is the focus of the social studies departmental site of Springville High School, Springville, Utah, which is found at www.shs.nebo.edu. Students and parents find a descriptive listing of classes and information related to AP exams. There is also a "showcase" of student projects currently under construction, as well as links to community resources.

Many schools are beginning to publish newspapers or newsletters on the web. Student articles dealing with social issues are submitted and published via this mechanism. Links from social studies classroom or departmental pages could lead parents or interested parties to these products as well.

Ricki Peto of Pasco High School in Washington has maintained a social studies classroom page that enhances students' projects and cultivates communication with students throughout the world. Her students produce projects while collaborating with community members and foreign students. One current cross-cultural project involves her students and high school students in Japan and Canada. Students at all three locations created web pages about themselves, "portfolios," in order to get to know each other. The students created an on-line scavenger hunt based on the portfolios and communicated it via e-mail. Then students from the three locales created an "adventure game" in which the player searched for a "plan for peace." In another published project of interest, students interviewed a family member or member of the community, researched events surrounding their lives, and published the results on the web.

Even though there is a trend toward producing websites for the classroom, this project is not for everyone. Many teachers have limited technological background and find that time to learn about the technology is short. Before you rush to judgment, however, note that not every on-line classroom is led by a computer wizard. You might become a supportive web page mentor after producing something exciting. As one former preservice teacher said, "I was a little bit intimidated when we started the process ... and then I was discouraged when things didn't go as planned ... but that all disappeared when I saw my first page on the web and I realized I could do it."

Resources
Web Page Design
Calkid. HTML 101, 1997: *www.geocities.com/Athens/Acropolis/5969/index.html*
World Wide Web Consortium:: *www.w3.org/Style*
HTML tutor: *hakatai.mcli.dist.maricopa.edu/tut/intro.html*

Tools
www.uwtc.washington.edu
Donnie Garvick, Teach Me Tutorials *HTML, 1997: *www.geocities.com/Athens/Forum/4977/index.html*
The Webmaster's Reference Library. Mecklermedia Co., 1998. *webreference.com*
CyberWeb SoftWare, The Web Developer's Virtual Library1997. *www.stars.com*
Barebones: *www.werbach.com/barebones*
Netscape: *home netscape.com/assist/net_sites*

Web Graphic Sites
Clip Art Universe: *nzwwa.com/mirror/clipart*
Clipart: *www.clipart.com*

Colors
www.columbia.edu/acis/documentation/color.html

Locating School Websites
American School Directory Computers for Education, Inc., 1997. *www.asd.com*
Bright Sites, South Central Regional Technology in Education Consortium, 1997. *scrtec.org/bright_sites*
Global SchoolNet Foundation: *www.gsh.org/fetc*
International School Registry, 1998. *web66.umn.edu/schools.html*
Yahoo!: *dir.yahoo.com/Education/K_12/Schools/Elementary*

CHAPTER 4

TEACHING HISTORY

C. Frederick Risinger
College of Education
Indiana University

I have often said this at presentations to groups of educators and in published articles, but it is worth saying again: "No subject area in the curriculum is affected more by the growth of the Internet than the social studies." Although it is impossible to quantify with any accuracy, it seems to me that anywhere from 75 percent to 85 percent of websites available on the World Wide Web (WWW) have relevance to one or more of the subject areas typically associated with the social studies curriculum. This is true particularly of history and political science. From early prehistory to events as recent as this morning's headlines, the Internet provides information, primary sources of every variety, pictures, maps and other graphics, analysis, and opinion. Students and teachers may access the web to read letters written by a homesick Iowa farm boy, describing the carnage after a battle near Vicksburg (www.civilwarletters.com/home.html), see pictures of the children and pets who have lived in the White House (www.whitehouse.gov/WH/kids/html/home.html), or contemplate theories about why the Mayan civilization fell (www.learner.org/exhibits/collapse).

I have argued in the past that the Internet is going to change history (and all social studies) instruction and learning dramatically. Some teachers and other educators have written to tell me that using the web is just another educational fad. Like programmed instruction or simulation games, they say it will either disappear or, after a brief flurry of popularity, fade into a seldom-used instructional technique. They are wrong, and here are two reasons why. First, most previous educational innovations were completely controlled by teachers. Teachers decided whether or not to use "Dangerous Parallels," an excellent simulation game about the Korean War. Teachers chose to use the "Flipatron," an extensive series of colored overhead transparencies, associated with Ted Fenton's inquiry approach, that helped teach historical and geographical content. But as former NCSS president Howard Mehlinger pointed out, the rules have changed. "It is no longer necessary to learn about the American War of Independence by sitting in Mrs. Smith's classroom and hearing her version of it. There are more powerful and efficient ways to learn about the Revolutionary War, *and they are all potentially under the control of the learner.*"[1] Students now have ready access to historical information—including primary sources and historical interpretation—that was available only to scholars in the recent past.

Second, even those teachers who choose not to use the Internet or encourage its use by students will find that the technology still affects their instructional lives. Every textbook publisher sees the writing on the wall. Market forces will push them toward a fundamental restructuring of textbooks. Future history textbooks may look like a small (80- to 120-page) "handbook" that provides a chronological outline of U.S. or world history. The real "meat" of history may be on CDs (or DVDs or a future format) or more likely on some sort of website, established and managed by the publisher. Instead of purchasing a 600-page, nine-pound textbook, schools or students will purchase access to resources. Of course, these changes will occur gradually over a decade or more; but it is unlikely that teachers will be able to avoid the impact of the web and its future incarnations for very long.

And why should they want to avoid them? Using the web can add extraordinary resources to the classroom or to individual teachers and students. The story of Pompeii has always been interesting. When I taught world history during the Cold War in the 1960s, my students made comparisons between the end of Pompeii and what might happen in the event of a nuclear attack on the United States. But their old textbook, *The Story of Nations*, with its black-and-white pictures of an indefinable Pompeian fresco did little to give them a true sense of the beauty and resources of that wealthy Roman trading town. But by logging onto the Discovery Network's website (www.discovery.com/online.html), students see the beautiful mountains behind the town, see reconstructed faces of the citizens (many Pompeii residents were of African origin), and read a fictionalized (but based on recent research) account of one man's day when the city was buried. With one mouseclick, students can see and hear a RealPlayer video about a Pompeian invention attached to horse-drawn wagons that foreshadowed the automobile speedometer. Every turn of the wheel moved a cog that dropped a pebble into a bucket after each carefully calibrated Roman mile. There's even an audio/video recreation of the volcanic ash burying a Pompeian villa. *The Story of Nations*, even with what I considered pretty good teaching, was never like this.

I recently participated in a planning meeting for an educational conference. We wanted to attract a broad group of pre-K–12 teachers and administrators and were discussing what topics and themes would encourage them to attend. My eyes glazed over at the "hot topics"—relatively new terms such as "authentic assessment," "coaching," "curriculum alignment," "constructivism," "multiple intelli-gences," and other issues of brain research, mixed in with older terms such as "standards," "decision making," "meeting the needs of all learners," and even "discovery learning." Suddenly, I sat up straight. I had been thinking of this chapter and realized that all of these theories and ideas can be discussed in the context of using the Internet to teach history. In an era of near-frenetic educational reform, technology—especially the Internet—can provide one avenue for all social studies educators. For teachers struggling with aligning curriculum content with state or national standards, the web provides a myriad number of sites to "fit" even the most specific content statement. For those working with Howard Gardner's theory of multiple intelligences or designing activities to meet the needs of all learners, the Internet has websites for helping integrate music and history or providing pictures and other graphics to make a historical event, such as daily life in the Roman Empire, more relevant. Others who believe that the constructivist theory of learning should form the basis for curriculum design and instruction can find support from the noted historian Daniel Boorstin, who opened a book with the sentence, "The historian is both discoverer and creator."[2]

Although I sincerely believe that the Internet—and what the Internet will become in the next decade—can and will alter dramatically how most history teachers will teach, I also acknowledge that it is basically one more "tool" in the teacher's tool kit. But it is an amazing tool—far more significant than the overhead projector or even educational films. Let us take a look at some of the ways that classroom history teachers can use the Internet.

Search Engines

Some teachers argue that the web is unusable in the classroom because of the millions of web pages and the perceived difficulty in finding what is useful and relevant information. However, I believe that finding the information or sources you want is easier than searching a major library or doing a search of ERIC, the government-sponsored educational database. Most experienced Internet users will go directly to a search engine and find the information that meets their specific needs. Finding what you want has become easier in many ways, yet a bit more cumbersome as more and more organizations, individuals, and agencies put their information on the web. Peterson has estimated that there are forty-nine search engines available for public use.[3] On another site, I found more than sixty listed. Some of these are "primary" search engines, and others are "niche" search engines, which focus on a specialized segment of the web. Only about six or eight, however, are widely used. They include

Alta Vista, Excite, HotBot, InfoSeek, Lycos, and WebCrawler. I have tried most of them, including the metasearch engines, such as MetaCrawler. This engine searches several of the other major search engines, eliminates the duplicates, and presents you with a combined list. I always come back to Alta Vista. It loads quickly for me (even on my 28.8 modem at home), has fewer advertisements, and is easy to use. All of the major search engines have some form of advanced search techniques, some of which allow you to use Boolean searching. Many engines (including Alta Vista), however, allow you to type in a simple question. The question "Where can I learn about teaching history?" yielded more than seven and a half million hits. The phrase *teaching history* came up with a more reasonable 4,900. You can usually tell from the brief descriptive listing if a site will be helpful. And each useful site probably has a list of links that are also relevant to your needs.

Teacher Resources

Most teachers begin to integrate the use of the Internet into their teaching by using it as a teacher resource. There are two reasons why it is the easiest and safest starting point and also the least expensive because it requires only one computer for the teacher, either at home or school). First, teachers do not have to be concerned about students roaming around on "hate sites" or viewing pornographic sites. Second, teachers still maintain control over the selection and use of the Internet resources. This second aspect might be more important than some teachers think. For example, The Learning Channel recently aired a show that provided convincing evidence that the earliest Americans arrived much earlier than previously thought and were of African and Australian origin, rather than Asians who migrated across the Bering Strait. This information is also on the channel's website (www.tlc.com) and directly contradicts what most U.S. history textbooks and teachers say about the first Americans. I have observed classes during which students challenged a teacher or a textbook with information they obtained from the Internet. Most teachers welcome such student initiative, but others do not. Although I certainly do not support the use of the Internet as a teachers-only resource, it is a consideration. Of course, teacher resource sites might be excellent sites for students, too.

Teacher resource sites can include (1) sites that provide primary sources such as letters, official documents, and speeches; (2) commercial sites maintained by textbook publishers, producers of educational materials, and television channels, such as The Discovery Channel; (3) sites that feature lesson plans and teaching strategies; and (4) those that provide maps, paintings, political cartoons, charts, and other graphics. Some sites combine all of these resources. One of the best sources for U.S. history is the Library of Congress's American Memory site (lcweb2.loc.gov/ammem/ammemhome.html), which offers more than fifty historical collections of documents, pictures, and other graphics. With a color printer or a copier that can make transparencies, teachers can bring resources to the classroom that were never available in the past. The list includes topics such as "Documents from the Continental Congress and the Constitutional Convention, 1774-1789" to "Baseball Cards, 1877-1914" to "Votes for Women," selections from the National American Woman Suffrage Association Collection, 1848-1921. Several of the collections include audio recordings, such as the "Voices of the Dust Bowl" or "American Leaders Speak: Recordings from World War I and the 1920 Election."

Commercial Sites

Commercial sites should not be overlooked just because they are trying to sell you something. Frequently, they provide teachers with excellent maps or other resources. One of the best commercial history websites is "Eyewitness" (www.ibiscom.com), which should gladden the hearts of those teachers who believe that primary documents should be a part of every historical topic. From "The Burning of Rome" to young Mary Jemison's abduction by Native Americans in 1755 to Corporal E. C. Nightingale's frightening eyewitness account, from the battleship *U.S.S. Arizona*, of the Japanese attack on Pearl Harbor in 1941, the words from those who were there truly make history come alive. This site even has audio clips now in a section titled "Voices of the 20th Century."

On the site of the textbook publisher McDougal-Littell (www.mcdougallittell.com), more than thirty map and other graphic transparency masters, ranging from "Ancient Cultures of North America" to "The Progressive Era" to "The Persian Gulf War: 1990-1991" can be downloaded free. Many are in color and include student activity worksheets. The History Channel (www.historychannel.com) is another helpful commercial website. It promotes its own programs and those of its companion A&E channel, but it also includes useful information for teachers such as a "Today in History" feature and many well-designed classroom guides. The guides include vocabulary words, student objectives, discussion questions, and extended activities. Using the appropriate History Channel program would make the lesson more effective, but a teacher more comfortable with a textbook and classroom discussion can use the guides as well.

Lesson Plan Sites

The History Channel's "classroom guides" are really lesson plans; its website is one of many that provide lesson ideas or complete lesson plans on just about any historical event or issue. Some are very good and use higher-order thinking skills, cooperative grouping, and a variety of instructional strategies. Many others are lifeless and uncreative. Yet even a boring, workbook-type lesson plan can stimulate the imagination of a creative teacher.

Some of the best lesson plan sites are those associated with a teachers' institute, college/university, or conference. Often, the student activities center on a theme. The plans also seem to be more creative and likely to heighten student interest. One of the most comprehensive sites for lesson plans and instructional activities is maintained by Marty Levine, an education professor at California State University in Northridge. Levine has collected lesson plans and links to other sites including literally hundreds of lesson plans and student activities, encompassing all grade levels and just about all history and social studies topics. Some lessons are merely brief outlines, but they examine topics such as "Critical Thinking in the Primary Grades," and The Silk Road in Ancient China, an interactive lesson for middle school students. One particularly outstanding lesson, "Comparing and Contrasting the Individual Experience of African Americans in the 19th Century," is based on Depression-era Work Projects Administration (WPA) narratives with former slaves. Students "interview" African Americans and compare and contrast the differing conditions of slavery.

R. Jerry Adams has collected links to lesson plans in all subject areas and at all grade levels at www.awesomelibrary.com/history.html. His selection of history sites is impressive, and some of the lessons, including a middle school lesson on ancient Egypt, would meet the criteria of the most exacting history teacher.

Students "Doing" History

Much of the excitement among history students and teachers results from the opportunity for students to do actual historical research and then "publish" their work on the web. Even at the elementary grades, students can work cooperatively and individually on projects, which are then displayed on the school's own website. Third-grade students in tiny Loogootee in southern Indiana are about as far from China as they can get, yet they have designed an interactive web page that not only illustrates their own learning but is interesting for anyone who uses it. You can view a slide show and take a test on it, learn how to make paper, and count from one to twelve in Chinese. The students used traditional sources of information, such as textbooks and the library, but designing and creating the web page features are excellent examples in applying constructivist learning principles.

Princeton High School near Cincinnati does an outstanding job of integrating the Internet throughout its curriculum. From exploring extinct species in science to studying Indonesian music, Princeton's students frequently use computers and the web. The social studies department, chaired by Tim Dugan (a contributor to this volume) leads the school's efforts. Dugan promotes the WebQuest concept, in which students solve a mystery or research a problem, using the web as a primary resource.

The students' goal is to "create knowledge," again following the constructivist approach to learning. Dugan's student project on "Researching Ancient History" is a model of combining the innovative medium of the web with more traditional student assignments.

For More Information

The websites and related learning activities described above are just a small sample of how the Internet can help you teach history. As my search indicated, innumerable websites have something to do with history teaching and learning. The only way to find those that meet your needs or the needs of your students is to explore on your own. Below I have selected five websites in three different categories: General Sites for Teachers, U.S. History, and World History. They are not necessarily the "best" sites, but they do have content, features, or examples that I believe make them worth your time.

GENERAL SITES FOR TEACHERS

Teaching with Historic Places (www.cr.nps.gov/nr/twhp/descript.html). This site, sponsored by the National Park Service, offers some wonderful lesson plans, guidelines, and hints for you and your students to create your own history lessons, as well as your professional development activities. Several of these lessons have been published in the NCSS journal, *Social Education*, but the website offers many more.

WWW Services for Historians (grid.let.rug.nl/ahc/hist.html). The Association for History and Computing (AHC) sponsors this site. It is also a list of links to other websites, but many of these are directly related to teaching history with computer technology, particularly the Internet. This site is for serious historians, although many of the links may appeal to students, too. It includes specialized sites on topics such as African history and links to electronic magazines of history, available only on the Internet.

Links for the History Profession (www.oah.org/announce/links.html). Sponsored by the Organization of American Historians, it includes links to college-level history departments around the world and many excellent archival locations.

In-Sites for Teaching History and the Social Studies (members.tripod.com/ozpk/history.html). Unlike the "professional historian-oriented" sites above, this one is designed for history teachers in elementary and secondary schools. Accordingly, when you look at their recommended "classics and the ancient world" section, you'll find a link to *The Olympic Games in the Hellenic World* (devlab.dartmouth.edu/olympic). This site seems to have made a special effort to include links to web pages that might have interest-heightening content for students at all grade levels.

The National Council for History Education (www.history.org/nche). "Promoting the importance of history in schools and society" is this organization's goal. Both professional historians and teachers at all grade levels belong to and participate in this group's activities. It has links to many other useful sites. The group sponsors conferences, such as the Kids Learning History meeting, a conference especially for elementary and middle school teachers.

WORLD HISTORY

Collapse: Why Do Civilizations Fail? (www.learner.org/exhibits/collapse). This is one of the more creative and useful sites that I have found. Part of the Annenberg/Corporation for Public Broadcasting project, it offers several other interactive multimedia programs. Teachers interested in the WebQuest or "Mysteries in History" approach can easily use this. Focusing on civilizations as diverse as the Maya, the people of Chaco Canyon (NM), Mesopotamia, and Mali, the site discusses what is meant by societal failure and the interaction of internal and external forces that are involved.

E-Conflict's World Encyclopedia (www.emulateme.com). This site would be particularly useful for those teachers at the upper elementary and middle school levels, who often teach regional studies courses. Students are expected to learn about history, but also about the economics, culture, and geography of regions and nations. You can search individually by country, take a factually oriented world quiz, and see the flag and hear (with an audio reader) the national anthem of each nation.

Women in World History Curriculum (www.womeninworldhistory.com). This interactive site, "for teachers, teenagers, parents, and history buffs," has some well-developed classroom activities, lesson plans, and reviews of classroom resources. The "Words of Wisdom" section, with quotes from women, including Catherine the Great and Margaret Thatcher, might especially help heighten interest among female students.

World History Compass (www.SchillerComputing.com/whc/index.htm). From "A Brief History of Albania" to the impact of the Vikings on British history, every point on the world's compass is included here. It is one of those basic informational sites that many school libraries include in the bookmarks/favorites file for their students.

The World History Association (www.hartford-hwp.com/WHA/index.html). Designed primarily for secondary and college-level world history and world civilization teachers, the site includes professional development information and many outstanding links to other websites. It also offers syllabi and even full-length texts from courses around the country and world.

UNITED STATES HISTORY

Been Here So Long: Narratives from the WPA American Slave Narratives (newdeal.feri.org/asn/index.htm). Between 1936 and 1938, more than 2,000 former slaves were interviewed by historians and others working for the WPA. The site has great potential for using primary documents in the classroom and for helping students learn how to conduct interviews.

The Library of Congress Exhibitions (lcweb.loc.gov/exhibits). I have mentioned the superb American Memory site earlier. Teachers and students, however, can access current and past major exhibits that are certain to provide stimulating, interest-heightening information and graphics. To be able to return to the outstanding exhibit "1492: An Ongoing Voyage" or "The African American Odyssey: A Quest for Full Citizenship" and use their resources in the classroom is one of the wonders offered by the Internet.

History Buff's Home Page (www.historybuff.com/index.html). This site is devoted to press coverage of events in U.S. history. It includes an extensive, searchable library with categories ranging from the Civil War to Journalism Hoaxes to Baseball. It has several items that teachers will find useful and students will find delightful. They include history crossword puzzles, a historic voices library, and recommendations on collecting and using newspapers in the classroom.

Creating On-line Materials for Teaching United States History (etext.lib.virginia.edu/history). This site includes a series of posters, documents, photographs, and political cartoons arranged chronologically through U.S. history. Compiled by teams of history professors and classroom teachers are links to teaching units developed by the Creating On-Line Materials Workshop at the University of Virginia in 1996. If I were teaching U.S. history using a multimedia approach, this would be one of my favorite sites.

History Matters (historymatters.gmu.edu). Social history is still given short shrift in many history textbooks and curriculum guides. Yet students clearly enjoy learning about how average people worked and played. A product of the American Social History Project, this site focuses on the life-styles of ordinary Americans and uses instructional materials, primary documents, and discussion groups. Most of the materials cover history from the Reconstruction Era to the present.

Vietnam: Echoes from the Wall (teachvietnam.org) This site offers resources and information about the Vietnam era. Created by the Vietnam Veterans Memorial Fund, it has a strong commitment to providing materials and a discussion forum for both teachers and students.

Endnotes

1. Howard Mehlinger, *School Reform in the Information Age* (Bloomington, Ind.: Center for Excellence in Education, 1995).
2. Daniel J. Boorstin, *Hidden History: Exploring Our Secret Past* (New York: Harper and Row, 1987).
3. Richard E. Peterson, *Harvesting Information from the Internet Using Search Engines* (Honolulu: University of Hawaii, 1999). (Web document).

CHAPTER 5

THE VIRTUAL TOUR

Eileen Giuffré Cotton
Professor of Education
California State University, Chico

Imagine sitting in on a class of eleventh-grade students where a small group is leading a virtual tour of Washington, D.C. Group members are giving a creative PowerPoint presentation highlighting what they have learned during the semester. The presentation captures the meaning of democracy in the United States. It has pictures and explanations about the three branches of government and about other important national resources: the House of Representatives, the Senate, the Supreme Court, and the Library of Congress. It showcases the value of freedom by exploring our national monuments, those to presidents and events that define our history and culture, such as the Lincoln Memorial, the Jefferson Memorial, and the Vietnam Memorial. The presentation ends with a reflection on what freedom and democracy mean to the presenters in the group and a round of questions from their peers. You can accomplish this in your class by having your students create and view virtual tours.

Example: High School Level Teaching Suggestion—Washington, D.C., Virtual Tour
For the culminating unit in U.S. Government, your students create a virtual tour of the nation's capital to showcase and celebrate what they have learned. They will present their virtual tour to their classmates using PowerPoint or HyperStudio presentation software, paired with a word-processed written document. After dividing your class into groups of three or four, have each group of students create a virtual tour that includes three to five of the following elements:

■ Information and discussion about the Legislative Branch of Government

■ Information and discussion about the Executive Branch

■ Information and discussion about the Judicial Branch

■ Information and discussion about five U.S. monuments to freedom located in Washington, D.C.

■ Information and discussion about cultural and aesthetic pursuits found in the area

■ Information and discussion about the geography of the area

■ Information and discussion about some of the historical events that have occurred in Washington, D.C.

■ Information and discussion about something that appeals to them

The virtual tour is assessed on the following elements: Ideas and content, response to their three chosen elements, organization of the presentation, use of graphics, creativity, cooperation, and mechanics (see below for a rubric). The following URLs can be bookmarked for your students to start them on their trek. They can search for other relevant URLs on the topic too.

Virtual Tour of Washington, D.C.: www.csuchico.edu/educ/c11.html

Yahoo!: dc.yahoo.com

National Capital Parks: www.nps.gov/nacc
   view all the parks and monuments in the federal area

City Net: Washington, D.C.: www.city.net/countries/united_states/
   district_of_ columbia/washington
   directory to more D.C. websites

Clickable Map of Washington, D.C.: sc94.ameslab.gov:80/TOUR/tour.html

The White House: www.whitehouse.gov

The House of Representatives: www.house.gov

The Senate: www.senate.gov

The President's Cabinet: www.whitehouse.gov/WH/Cabinet.html/cabinet_links.html
   explanation of each cabinet office and who holds the office

The Library of Congress: www.loc.gov

The Smithsonian Institution: www.si.edu

Why a Virtual Tour

With a virtual tour, you set a task for your students to accomplish, you give them guidelines for accomplishing the task, and, finally, you give them an opportunity to share their accomplishment with others. It is a good lesson that reinforces previous learning and skills needed to use the Internet. It also assesses the amount of knowledge they learned during the semester about a particular topic.

A virtual tour is an Internet way of taking a firsthand look at the people, customs, sites, sounds, and life-style of a place without actually going there. Although books and regular print media are very much a part of our curriculum, and are used to discover "static" information about a location, the resources found on the Internet are used to discover "dynamic" information about what is happening now. The "nowness" of the Internet makes a virtual tour an ideal way for students to learn about a target location or theme as it relates to them today. In the above tour, your students can follow the "birth" of a law as it is worked through Congress and finally signed by the president.

Creating a Virtual Tour

You can use a virtual tour in several different ways. Teachers at all grade levels can design a virtual tour to any destination by using relevant websites to introduce a unit of instruction. This visual introduction via the web shows students what will happen in that subject-matter area for the next few sessions and acts as a motivational "hook" to increase interest in the topic.

Start out with an easy virtual tour lesson to introduce your students to the concept. Then progress to more difficult lessons as they gain proficiency. For beginners, after you determine the curriculum area and the lesson you want to accomplish, use a browser like Netscape or Internet Explorer to bookmark a specific set of websites that your learners will visit. At these websites, your students collect information according to a predesigned set of questions. After they have collected and organized the information, they prepare a report or presentation. This way the teacher guides the virtual tour, but the students develop a sense of ownership of the project by collecting, writing, and presenting the information in a specific format.

As students become more familiar with the Internet and use consistent search strategies, they can expand on the bookmarks recommended by the teacher, and add other websites. By searching for other websites that relate to the topic and incorporating that information into the final report, the students create new knowledge, thus further reinforcing what you want them to learn.

Last, when students have gained proficiency at using the World Wide Web, they can design their own virtual tours. This is a constructivist project that builds information retrieval, reading, writing, thinking, and collaboration skills, just to name a few.

Whether teacher-designed to introduce a unit of instruction, teacher-guided to reinforce specific skills and knowledge, or student-designed to showcase skills, knowledge, and ability, each virtual tour creates a unique and personal learning experience for the student. Interacting and working with the information found on the Internet require ways that are a bit different from dealing with traditional print or text information.

Elements of a Virtual Tour

The ability to travel in cyberspace to explore or discover one or many facets of a location is possible with a bit of planning. What follows are some possible virtual tours you can take your students on, as well as ideas for virtual tours they can create on their own.

A well-planned virtual tour has three basic elements: (1) A statement of purpose, (2) a definition of the outcome you want your students to accomplish, and (3) clear assessment guidelines, so your students know what to expect before they either take or create a tour. These elements do not have to be long or complicated, but they do need to be in place.

STATEMENT OF PURPOSE

If you want your students to take a virtual tour, you must have a purpose for the lesson. Are they going on a class-sponsored field trip to the locality? Are they going to plan their dream vacation? Are they supposed to get an understanding for the people and the culture of the locality? You have to decide on a purpose, then take it from there.

Successful Internet lessons are self-directed and constructivist in nature. As such, the role of the on-line teacher is that of "guide on the side" rather than "sage on the stage." As a guide, you develop a rationale or purpose for the lesson that will make it meaningful to your students and necessary to your curriculum. Because there are many different routes to take on the Internet, you must be prepared for a variety of solutions to an assignment. Instead of thinking of this as frustrating, think of it as refreshing. The motto of one Internet instructor I work with is "There are many ways to peel an orange; I just want you to peel it."

DEFINITION OF THE FINAL PRODUCT

Second, the students must know what they are to produce as a result of the virtual tour. Do you want your students to write a report? Create a PowerPoint or HyperStudio presentation or portfolio? Bookmark and explain ten important websites? Create a travel brochure? Or develop a video production? Whatever end product you choose, you must ensure that your students have the skills to construct it. Again, because there are many possible routes to success when the World Wide Web is used as a curriculum resource, there are many opportunities to develop "other" products.

ASSESSMENT

Last, your students must know how they will be graded or assessed on the total project. Part of World Wide Web teaching is authentic assessment. As your students work, you have visual proof of what they are doing and how they are doing it. To make them accountable, however, you must develop some type of assessment rubric that will encourage your students to create a useful learning document—not only for themselves but for the other people in the class, too.

The rubric that was successfully used for the Virtual Tour of Washington, D.C., is presented on page 36. The rubric addresses three levels of expertise: Exemplary, Proficient, and Not Yet. Students receive ratings for the ideas, content, and organization of the written and multimedia presentations, graphics, creativity, cooperation, and mechanics.

Virtual Tour Examples

You can use a virtual tour in a classroom in other ways. At the elementary level, a learner might be going to visit a relative in a large city. When she takes a virtual tour by traveling in cyberspace, she can see

Field Trip Rubric	_Exemplary_	_Proficient_	_Not Yet_
Ideas and Content of the Written Presentation	▪ Ideas are clear ▪ Enough details ▪ Holds attention ▪ Responded to three elements very well	▪ Ideas somewhat clear ▪ Some details ▪ Responded to two of three elements well	▪ Unclear ideas ▪ Details broad, general, vague ▪ Did not respond to three elements
Organization of Multimedia Presentation	▪ Very good introduction ▪ Smooth, easy pace ▪ Good placement of details ▪ Strong conclusion	▪ Good introduction ▪ Some trouble following pace ▪ Some details, but out of order ▪ Good conclusion	▪ Introduction boring and/or hard to follow ▪ Wanders aimlessly ▪ Stops abruptly or drags on
Organization of Written Presentation	▪ Very easy to read ▪ Follows multimedia presentation well ▪ Can "stand alone" without multimedia presentation	▪ Easy to read ▪ Wanders from multimedia presentation once in a while ▪ Needs multimedia presentation to clarify some issues	▪ Very hard to read ▪ Does not follow multimedia presentation ▪ Cannot "stand alone"
Graphics	▪ Reflects research ▪ Follows a plan and coincides with the virtual tour ▪ Carefully and neatly executed	▪ Reflects some research ▪ Shows some planning ▪ Most are carefully and neatly executed	▪ Does not reflect research ▪ Not planned ▪ Not carefully or neatly executed
Creativity	▪ Reflects exemplary work that shows style, humor, and zest	▪ Reflects good workmanship but lacks the zest of a truly creative virtual tour	▪ Monotonous ▪ Tedious
Cooperation	▪ Group shared its workload and managed problems that arose in a way that advanced the group goal	▪ Group managed problems that arose in a way that advanced the group goal, but a few people did most of the work	▪ One person did most of the work and/or problems that arose were not managed in a way that advanced the group goal
Mechanics	▪ Correct spellings ▪ Punctuation works with sentences ▪ Correct grammar ▪ Easy to read aloud ▪ Varied sentence length	▪ Most spelling correct ▪ Most punctuation works with sentences ▪ Mostly correct grammar ▪ Most parts easy to read ▪ Some varied sentence length	▪ Spelling faulty ▪ Punctuation doesn't work with sentences ▪ Grammatical problems ▪ Awkward to read aloud ▪ Short, choppy sentences

the place, hear the sounds, and meet some people. By visiting several websites for an "Internet" town, she can have an idea what to expect when she finally arrives at Aunt Mary's home.

VISITING NEW ORLEANS

Not too long ago, I was going to New Orleans. Before I flew there, I took a virtual tour of the "Big Easy" to get an idea what to expect. I found out about the Jazz Festival, where to stay in the French Quarter, the best restaurants for Cajun food, the important historical sites of the city, where to get my palm read, and more. I also learned about the convention center, the streetcar lines, and the weather. I looked up extended weather forecasts to plan my wardrobe, and I ordered my airline ticket on-line. I did all of this without leaving my home! When I arrived in New Orleans, I knew exactly what to do, where to go, and what questions to ask. It was ideal! The only drawback to the actual tour was the humidity. Various weather websites related that the humidity was going to be high, but they did not truly prepare me for warm, damp late spring days. By the way, the current WebCrawler (www. webcrawler.com) search for New Orleans gives more than 50,000 hits, which is too many, so I listed just a few below:

> The Best of New Orleans: www.bestofneworleans.com
>   Everything worth knowing about New Orleans
> Yahoo!: www.yahoo.com
>   In search window type "New Orleans"
> The Historic New Orleans Collection: www.hnoc.org
>   On the history of the French Quarter
> Greater New Orleans Area: Louisiana Tourism: www.louisianatravel.com/where_to_go/
>   greater_new_orleans/index.html
>   A regional guide to the area

A good resource for "virtual field trips," "electronic field trips," or "virtual tours" is Yahoo! at www.yahoo.com. When you scroll to the bottom of the Yahoo! home page, you will see several virtual tours to various countries and metropolitan areas in the United States—some of these are written in the language of the country. If you scroll to Yahoo! Metros, you will find pages for Atlanta, Austin, Boston, Chicago, Dallas/Fort Worth, Los Angeles, Miami, Minneapolis/St. Paul, New York, San Francisco Bay, and Seattle. A word of warning: Please visit the websites before assigning them to your students. You might not want to introduce some of the site information to your students at this point in time.

Internet Inquiry as Virtual Tour

You can have your students go on a teacher-guided tour or a student-guided tour to a location. As an example, here are just a few of many ways to take a virtual tour of China. With teacher guidance, a beginning virtual tour might ask students to choose five places they want to visit in China, find out information about each place, and prepare a bookmarked web tour with a written narrative. Students who have a specific question about China can use the "Internet Inquiry" approach designed by Leu (1998). This student-guided learning project has the student setting up a contract, planning meetings with his or her teacher, and producing a product, which has a solution to the original question.

Middle School Level Teaching Suggestion—An Internet Inquiry about China

Have your students research a question about China. The question can be simple or complex, such as "What was the importance of the Imperial City in Ancient China?" or "What will be the impact of recent flooding in China on peasants?" Have your students ask their question and determine a starting place on the web and in books where they can find some possible solutions. Let them set up at least three individual conferences with you during the contract time, at which time you discuss the question and the progress that each student is making with a solution. When the question is answered, the student presents the result to the class as a written paper, oral presentation, or media presentation. For an Internet inquiry virtual tour of China, try these URLs:

> The Forbidden City: www.chinavista.com/beijing/gugong/ !start.html
> A Virtual Tour
> China the Beautiful: www.chinapage.com/china.html
> A look at Chinese art and literature
> Chinese History: A view from Taiwan: darkwing.uoregon.edu/~felsing/cstuff/history.html
> Chinese Culture: hanwei.com/culture/oldindex.html
> Map of China (mainland): www-chaos.umd.edu/history/chinamap.gif
> History of China: www-chaos.umd.edu/history/toc.html
> Table of contents to many pages of information on China
> The Art of China Home Page: pasture.ecn.purdue.edu/~agenhtml/agenmc/china/china.html
> Looks at the art and culture of China (beautiful website)
> Six Paths to China: www.kn.pacbell.com/wired/bluewebn/fr_History.html
> Great WebQuest lesson for students

All virtual tours are informative and useful. Which type is the most appropriate depends on your class. It could be the teacher-designed virtual tour for new Internet users or the student-designed virtual tour for experienced "webbies."

The ABC Book as Virtual Tour

Have your elementary level students create a virtual tour of a country by writing an A-B-C Book. The A-B-C Book is a way to learn basic information about the alphabet or about the topic. Using the formula at this level is a good way to introduce students to a country or a region while they learn "alphabetical" facts and information.

ELEMENTARY LEVEL TEACHING SUGGESTION—THE A-B-CS OF CANADA

Fifth- or sixth-grade students studying Canada create an A-B-C book on the places, people, and culture of Canada. Groups of five students each create an A-B-C book on Canada. Each member of the group is responsible for finding out information on five (or six) letters of the alphabet. They search the web and traditional text materials for Canadiana. Each page of the book must represent one letter of the alphabet, a picture of something "Canadian" that represents that letter, and an explanation of the picture. When each group has collected twenty-six pictures, facts, and explanations, the group members create an illustrated A-B-C book of Canada, which they present to another class. After they have published their books, they place them in the school library for general circulation. The assessment is based on completeness and accuracy of the collection of pictures, facts, and explanations; mechanics; group cooperation; Internet usage; and sharing with another group. Below are some URLs for this virtual tour:

> Yahoo of Canada: www.yahoo.ca
> Shows websites about Canada in French and English
> The Flags and Arms of Canada: www.cs.cmu.edu/Unofficial/Canadiana/CA-Flags.html
> One for each province and territory
> About Canada: canada.gc.ca/canadiana/cdaind_e.html
> Explains the symbols that help establish Canadian identity
> Symbols of Canada: canada.gc.ca/canadiana/symb_e.html
> Explains the meaning of the name, the national anthem, etc.

The Canadiana Resource Page: www.cs.cmu.edu/Unofficial/Canadiana/README.html
  With facts and information from a newspaper point of view

Tour Canada Without Leaving your Desk: www.cs.cmu.edu/Unofficial/Canadiana/
  Travelogue.html

Canadian Government Information on the Internet: dsp-psd.pwgsc.gc.ca/dsp-psd/
  Reference/cgii_index-e.html

Natural Resources Canada: www.nrcan.gc.ca/homepage/toc_e.shtml
  For information about the land and resources

Unusual Virtual Tours

The virtual tours described above are for specific geographical locations. Not only can you have your students visit cities, counties, states, countries, and continent; they can also visit planets (The Nine Planets at seds.lpl.arizona.edu/billa/tnp or Stars and Galaxies at www.eia.brad.ac.uk/btl/sg.html or Welcome to the Planets at pds.jpl.nasa.gov/planets). Your students can also create a virtual tour for "Around the Block" or "Our School" or the "Fire Escape Route/Evacuation Plan for My House." The first and second graders in a school where I work are studying their community. With the help of a digital camera and walking field trips, the children are taking pictures of their immediate school neighborhood. When they return to the classroom, they download each photograph to the classroom computer and describe it in writing. The neighborhood houses, businesses, and services will be pictured, described, and placed on the web. They are on the way to creating a virtual tour of the immediate community for others to view and enjoy. These students can read what their classmates write about each picture, further reinforcing reading, writing, and thinking skills, along with their basic geography knowledge. In addition, they are very excited to see pictures of their school bus and homes on the web.

If you are studying manufacturing, say for the purposes of creating a fund-raising event like a cookie sale, your students can "tour" several manufacturing sites on the web. After studying the aspects of manufacturing a product, the students develop their own manufacturing process for the purpose of making cookies. To get an idea about manufacturing, they can visit the Jelly Belly factory at www.jellybelly.com or a Dominos Pizza Store in Florida at dominos.gator.net (click on cybertour).

Students can study art on-line by virtually touring world-famous museums. While there, they can collect knowledge about the artists who painted the masterpieces. A good place to start is the Louvre at www.louvre.fr, but don't forget the museums listed below either because they have much to offer.

Art Institute of Chicago: www.artic.edu
The Metropolitan Museum of Art, New York: www.metmuseum.org
The San Francisco Museums of Fine Arts: www.thinker.org
  See 70,000 images on-line

Also, do not limit yourself only to art museums. Students can go on virtual tours of scientific or historical museums, too. Great places to explore virtually include the Franklin Institute of Science at sln.fi.edu/tfi/welcome.html, Resources at The Smithsonian at www.si.edu/resource/start.htm, Exploratorium Home Page at www.exploratorium. edu, or the Florida Aquarium at www2.sptimes.com/Aquarium/Default.html.

Students may develop virtual tours of strange and unusual places or things. They can take a virtual tour of a boy's wallet on the web. This tour describes more than forty different items (www.mu.org/~doug/wallet). How about having your students develop a virtual tour of a school desk or a closet or a cabinet, a schoolroom, or a backyard? This type of virtual tour probably has a different purpose than previous tours. Writing skills, imagination, creativity, and the like are what it emphases.

The WebQuest Virtual Tour

One of the more interesting virtual tours is a WebQuest, which is a type of student-guided virtual tour designed by Bernie Dodge (1997). See edweb.sdsu.edu/webquest/webquest.html for more information. With a WebQuest, students must solve a problem. It can be a simple problem, like "Mine the web for five places you want to visit. Find out everything about those five places and prepare to share your findings using HyperStudio or PowerPoint with the class." It can be a very difficult problem, such as the "Ambassador to Mexico WebQuest" found at www.csuchico.edu/educ/c14.html, which this author developed. Here the students must prepare their teacher for a stay in Mexico where she will be the new "Special Ambassador." They must give her as much up-to-date information as they can find about the culture, history, languages, geography, politics, government, cuisine, and music of Mexico. When they complete this WebQuest lesson, the students have a better idea about Mexico, and the new "Special Ambassador" has good information to use to get started out on her new job. Although a WebQuest can be complicated, it is rewarding to the students, and they do have a lot of fun learning about their topic along the way.

Give your high school students this question to answer: *What are the various impacts of building the Three Gorges Dam?* Several small groups of students study the problem by focusing on the region's geography, history, economy, ecology, and politics. Each group then coordinates and cooperates with the other groups to create a comprehensive report that explains the social, geographic, economic, historic, and aesthetic impact of the dam, not only on China but on the world. You may wish to have students view the URLS listed previously.

There are many places on the web that explain the process and give examples of WebQuests. A few are mentioned below:

Kathy Schrock's WebQuest Guide: school.discovery.com/schrockguide/webquest/webquest.html

Kathy Schrock's WebQuest Slide Show: www.capecod.net/schrockguide/webquest/wqs1.htm

WebQuest Design Process by Bernie Dodge: edweb.sdsu.edu/webquest/Process/WebQuestDesignProcess.html

As you can see, the field trip has gone electronic. No longer do you need to order the school bus weeks in advance. Nor do you need to gather permission slips or beg for parents to donate their time to transport your students to far-away locations. With an on-line computer, you can take your class on journeys around the street or around the universe. They can study a location with either teacher guidance or student guidance—or a combination of both. They can discover answers to questions and possibly find new solutions to old problems. With well-planned lessons that have a purpose, coupled with selected websites, details about an end product, and a way to assess student achievement, your students will want to take plenty of virtual tours to enhance their learning.

Selected References
Cotton, Eileen G. *The Online Classroom: Teaching with the Internet.* 3d ed. Bloomington, Ind.: ERIC/EdInfo Press, 1998.
Dodge, Bernie. The WebQuest Page. Available on-line at edweb.sdsu.edu/webquest/webquest.html, 1997.
Leu, D. J., and D. D. Leu. *Teaching with the Internet: Lessons from the Classroom.* Norwood, Mass.: Christopher-Gordon Publishers, 1997.

CHAPTER 6

TEACHING GEOGRAPHY

Cheryl L. Mason
University of Virginia
&
Marsha Alibrandi
North Carolina State University

Walking down the aisle of the local grocery store, I spied a neighbor and her nine-year-old, Sarah. Sarah was scurrying up and down the aisles, recording the prices of items, such as a pound of sugar, one egg, and a pound of peanut butter.

"What are you going to do with the prices you are writing down?" I asked Sarah.

Clutching her clipboard tightly, she confidently announced, "Tomorrow in school, we are going to average everyone's price lists. Then we're going to add our prices to the Global Grocery List!"

Thinking that this was a clever way for Sarah's math teacher to have her students practice averaging numbers, I asked her to come by for a visit later in the week to report the average food prices for our city. She seemed pleased with this and asked if I would also like her to bring the average food prices of cities around the world?

"Of course, I'd love to see those, too, Sarah, but how will you get averages from other cities?" I asked her.

Assuming that I should know the answer to this question, she looked puzzled when she answered, "You know, the Global Grocery List!"

Sensing that I had not heard of the Global Grocery List, Sarah's mother explained to me that this was a web-based project that allows students from around the globe to share and compare their grocery lists with each other. I later visited this project on-line, and learned it was actually much more than that. The data that students from around the globe submit to the Global Grocery List are stored in a searchable on-line database. Each school, submitting its grocery list, also submits its latitude and longitude coordinates. Exploring this on-line project made me realize that Sarah's grocery list was much more than a math lesson—this was also a geography lesson!

The Global Grocery List (landmark-project.com/ggl.html) is one example of a web-based geography project that allows us to teach geography in a way that we could not do before the advent of the Internet. The Internet enables teachers to introduce many innovative practices into the geography curriculum. With the hundreds of millions of electronic pages that are already on-line, and the million or so that are added everyday, the list of websites that can be used in our geography classes is astronomical. Because there are so many resources on-line for the geography teacher, we have selected a small sample of quality web pages and classroom activities to present in this chapter. The sites we highlight have been selected on the premise of two criteria:

- ■ Will this use of the Internet enable students to do something they couldn't do before?

- ■ Will this use of the Internet enable students to do something they could do before, but better (Harris 1998)?

Telecollaboration: Elementary School Examples

Providing elementary students with the opportunity to work with and learn with others from around the globe allows students to experience rich geography activities. Harris (1998) defined "telecollaborative" learning activities as those in which the primary focus of student learning is on collaboration with peers or other individuals in different locations. The web projects we highlight in this section provide students with the opportunity to learn about people, places, and regions via telecollaboration. Harris classifies telecollaborative activities into three genres: Interpersonal Exchanges, Information Collection and Analysis, and Problem Solving. We define each genre and provide examples of classroom applications.

1. INTERPERSONAL EXCHANGES

These activities are those "in which individuals talk electronically with other individuals, individuals talk with groups or groups talk with other groups" (Harris 1998, 18). An example of an interpersonal exchange activity is ePALS Classroom Exchange (www.epals.com). This web-based project allows teachers and students to link with more than 13,000 classrooms in 100 countries from around the globe. Teachers register their class through an on-line submission form and then use the ePALS search engine to select a class with which to collaborate. Once a match is made between two classrooms, teachers may design learning activities that allow their students to learn more about everyday life in another state or country. For example, students from two school locations could be asked to record their activities every hour. The collection of their day's events is then compiled and shared with each other via the ePALS exchange. The teachers at both schools then design a series of activities that have the students note the similarities and differences of daily life between the two geographically disparate locations. Additionally, students locate their ePALS location on the map and hypothesize why such similarities and differences exist.

Other examples of interpersonal exchange projects include the following:

- **E-mail around the World** (www.siec.k12.in.us/~west/proj/mail/index.html)
  More than 13,000 students last year sent and received 100 e-mail messages to classrooms around the globe. Their messages included interesting information about their communities and directions for identifying their location on a map. As they receive e-mail messages, students print and post each and connect a piece of yarn from the message to the sender's location on a map.

- **Electronic Postcards** (www.schoolworld.asn.au/geocard.html)
  Students create electronic postcards that accurately represent their community with both graphics and text. The class downloads a "mailing list" from the Electronic Postcards project and mails the postcards to the schools on the list. Once a class has received postcards from other schools, the students and teachers display them in a creative way and record what they have learned from their peers around the globe. This information is then submitted to the project gallery for all to view.

- **Weather Watch** (www.schoolworld.asn.au/weather.html)
  Classes from around the world record their local weather and submit it to an on-line data base. The project then pairs classrooms in different climatic zones so those students can analyze and discuss global comparisons between their school and the other's results. Additionally, all weather reports are posted so those teachers can design lessons that go beyond comparing climatic zones.

2. INFORMATION COLLECTION AND ANALYSIS

These activities are those that "involve students collecting, compiling, and comparing different types of interesting information" (Harris 1998, 33). For example, an information collection and analysis activity is "Find the Rabbit!" (chesterfield.k12.va.us/~chester). Students follow clues to track Chester, the Beagle, throughout the state of Virginia as he searches for the "rabbit." Students and teachers post new clues each week. Clues may include latitude and longitude or significant cultural or physical features. Using their map skills, students compete to identify Chester's location. Once they locate Chester, students send digital postcards to Chester depicting significant attributes of his location. Classroom maps may be posted that track Chester's weekly travels.

Other examples of information collection and analysis include the following:

■ Virtual Jamestown (vcdh.virginia.edu/vcdh/jamestown)
This digital history project allows students to explore the physical and cultural geography of the Jamestown settlement and "the Virginia experiment." Virtual Jamestown includes primary documents such as laws, census data, art, historical and modern maps, and QuickTime Virtual Reality (QTVR) panoramas of the current fort and site. Accompanying curriculum materials are included.

■ Cross the Empty Quarter Expedition (www.alwaysadventure.net)
Students follow three explorers on an expedition to cross The Empty Quarter of Arabia. As these explorers attempt to cross the world's largest sand desert, they communicate with students via e-mail, digital postcards, and digital videos. A series of curriculum materials is included to help guide the students as they track the explorers' daily ventures.

■ Multicultural Calendar (www.kidlink.org/KIDPROJ/MCC)
Students from around the globe contribute to this on-line data base of holidays and festivals around the world. Information included for each entry may include recipes, historical background, and traditions that describe how these special days are celebrated. Students can search the existing archive by month, holiday, keywords, or author.

3. PROBLEM SOLVING

These activities promote critical thinking and problem-based learning. Problem-solving structures include the GeoGame Project (www.gsn.org/project/gg/index.cfm). In this project, students work together to master geography terms and to read and interpret maps, as they develop a heightened awareness of geographical and multicultural diversity. Students must submit fifteen pieces of information about their city, such as a URL for their city, state, province, or country; longitude; latitude; time zone; population; January weather; average high temperature; average low temperature; January clothing; land forms; tourist attractions; and famous features. Once students have entered the data about their city, they may select data that another class has entered. Students are then given the charge to discover the location of the unknown class. GeoGame provides links to map resources as well as currency, language, measurement, and time conversions.

Other problem-solving activities include:

■ International Schools CyberFair (www.gsn.org/cf/index.html)
The International Schools CyberFair '99 is designed to strengthen the bond between schools and their local communities. Schools develop web-based projects based on one of eight different categories: (1) local leaders; (2) community groups and special populations; (3) businesses and organizations; (4) local specialties; (5) local attractions; (6) historical landmarks; (7) environmental awareness and issues; or (8) local music/art forms. Students and teachers access these displays to learn about communities across the globe.

■ The Geo-Mystery Project (www.hern.hawaii.edu/hern96/pt053/GEOMYstery/geomys.html). Two primary questions are at the crux of this project: What is unique about where you live? and What is unique about a place? To answer these questions, students select a location and develop a web-based description of this place. The description must include latitude and longitude coordinates, and may also include digital photographs, drawings, or text. Using the student-generated clues, other students then attempt to identify the location.

■ Flat Stanley Project (www.schoolworld.asn.au/flatstan.html)
Join author Jeff Brown's Flat Stanley as he travels from classroom to classroom around the globe. Students create a paper version of Flat Stanley and send it along with a letter that includes information that describes their community, such as weather, latitude and longitude, population, special descriptors, and seasonal activities. These letters serve as an excellent resource to learn about communities around the globe.

Geographic Information System: Middle School Examples

A call comes in to a town water department. The caller, quite hysterical, breathlessly describes a gushing water main struck by a bulldozer. The operator asks, "What's your location?" "Honeysuckle and West 17th!" The operator consults a computerized map of the city, locates the water main, hydrants, and connections, and then contacts a dispatcher. Searching the board for the response vehicle nearest the location, the dispatcher orders, "Immediate response, possible broken main, Honeysuckle and 17th!" From there, the dispatcher instructs the responders exactly which sections of the water pipe to shut off temporarily, and repairs begin.

The computerized maps used to locate the water main and the response team are part of a system known as a GIS (Geographic Information System). GIS is a small acronym for a powerful set of tools. GIS can translate data from multiple data bases—say, street addresses, water distribution systems, and water hydrant locations—and relate this information to a map. For an introduction to GIS, visit the on-line demonstrations at www.esri.com.

The most familiar GIS maps are those seen on television weather forecasts. The information represented on the weather map screen comes from digital satellite information; satellites do not send "pictures" per se; they send digital data that is translated through a GIS into a spatial map format. Those digitized cloud patterns that are generated and repeatedly shown to move across the map are digital images in a special spatial information system.

Like televised weather maps, GIS mapping applications are used in more and more government agencies, businesses, and industries every day. With their imaging capabilities taken for granted and readily understood from the visual presentation, the application is rapidly becoming of interest to educators. GIS will probably be as extensively used in the near future as word processing is today. Because of the rapid growth of applications, and because students with GIS skills can command wages even in their high school years, the integration of GIS in education is imminent. More information about undergraduate GIS programs and GIS jobs may be found at www.plangraphics.com/doclist/schools/schlsud/schudi.html and www.gis.umn.edu/rsgisinfo/jobs.html.

Maps are built in "layers." In hand-drawn mapping, the layers usually represent the different colors found on a map, as in topographic quadrangle maps that show land contours in brown, water in blue, vegetation in green, and the built environment in black, red, or purple. To print such maps, the required four-color separation in some ways determined how the information was "layered." A GIS map can correlate many more "layers" of information, and can do so in adjustable zoom-in and zoom-out scales in seconds electronically. Some GIS programs can vary the angles at which a map or graphic is represented from the standard bird's eye view to a more oblique view, and others can rotate and transform images to produce 3-D modeling and in other ways as well.

The development of GIS applications and software coincides with the study of geography. For example:

▌ Census Bureau data are used to generate all manner of census information maps to compare national, regional, state, municipal, and block statistics and population information. (www.census.gov)

▌ Cultural features at historic and archaeological sites can be digitally mapped and displayed as areas for preservation: www.execpc.com/~dboals/arch.html, www.links2go.com/topic/Archaeology, www.ercomer.org/wwwvl/alphabetical/index.html, and anthrotech.com/resources.

▌ Transportation mapping at every level is digitized, and distribution networks are digitally mapped.

▌ Utilities distribution networks and infrastructure are mapped digitally. These can be linked to automatic censoring and monitoring systems for locating emergency conditions:
  EPA Surf Your Watershed: www.epa.gov/surf
  Maps on Demand: www.epa.gov/enviro/html/multisystem_query_java.html
  Drinking Water Program: www.epe.be/epe/waterpartners/dwpgis.htm
  GIS for Water and Wastewater Utility Mapping: www.cowi.dk/div3%5F1%5F10.htm
  GREEN Net Watershed Links: www.igc.apc.org/green/resources.html
  GIS Data for Water Resources: water.usgs.gov/public/GIS/index.html

▌ National Parks, historic sites, wildlife areas, and other public lands are digitally mapped, as are specific resources in each of these areas. Physical landmark features, culturally significant features, artifacts, habitats and migration zones, recreational resources, and thousands of other features of historic, geographic, economic, cultural, social, and political interest are in the process of being digitally linked to mapping applications.
  National Park Service: www.nps.gov
  Teaching With Historic Places: www.cr.nps.gov/nr/twhp/descrip.html
  Links to the Past: Tools for Teaching: www.cr.nps.gov/toolsfor.htm

▌ U.S. Geological Survey (USGS) data have been digitized—the familiar topographic quadrangle maps are a tiny fraction of the USGS data that have been converted (www.usgs.gov). State agencies exchange state resource data with local agencies to identify all manners of tax map information: parcels, streams and rivers, flood zones, infrastructure, environmental information, and land use, to mention a few.

▌ Remote sensing and aerial photography can be integrated into GIS to produce detailed information on vegetation and human impacts as well as natural impacts. Across the North American continent, USGS satellite images are taken of areas of the earth's surface every two weeks. Data from satellite imagery is routinely being converted into map formats. For example, visit the following:
  United States Geological Survey: www.usgs.gov
  Global Hydrology and Climate Center: wwwghcc.msfc.nasa.gov/ghcc_home.html
  Downloadable Satellite Images, selected regions: members.aol.com/landsatcd/
    MOREHTML/nalc.html
  Microsoft Terra-Server: www.terraserver.microsoft.com
  Discovery Channel's "Earth's Past" site: discoveryschool.com/spring99/programs/
    earthspast/index.html

GIS in the Middle School

There are four conditions that more readily support GIS integration. First, integrating GIS requires an understanding of spatial, geographic, and cartographic concepts. Second, all successful GIS implementation in schools is done collaboratively; working with an Instructional Technology teacher is strongly suggested. Because this is an integrative information system, not a "plug-and-play" software application, teaming up is not only recommended but also necessary—and more fun! Third, access to PC-based computers and the Internet is critical. Fourth, using a problem-based approach is the best context for using GIS. Because it is a set of tools for integrating and analyzing information, having data to analyze is a better approach than simply learning the application.

There are now school projects using GIS applications that have websites describing and demonstrating activities and applications, such as the following:

- Powerful School Programs (www.esri.com/industries/k-12/hrschl.html)

- ESRI Lesson Packs (www.esri.com/industries/k-12/lessons.html)

- Links to Powerful Educational Projects (www.esri.com/industries/k-12/hrproj.html)

A team of middle school teachers at Ligon Gifted and Talented Magnet Middle School in Raleigh, North Carolina, has been working with GIS for two years in an elective course arrangement. The course has evolved from a one-quarter offering to a multiple-quarter elective taking advantage of various local "data layers" as the bases for problem and project applications. Visit the Ligon Middle School's GIS course at www.ncsu.edu/midlink/gis/courseoutline.htm.

In addition to the samples of projects demonstrated on the website cited above, the students are working on a web archive project and a habitat project in conjunction with a zoo that has radio-collared a group of elephants in Cameroon in West Africa. The zoo, with no available GIS lab, is thrilled with the middle school students' contribution to a project that would have been mapped essentially by hand. Using available map "layers" and assistance from ESRI Schools and Libraries, the teachers and students are mapping the movements of the animals they have come to know by name, even while thousands of miles away. Most important, the students are having authentic experiences, contributing a service to the zoo, and establishing relationships with scientists and veterinary school professors and graduate students.

Another example from Ligon Middle School is the Web Archive Project. Students have interviewed alumni of the school, formerly a Historically Black High School, and developed data bases of the alumni. Using the web and GIS mapping, the students are developing spatial analyses of the Historically Black community and linking this information to an on-line archive of photos and oral history videos. The project has led to recognition of the school and an installation of two permanent preservation exhibits— one in the school itself and one on school grounds—linking it to a municipal "Millennium Trail."

These types of projects highlight the potential of GIS in geography education—students contribute to their communities through their facility with technology. They integrate learning in real applications worthy of community pride and preservation, and they learn skills that enable them to command desirable positions at either entry level or beyond.

As GIS has co-evolved with the web, the amount of information available for integration into GIS formats has multiplied. While early pioneers of GIS in K–12 classrooms struggled with user unfriendly software and hard-to-get data, those looking to investigate and integrate GIS at the turn of the century have far more advantages with applications and hands-on demonstrations available at several websites, such as oddens.geog.uu.nl/index.html.

Map Collections: High School Examples

The Internet is home to thousands of interactive maps that are changing the way we teach and learn geography. One such collection of map resources is the Geospatial and Statistical Data Center

(GeoStat) at the University of Virginia (fisher.lib.virginia.edu). The center is host to data sets and electronic maps that can be manipulated and interpreted by students. For example, digital copies of the 1988 and 1994 county and city data books are on-line, and present an array of demographic, social, and economic conditions for U.S. counties, cities, and states. Access to this information enables teachers and students to customize data and explore a variety of topics that are not typically available with textbook maps. Students can use this data to create maps that allow them to interpret the data and draw comparisons over time and between regions.

GeoStat also hosts the Domestic Data Investigator (DDI), which posts data sets from the County Business Patterns and Regional Economic Projections. These data sets hold an abundance of authentic data that students can manipulate to create maps, ranked lists, and descriptive statistics. A publication of the U.S. Census Bureau, *County Business Patterns* reports business establishment information at county and state levels for the period 1977 to 1995. *Regional Economic Projections*, published by the Bureau of Economic Analysis, reports earnings, employment, personal income, and population information for industries at the state level from 1969 to 1993. It also includes projections for these data over the period 1998 to 2045.

Teachers can use these web-based resources to design activities in which students develop a fiscal plan for a particular county in their state. To prepare this plan, students first research the economic history of the particular county from 1977 to 1995. Students then construct a series of maps that provide a visual inspection of the county's economic patterns. Among the industry divisions they may track are agricultural services, mining, construction, manufacturing, transportation, wholesale trade, retail trade, service, finance, insurance, and real estate. Additionally, students must consider variables such as the number of employees and wages. These variables may be selected and layered on the web-based maps. After constructing a series of maps, students notice trends and forecast economic growth and development for a particular county.

The GeoStat center also hosts the USGS Digital Line Graph Data Browser. The data base has been produced by the U.S. Geological Survey to allow the user to create maps of selected data layers at state, multistate, or national level. For example, students can create a map of their state that displays information such as national forests, national parks, Bureau of Indian Affairs Indian Reservations, Department of Defense Lands, lakes and rivers, highways, railroads, airports, or national historic sites.

The GeoStat center also hosts the U.S. Historical Census Browser (fisher.lib.Virginia.EDU/census). The available data report the people and the economy of every county and state in the United States from 1790 to 1970. For example, students compare categories such as education, employment, agriculture, general population, housing, and business statistics. The table below illustrates a sample of state residents born in foreign countries in 1870 and 1960. Students may use this information to generate graphs and maps that help them visualize immigration patterns. Inquiry-based activities may follow, which help students understand why a particular state attracted more immigrants than another in any one year.

Residents Born in Foreign Countries

Year	Virginia	Texas	New York
1870	13,754	62,411	1,138,353
1960	151,506	1,027,487	7,273,250

The World Wide Web is home to numerous other interactive mapping sites. Among some of our favorites are the following:

▌ The National Imagery and Mapping Agency (www.nima.mil).
Includes maps of many foreign countries in various scales. Strategic areas during World War II are covered, as is much of the British Commonwealth.

■ CIA for Kids (www.cia.gov/cia/ciakids/safe.html)
Geography trivia questions for students are one of the highlights, along with maps of foreign countries and world regions. These maps are primarily intended to show political boundaries rather than topographic. Some demographic information, such as data on religious or ethnic groups, is included. A link to the CIA World Factbook is provided.

■ National Geographic's Map Machine (www.nationalgeographic.com/resources/ngo/maps)
National Geographic publishes facts, profiles, and flags for each country. The site also includes an interactive atlas, physical maps, political maps, star chart, satellite imagery, and printable maps.

■ MapBlast (www.mapblast.com/mblast/index.mb)
Users are able to make maps of a location by street address and gather information, such as local weather conditions and points of interest. Maps may also be downloaded to the PalmPilot or Windows CE device.

■ Outline Maps (www.eduplace.com/ss/ssmaps/index.html)
Published by Houghton-Mifflin, these outline maps are on-line for teachers to print or download for use in activities, reports, or stories.

Each of the web resources and classroom activities that we have presented here empowers teachers to teach geography in a way that we could not do before the Internet. Using these resources, students engage in content-rich, inquiry-based activities, which help students to develop technology-rich geography skills. We hope you integrate these resources into your curriculum and open your geography classroom to the world!

Geography Websites
Association of American Geographers (www.aag.org). Grant opportunity links, careers and jobs in geography, publications, and more.
National Geographic Society (www.nationalgeographic.com). Geography Standards; Geography for Life; atlas, forums, expeditions, publications, and more.
National Council for Geographic Education (www.ncge.org).
Geographic Education National Implementation Project (GENIP) (www.ncge.org/genip/index.html).

References
Harris, J. *Virtual Architecture: Designing and Directing Curriculum-Based Telecomputing.* Eugene, Ore.: International Society for Technology in Education, 1998.

CHAPTER 7

CREATING TELEDEMOCRACY

Bruce Larson
Western Washington University
&
Timothy A. Keiper
Western Washington University

Proponents of computer technology believe it can increase civic participation, provide communication for citizens across boundaries of time and space, and offer an unmediated form of communication. In this chapter we describe the use of technology tools for creating "teledemocracy" in social studies classrooms. Teledemocracy is a way for students to explore and examine perennial issues, then take social action. Although teledemocracy prepares students to hold the "office of citizen," it is not a mock or simulated experience. The Internet provides (1) a forum for the students to put forth their ideas to the global electronic community and (2) a tool for locating background information about legislation, political parties, and public officials at local, state, and national levels.

Teledemocracy

We live in an age in which media and computer technologies play increasingly prominent roles in many aspects of our lives. We can access information easily and communicate smoothly and effortlessly. Democratic participation is one of the many areas affected by the current information and technology expansion. This emerging technological form of democratic participation is often referred to as teledemocracy. Advocates of teledemocracy believe that modern technology can increase civic participation, provide communication for citizens across boundaries of time and space, and offer an unmediated form of communication. Teledemocracy is an outgrowth of liberal democracy; it helps sustain a "marketplace of ideas" and "aggregate individual preferences into a collective choice in as fair and efficient a way as possible" (London 1995, 50).

Supporters of teledemocracy highlight many ways in which this form of communication enhances liberal democracy: it creates a direct link between citizens and the government, ensuring the accountability of representatives; it provides a mass feedback system, giving representatives instant public opinion; it facilitates direct public participation through plebiscitary devices and direct interaction between citizens and policymakers; its electronic networks provide excellent means for creating political agendas; its new technologies create new ways to educate the electorate on important issues; and it creates an excellent information source (London 1994; Winford 1997).

The Internet may hold potential as one of the most rapidly expanding branches of teledemocracy. Regarding democratic participation, it is credited with providing the same enrichment that it has given to many other aspects of our lives. The Internet has allowed greater access to information, created smooth communication across time zones and geographic areas, given forums for people with common interests to discuss issues, and, overall, increased democratic participation.

Teledemocracy Applications in the Social Studies Classroom

In this chapter, we explore three avenues along which the Internet could serve as a tool for encouraging teledemocracy in the classroom: (1) the Internet provides sources for public information; (2) students can engage in electronic discussions; and (3) political participation may be facilitated.

SOURCE OF PUBLIC INFORMATION

One Internet use is to provide students and teachers with a variety of information resources. If students are to interact with others about public issues or democratic concepts, they need access to a variety of news sources. The Internet provides a way for the students and the teacher to gain information from and about political entities, such as legislation, political parties, and special interest groups. In addition, the Internet provides press releases and position statements from elected officials and on-line reports from a variety of news and information sources. Gathering information about important social and political issues can potentially tap into international sources.

ELECTRONIC DISCUSSIONS

Once the students gather information about issues, they can begin to engage in kinds of electronic interactions that are touted by those supporting teledemocracy. Discussion provides one of many possible ways for citizens to interact. A central characteristic of a democratic community, in addition to the free election of representatives, is the formulation of policy through free and open discussion (Bridges 1987). Such discussions can be characterized by "creativity, variety, openness and flexibility, inventiveness, capacity for discovery, eloquence, potential for empathy and affective expression" (Barber 1989, 355). Discussion with these characteristics becomes a process that promotes understanding and improved perspectives on issues (Mathews 1994; Parker 1996). Democratic citizens must participate in what Barber (1989, 355) calls "self governance." Self-governing citizens engage in "public forms of thinking, and participate thoughtfully in the whole spectrum of civic activities." The Internet provides students with access to democratic processes such as using teleconferencing with community or political leaders, using the immediacy of e-mail to communicate with public officials, and creating on-line class forums. On-line class forums show particular promise, because they are a type of discussion—an electronic discussion that enables students (citizens) to interact with each other about important issues.

POLITICAL PARTICIPATION

"Social studies is the integrated study of the social sciences and humanities to promote civic competence" (NCSS 1994, vii). The goal of the social studies curriculum, then, is civic competence. "Social studies helps young people develop the ability to make informed and reasoned decisions for the public good as citizens of a culturally diverse, democratic society in an interdependent world" (NCSS 1994, vii). This means preparing children to hold the office of citizen in a society organized under the democratic ideal that citizens share in ruling. Part of this is attained through participation in the political process. Through opportunities to extend beyond traditional limitations of time and space, students are able to interact with a broader audience than their classmates, community, or region. The Internet might facilitate forms of participation through political actions such as on-line polling of the electronic "community," signing, or distributing on-line petitions, "virtual voting" about issues, and writing and submitting articles to the newspaper electronically.

Classroom Models

In this section we present three specific examples of teledemocracy, which could serve as models, and suggest how the Internet might encourage teledemocracy in elementary, middle, and high school classrooms.

ELEMENTARY SCHOOL

At the site of the U.S. Environmental Protection Agency's Explorers Club, located at www.epa.gov/kids, elementary-level students of varying ages can gather information on environmental issues that have an impact on their community. The site discusses issues such as air pollution, water quality, garbage and recycling, and the care of animal and plant habitats. Students may explore their environment and discover ways to participate in its protection. More specifically, consider the topic "water quality," using the three avenues for encouraging teledemocracy as outlined above.

❚ Sources of Public Information
This site provides information related to the topic and an opportunity to learn through the use of various educational games. A student can search a data base of more than 38,000 documents and discover water quality information specific even to a region of a county. Students living near the university in Whatcom County, Washington, learned that, on a scale of 1 to 6, the quality of water in the county is rated a 5. Unfortunately, a score of 6 is the worst. County maps provide watershed locations, and graphs and charts provide easy-to-gather information.

❚ Electronic Discussions
Students have the opportunity to discuss this issue not only with classmates but also the electronic community via the on-line bulletin board for school children found at this site. Via e-mail, students discuss the quality of their water with elected representatives and community leaders, or directly with another classroom in another part of the country or world. Several sites listed at the end of this chapter have useful contact information to help promote this discussion.

❚ Participation
Moving beyond research and discussion, students in the Northwest participate in environmental protection through developing local projects that support clean water, such as painting "Drains to Salmon Habitat" by street runoff drains. These student-initiated ideas are then posted at this website to encourage other students to become involved in their communities. Furthermore, students are encouraged to write letters to their state representatives via e-mail or to electronically submit op-ed pieces to various newspapers based on their research findings. A page on the KidsWeb site, designed for elementary-level web users and located at www.npac.syr.edu/textbook/kidsweb/government. html , shows where comments can be sent to government agencies via e-mail.

MIDDLE SCHOOL

A nice opportunity for middle school students is the UNICEF site, Voices of Youth, found at www.unicef.org/voy. At this site, students are encouraged to take part in on-line discussions as well as to take part in a series of global learning projects related to current issues. Teachers may also enjoy the forum discussing the use of the Internet to enhance discussion of global issues.

In one portion of the site, titled "The Meeting Place," students confront issues that affect children. Current topics of discussion include "Children and Work," children working in factories, on farms, in homes, and on the street; "The Girl Child," a girl's path from prebirth to adulthood; "Children's Rights," every child's right to health and education, to be safe, and to be heard; "Children and War," how war and armed conflict affect children; and "Cities and Children," children in today's fast-growing cities. Each of these discussion topics has an index page that students can use to obtain general information or images dealing with the topic prior to engaging in discussion. For example, the "Children and War" index page includes powerful drawings made by children who have experienced war in the former Yugoslavia.These drawings, along with photos of children in war zones and statistics related to the topic, lead the students to an easy-to-use on-line discussion forum.

In another portion of the Voices of Youth site, titled "The Learning Place," teachers partner their students with groups elsewhere in the world. Through Voices of Youth on-line classrooms, groups of similar ages or grade levels meet to carry out projects and discussions. These projects could easily include important topics of relevance to middle school students.

Sites such as this one can be powerful tools to enhance democratic discussion with students from a variety of global perspectives. The reality, however, is that commonly these sites are underused and discussion is limited. Students may become uninterested because of the lack of interaction. It may be helpful to contact other classrooms directly with the intent of engaging them in a particular topic of discussion at this site. This may ensure posting on a regular basis, thereby ensuring more interaction.

HIGH SCHOOL

The Bergen County Leaders Forum located at www.bergen.org/AAST/Projects/Forum/index2.html is an example of a high school student-produced website that allows a community to examine issues of local interest and engage in dialogue with local leaders. This site also incorporates an on-line poll on several issues currently facing Bergen County residents.

To engage in an informed discussion of these local issues, users of this site are referred to several sources of public information. The local newspaper, *The Record*, has a number of on-line articles related to relevant local issues. Those items that relate to broader national issues have web links to sources of public information offering various perspectives. Another source of information by students from the local high school consists of persuasive papers that the students wrote for on-line publication.

Through this website, communication has been promoted between the community and a number of local leaders. Real-time chat sessions are regular features of the site. Two discussions noted by the site developers were with the North Bergen Fire Captain on the "Issue for the Day," and a "heated" discussion with a county executive on Bergen County Blue Laws. In addition, the community is invited to post comments related to a variety of issues on the Web Board, the equivalent of the sixteenth-century church door.

This site encourages a form of political participation not only through the electronic discussion component but also through the use of on-line polls. Users choose a topic of local concern and register their opinion at the site-generated polls. For example, related to the local issues "Blue Laws," the user is asked to respond to the question, Should people in Bergen County be allowed to shop on Sundays?

The Bergen County Leaders Forum is an example of student-generated teledemocracy. Not only do students have the opportunity to participate in the democratic process; they may create a mechanism by which others can participate. Because this site is intended for a local audience, it would have limited appeal to high school students in other parts of the country. This site, however, could serve as a useful model for other interested student web developers as a community service project. Be certain that to produce a similar site, a great deal of technical support from the local district would be required.

The use of the Internet in classrooms has potential for a type of democratic participation that transcends time and place. This type of participation, which we have labeled teledemocracy, relies on the Internet. In this chapter, we identified how social studies teachers might use the Internet to gather information, engage in electronic discussions, and participate in a limited form of politics. Viewed this way, the Internet becomes a tool that teachers can use with their students to extend student learning and application of course content beyond the classroom.

References

Barber, B. "Public Talk and Civic Action: Education for Participation in a Strong Democracy." *Social Education* 53, no. 6 (1989): 355-56, 370.

Bridges, D. "Discussion and Questioning." *Questioning Exchange* 1 (1987): 34-37.

London, S. "Electronic Democracy: A Literature Survey." A paper prepared for the Kettering Foundation, Dayton, Ohio, March 1994.

London, S. "Teledemocracy vs. Deliberative Democracy: A Comparative Look at Two Models of Public Talk." *Journal of Interpersonal Computing and Technology* 3, no. 2 (1995): 33-55.

Mathews, D. *Politics for People*. Baltimore: University of Illinois Press, 1994.

National Council for the Social Studies. *Expectations of Excellence: Curriculum Standards for Social Studies*. Bulletin 89. Washington, D.C.: NCSS, 1994.

Parker, W. C. "Curriculum for Democracy." In *Democracy, Education and Schooling,* edited by R. Soder, 182-210. San Francisco: Jossey-Bass, 1996.

Winford, G. M. *Democratic Participation through Teledemocracy*. Tech Rep. No. 2. Bellingham: Western Washington University, Institute for Civic and Social Education, 1997.

CHAPTER 8

CIVIC EDUCATION

Bruce Larson
Western Washington University
&
Angie Harwood
Western Washington University

The Internet provides a multitude of avenues that enable civics educators and their students to explore the world of government and politics. Through accessing a wide array of information, exploring simulated government activities, and communicating with others about issues, students can use the Internet to participate in civic activities and events in several unique ways. Furthermore, the Internet offers opportunities for teachers to meet the civics performance expectations set forth by the National Council for the Social Studies (1994) and the Center for Civic Education Framework (1994). In this chapter, we focus on how civic education, including participation in community projects, service-learning, and the exploration of perennial issues, can be enhanced through Internet use. We address how teachers can use the Internet to help meet civic education standards and present teaching ideas to be used in elementary, middle, and high school classrooms. We also include several websites that are helpful for civics educators, including general civic education, government, and news and information sites.

Meeting Civics Standards through Internet Use

Each teaching idea included in this chapter is an example of how the Internet can be effectively used to enhance students' acquisition of participatory citizenship skills. The lessons are designed to help civics and government teachers meet standards set forth by national organizations and state departments of education. In the following paragraphs, we review national standards and explain how the Internet can be used to address them.

The National Council for the Social Studies Curriculum Standards (1994, 8) provide guidelines for citizenship education. The importance of having students connect knowledge, skills, and values they learn to civic action is stressed in the introduction, with a focus on acquiring information and manipulating data, developing and presenting arguments and policies, and participating in groups. The teaching ideas presented in this chapter address each of these skills through using the Internet to acquire information, explore avenues of participation, and provide background for proposing public policy statements. In addition, three of the thematic strands presented in the NCSS Standards are directly related to civic education and are easily connected to each of the instructional ideas presented in this chapter. The interactions of **INDIVIDUALS, GROUPS, AND INSTITUTIONS** (Theme **V**) can be examined through searching for types of organizations and information on the Internet and through creating and implementing community service plans as students explore varying positions on public policy issues. **POWER, AUTHORITY, AND GOVERNANCE** (Theme **VI**) can be explored as students determine what public policies exist, who makes the policies, and how policies affect their community. Finally, through using the Internet in each of our teaching examples, students gain a deeper understanding of **CIVIC IDEALS AND PRACTICES** (Theme **X**). Each teaching example provides an avenue for active involvement in the community and allows students to explore their role in making a positive difference to society. The following sections of the chapter present civic education teaching activities for elementary, middle school, and high school classrooms.

Elementary-Level Civic Participation Activities: Community-Based Projects

Across the country, elementary students have been involved in projects that make a difference in their local community—projects that require service and the spirit of volunteerism. For example, in the Bellingham, Washington, area, one class has adopted a road as a beautification project. Another class has made friends at the senior center. Projects such as these are vital elements in the development of well-rounded citizens: citizens who possess an understanding of community ideals as well as the ability to put those ideals into practice. This relates directly to the NCSS Standards (1994, 73), **CIVIC IDEALS AND PRACTICES** (Theme ❿), performance expectations j, which state that students should be able to "recognize and interpret how the 'common good' can be strengthened through various forms of citizen action."

Traditional community-based projects value a personal approach to issues. This approach values hands-on involvement and face-to-face contact with the local community, which requires movement beyond the confines of the classroom. At first glance, the electronic environment of the Internet may not seem well-suited to this approach. The challenge, then, is to use the Internet as a tool to enhance community-based projects without forcing students away from the benefits of a personal approach.

An example of this project type is Community Share Web: www.gsn.org/csw/index.html. In this example, students engage in an on-line community-based project by following a three-step process: (1) research a local issue; (2) produce a community-based website based on their research; and (3) submit the site to an on-line "community."

1. RESEARCH A LOCAL ISSUE

Students use the Internet and local sources to explore and describe one of eight aspects of their local community—(1) local leaders, (2) community groups and special populations, (3) businesses and organizations, (4) local specialties, (5) local attractions, (6) historical landmarks, (7) environmental awareness issues, and (8) local music and art forms. As with any research project, the teacher must provide guidance to aid the development of young researchers. Because of this, we include three web resources that may be useful for teachers:

> The Steps of the Research Cycle (Bellingham Public Schools): www.bham.wednet.edu/
> mod5.htm
> Evaluating On-Line Information (Western Washington University):
> www.wce.wwu.edu/sec/social/info.html
> Using Oral History (Library of Congress): memory.loc.gov/ammem/ndlpedu/lessons/
> oralhist/ohguide.html

A Step One Example. Students at University Park Elementary chose to explore a local environmental awareness issue, the Chena River Ecosystem, a small river running through Fairbanks, Alaska. The students determined if this was an area of environmental concern and noted special efforts that promoted a sense of awareness and action. To gather information and obtain equipment, they contacted the Fish and Game Department, the National Weather Service, the high school biotechnology program, Native elders, the University of Alaska, community members, and parents. The students used video and digital still cameras, scanners, computer software, libraries, books, museums, Probeware for measuring water quality, and oral interviews.

2. PRODUCE A COMMUNITY-BASED WEBSITE

Traditional classroom teachers have used the walls and bulletin boards of the school to display student work. The Internet allows an opportunity to remove the barriers of the classroom wall to "hang" student work on the electronic wall of the web. The benefits are twofold. Student-created web pages are published not only to provide a forum for students to describe their community, but, as importantly, because the community will benefit from considering the students' perspectives. A web-published project, such as the one described here, encourages interest in the community from both within and without the school culture.

As explained in other chapters in this bulletin, production of a website can seem daunting without adequate support. Basic requirements are server space, an ability to work with HTML documents, and perhaps a supportive technical adviser at your school!

A Step Two Example. The University Park Elementary School students created the Chena River Home Page located at www2.northstar.k12.ak.us/schools/upk/chena/chena.html. This site provides research information from the project. This includes photos, maps, interviews, student research papers, Internet links, letters, poetry, and much more.

3. SUBMIT THE SITE TO THE INTERNATIONAL CYBERFAIR

For many, the creation of a community-based website may prove adequate. Others, however, may find great value in sharing their site with the electronic community. These globally minded classrooms share their communities with students throughout the world and, in turn, have an opportunity for heightened awareness of many other cultures and communities. The Global Schoolhouse Network solicits entries into an international CyberFair contest, which encourages this global perspective. Specific instructions related to the submission process can be found at the Community Share website at www2.northstar.k12.ak.us/schools/upk/chena/chena.html. Project objectives, discussion questions, and activities are provided to start the process.

A Step Three Example. The Chena River Study by University Park Elementary School was awarded first place in the International Schools CyberFair'97 Environmental Awareness category. Part of the process required the class to reflect on the impact the project had made on the community. Their comments suggest not only a high degree of satisfaction with what was learned about this local ecosystem, but, perhaps more importantly, their delight and surprise at the parental and community involvement in the project. Their words best describe how involved and interested the community became:

> We were amazed at the amount of help and expertise that was offered to students and staff members…Parents with expertise in areas that are not generally discussed in school were able to share their knowledge with students and bring new perspectives to the forefront.

Middle-Level Participation Activity: Civics in Action through Service-Learning

Service-learning provides a way for middle school students to gain experience in "doing civics," and can be a powerful tool for helping students develop critical citizenship skills. The immediacy of local issues allows students to understand how they can have a concrete influence in the community and may help them to better understand the issues at a national or international level (Totten and Pedersen 1996). In this section we outline how the Internet and electronic communications can be used to enhance service-learning projects. We present a three-step approach to service-learning in which students prepare for the experience, engage in and reflect on service, and share an opinion on a public policy issue.

PREPARING FOR SERVICE-LEARNING

Prior to engaging in service-learning, students can use the Internet to research issues related to their service projects. The Internet is a storehouse that can lead students to national or international news reports about the issue, to local, state, and federal agencies, and to nongovernmental organizations. Exploring these sources enables students to engage in "reflective deliberation" (Avery, Sullivan, Smith, and Sandell 1996) by addressing the following questions:

- What is the issue, and why is it important?

- Who is interested in the issue, and why?

- What government regulations and policies exist with regard to this issue?

Using animal rights as an example issue, students locate information in the following ways. First, they can find out current news about the issue by using the web to locate state, national, and international news reports. National and international news can be located using either nt.excite.com or www.yahoo.com/News and searching for the topic name. Entering the term *"animal rights"* in either of these search engines will produce several hits to get students started on current events related to animal rights.

Nongovernmental organizations can also provide good background information for students. Two sites designed especially for kids are the National Wildlife Federation site, www.nwf.org/kids, and the Wildlife Conservation Society site, www.wcs.org. At each of these sites, students explore issues of wildlife habitats, zoos, wetlands, and water quality, in addition to the latest news about animals and conservation. Each site features a "Take Action!" button, which includes ideas for student projects. Accessing other sites such as www.animal-law.org, a clearinghouse for information on animal rights, www.hsus.org (the Humane Society of the United States), or www.wwf.org (the World Wildlife Fund) will help students learn who is interested in animal rights issues and give them insight into current controversies.

Government agencies are another source students can access through the Internet. If students enter *animal rights* at the searchable U.S. Congress website thomas.loc.gov, they can read related federal legislation. A state's Department of Fish and Wildlife is another good source of information about animal management issues (see the Washington State DFW site at www.wa.gov/wdfw as an example).

Prepared with background information found at these sites, students are now ready to turn to a final question, which will help them define a service-learning project: What is our interest in the issue, and how can service-learning help us to further explore it? Some students might want to study the situation of domestic animals by volunteering at the local humane society or licensing department, while others might be intrigued by conservation projects or by creating wildlife habitats in their area.

ENGAGING IN AND REFLECTING ON SERVICE

One of the primary components of service-learning is giving students the opportunity to reflect on their service. While students are engaged in service-learning, keeping on-line journals on a classwide listserve or posting e-mail reflections to the teacher are two ways technology can facilitate this process. In postings, students might describe their activities, note one or two things they learned during each visit, and raise questions they would like to answer the next time they go to their site.

As a culminating assignment for their service-learning project, students reflect on their experiences, reconsider the current issues, and communicate an opinion statement to others. Students may choose to write to other students their age, to local or national political leaders, or to the community at large. The Internet can be used to facilitate each of these types of communication.

Students who wish to share their positions with other middle school students could do so through writing an article for *Midlink Magazine*, an on-line magazine written and edited by middle school students, longwood.cs.ucf.edu/~MidLink. The Youth In Action network also sponsors an on-line forum specifically for students to communicate about service-learning projects, which can be found at www.mightymedia.com/yia.

Students who wish to communicate with local and national leaders can do so via electronic mail to their representatives. For helpful hints on how to write effectively to members of Congress, students can review protocol at www.sierraclub.org/misc/writecongress.html.

Students can also communicate their ideas with other members of their community by writing letters to the editor of their local newspaper. Once students compose and edit their letters in a word-processing program, they can e-mail the paper from Internet-connected classrooms or computer labs.

Finding background information on issues, reflecting on service-learning, and publishing opinions or sending opinions to public officials are three ways technology can increase the power of service-learning projects. For more information on the basics of service learning or on specific service-learning projects, we recommend browsing the National Service-Learning Cooperative Clearinghouse website at www.nicsl.coled.umn.edu.nslctext.htm.

High School-Level Civic Participation Activities: Perennial Issues in Headline News

An issues-centered curriculum has long been a philosophical foundation of social studies education. In a summary of research on issues-centered instruction, Hahn (1996) concluded that students who are encouraged to discuss issues and present their opinions are likely to have more positive attitudes toward politics and a greater tolerance of dissent. Ochoa-Becker (1996) defined three rationales for a social studies curriculum that is based on public issues: (1) to help students learn to become democratic citizens; (2) to engage students through the use of issues incorporating their personal interests; and (3) to help students engage in intellectual processes that contribute to reflective decision-making abilities.

In the section below, we describe an activity in which high school students connect current events to an underlying, "perennial" issue. Issues that transcend time and place are perennial in nature. These are the "big ideas" that cultures and societies have been wrestling with for a long time. These issues often underlie news events and current events. Current events hold the potential for being "case studies" of a particular issue. The lesson follows a four-step process: (1) Research a current event; (2) Produce a newspaper article, editorial, and political cartoon about this event; (3) Locate a newspaper article, editorial, and political cartoon about different news events that share a perennial issue with the current event; and (4) Publish student work. The class should be divided into groups of three, with each group working together to accomplish the goals for each of the steps in the lesson sequence.

RESEARCH A CURRENT EVENT

The teacher selects a current event related to a perennial issue addressed in the course curriculum. Students then search for more information about that event by examining other sources and conducting research on news service websites. The following list provides several possible starting points:

CNN Interactive: www.cnn.com
USA Today: www.usatoday.com
US News and World Report: www.usnews.com/usnews/home.htm
Newsweek: school.newsweek.com
The Associated Press: www.apalert.com
NewsLink: www.newslink.org/news.html
ABC News: www.abcnews.go.com

Students examine possible connections by brainstorming possible underlying issues. For example, a news account about the opening of a casino on a tribal reservation might be tied to sovereign rights or an account of a protest march might be linked to First Amendment rights. After students gain the necessary background information and understand this event and the perennial issue(s) related to it, they proceed to the second step.

PRODUCE A NEWS ACCOUNT

The student groups produce their own news account of this event—a newspaper article, editorial, and political cartoon. In it they follow a traditional journalistic approach by considering the questions Who? What? Where? When? Why? and How? By pulling from multiple resources, and from their research of the event, students attempt to provide the most accurate and up-to-date account of the event. Along with this account, the groups produce an editorial article in which they express an opinion about the news item. This will be facilitated if the event is controversial in nature, but the editorial may address ideas such as policy recommendations, interpretations of the news account, personal opinions of the news, and/or messages to members of the community. Finally, the group produces an editorial cartoon that represents the news event in symbolic and pictorial form. Every item in the cartoon symbolizes a real-world item. Students may rely on widely used symbolism (e.g., donkeys for Democrats, bulls for rising stock markets), or develop their own. Notice that the three news items they produce (the article, editorial, and cartoon) move from recounting the details to inference and interpretation of these details, which leads the students to higher levels of thinking.

LOCATE A SIMILAR NEWS ACCOUNT

During this stage, students examine other news events that appear to be related to their event because they share the same underlying perennial issue. These other events could be current, or they could be from particular eras in history. For example, to facilitate the exploration of a particular historical time period, the teacher might require the news event to be from the Reconstruction era, or some era that meets with the curricular objectives. The groups produce three artifacts that relate to the perennial issue: a newspaper article, an editorial article, and a political cartoon. These may all be related to the same event, or may be about three different events. However, they will all be related to the perennial issue. The Internet provides several excellent historical inquiry sites that serve as research tools for students:

News Accounts
Any of the news sites listed above

Editorials
Editorials on File: www.facts.com/eof.htm
Archives of local, national, and international editorials: www.4editorials.com

Editorial/Political Cartoons
Daryl Cagel's Professional Cartoonists Index: www.cagle.com/teacher
Cartoons for Your Classroom: Secondary School Educators Net Links
7-12educators.miningco.com/msub58cartoons.htm

Publish Student Work

Student work is published on a class-created current events website, and selected works are submitted to a local newspaper. Each group posts its account of the news event, editorial, and cartoon on the website. Each group also sets up "links" to the site(s) where the news account, editorial, and cartoon that share a common perennial issue might be located. In addition, the groups write a letter to the editor that explains how the current event is related to previous news events by a common, perennial issue. In the letter they provide insight into the current event by describing what they learned from their research about it, and about the other related events.

The classroom activities presented in this chapter provide examples of how civics education can be enhanced through Internet use. Elementary students engaged in community-based projects, middle school students taking action through service-learning, and high school students examining perennial issues can all benefit from the wide array of information available on the World Wide Web. Students can learn how to use the Internet to find information about issues, to participate in electronic discussions, and to communicate with classmates, community leaders, and other citizens. Each of these examples allows students to practice a variety of essential citizenship skills, including locating and assessing information, learning about current events, forming and communicating their ideas about public policy, and becoming actively involved in their communities.

Websites Supporting Civic Education
Previously published articles contain helpful lists of websites that will support civics education (Boldt, Gustafson, and Johnson 1995; Risinger 1997) and a list of websites for social studies education can be found at the NCSS website, www.ncss.org or socialstudies.org. We have chosen some sites from these lists and others. The Library of Congress and Thomas websites are excellent jumping-off points for study of the federal government. Each site contains numerous links to other sites of interest. Teachers and students are encouraged to explore the websites of their state and local governments, which often include helpful citizens' guides to state government and access to local and state representatives. These can typically be found by using a search engine and specifying your state's name followed by "state government." The following sites are of general interest to civics educators.

General Civics Education Sites
www.civnet.org: U.S. Information Agency: A source of international information on civics education
www.civiced.org: The Center for Civic Education: Civics standards, curriculum guides, and program descriptions
www.nagb.org: Site of 1998 National Assessment of Educational Progress civics frameworks
www.closeup.org: The Close Up Foundation
www.epn.org: Electronic Policy Network
www.americanpromise.com/home.html: The American Promise
www.nara.gov: National Archives and Records Administration

Government Sites
thomas.loc.gov: U.S. Congress
lcweb.loc.gov: Library of Congress (check for links to state and local governments)
www.house.gov: U.S. House of Representatives
www.senate.gov: U.S. Senate
www2.whitehouse/gov: White House
www.usacitylink.com/default.html: City Link
www.refdesk.com/factgov.html: Links to government sites
www.fedworld.gov: Links to government sites
www.statelocal.gov: Searchable state and local government information
www.washingtonpost.com/wp-srv/politics/govt/fedguide/fedguide.htm

News and Information Sites
www.cspan.org: CSPAN
www.psmedia.com: primary source site (world government's documents archive)
www.allpolitics.com: CNN/Time AllPolitics
www.discovery.com: Discovery Channel
www.pbs.org: Public Broadcasting System
democracyplace.org/~democracy/forum.html: Democracy Forum

References

Avery, Patricia G., John L. Sullivan, Elizabeth S. Smith, and Stephen Sandell. "Issues-Centered Approaches to Teaching Civics and Government." In *Handbook on Teaching Social Issues*, edited by Ronald W. Evans and David W. Saxe, 199-210. Washington, D.C.: National Council for the Social Studies, 1996.

Boldt, D. J., L. V. Gustafson, and J. E. Johnson. "The Internet: A Curriculum Warehouse for Social Studies Teachers." *The Social Studies* (May/June 1995): 105-12.

Carnegie Council on Adolescent Development. *Turning Points: Preparing American Youth for the 21st Century*. New York: Carnegie Corporation of New York, 1989.

Center for Civic Education. *National Standards for Civics Education*. Calabasis, Calif.: Center for Civic Education, 1994.

Hahn, Carole L. "Research on Issues-Centered Social Studies." In *Handbook on Teaching Social Issues*, edited by Ronald W. Evans and David W. Saxe, 25-41. Washington, D.C.: National Council for the Social Studies, 1996.

National Council for the Social Studies. *Expectations of Excellence: Curriculum Standards for Social Studies*. Washington, D.C.: NCSS, 1994.

Ochoa-Becker, Anna S. "Building a Rationale for Issues-Centered Education." In *Handbook on Teaching Social Issues*, edited by Ronald W. Evans and David W. Saxe, 6-13. Washington, D.C.: National Council for the Social Studies, 1996.

Risinger, C. Frederick. "Citizenship Education and the World Wide Web." *Social Education* 61, no. 3 (1997): 223-24.

Totten, Samuel, and Jon Pedersen. "Issues-Centered Curricula and Instruction at the Middle Level." In *Handbook on Teaching Social Issues*, edited by Ronald W. Evans and David W. Saxe, 237-46. Washington, D.C.: National Council for the Social Studies, 1996.

CHAPTER 9

ECONOMIC EDUCATION

Lawrence A Weiser
University of Wisconsin-Stevens Point
&
Mark C. Schug
University of Wisconsin-Milwaukee

Good teachers want to know how new technologies—like the Internet—can have effective applications in the classroom. Economics teachers are no exception. The Internet provides economics teachers with an excellent resource for locating timely, accurate economic and financial data as well as offering engaging learning activities for students of different grade levels.

In this article, we identify some longstanding problems associated with using technology to teach economics. One of the key issues has to do with data obsolescence. We describe a way of looking at resources on the Internet that involves the use of hubs, authorities, and content sites. With this framework, teachers can gain access to key sites on the Internet that are useful for the teaching of economics. We offer some immediate teaching activities that can be used now by teachers interested in economics. Finally, we close with a brief discussion on the future of teaching with the Internet and identify some of the potential problems.

Special Interests of Economics Teachers

Not all social studies teachers have the same interests regarding their use of the Internet. For example,

- History teachers have a special interest in locating primary source documents.

- Geography teachers have a special interest in locating maps.

- Government teachers have a special interest in securing the latest information regarding the formulation of government policy and pending legislation.

What might be the special interests of economics teachers?   We think they are of two sorts. First, high school economics teachers benefit when they have access to current, authoritative sources of data that can be conveniently used to illustrate widely accepted fundamental principles of economics. Second, economics teachers benefit when they are able to take advantage of the increasing supply of learning activities and simulations available on the Internet.

The Problem with Economics Textbooks

We know that social studies teachers tend to rely heavily on their textbooks. One recent study revealed that social studies teachers view their textbooks as assisting them with course organization, offering ancillary materials, enhancing student, learning, and providing complete coverage. Overall, teachers have confidence in textbooks. (Shaver 1979)

A frequent complaint among social studies teachers is that their textbook and ancillary materials are out-of-date. Textbook adoptions generally occur every five to seven years, depending on local school district policies. Textbooks themselves take years to produce. Usually, teachers are playing "catch-up" to find the most current information.

One difficulty of out-of-date textbooks is reflected in how authors and publishers illustrate basic points. A cursory examination of several high school economics textbooks suggests a reluctance on the part of authors and publishers to provide many graphs, charts, or tables that make use of current economic data—the latest quantitative information on international trade, new markets, inflation, unemployment, GDP, for example. This reluctance is understandable. Publishers would not want school districts to reject their textbooks because of their fear that the books would "age" too quickly.

Increasingly, textbook publishers as well as classroom teachers are turning to the Internet as a solution to data obsolescence. The Internet offers unique advantages to help the high school economics teachers update their textbook and ancillary materials with current and meaningful examples of economic data. The websites described below provide a wealth of information resources for teachers to illustrate economic principles and contemporary economic performance.

The Golden Oldies

Many economics teachers recognize that their discipline offers numerous opportunities to engage students in demonstrations, simulations, or other sorts of interesting learning activities. Consider the "Golden Oldies" of the high school economics course. "A Market in Wheat" is the name of an auction market simulation which has been widely used to demonstrate how the forces of supply and demand establish equilibrium price. Another classic is titled "Why Do People Trade?" Often affectionately referred to as "grab bag," this is a trading simulation that demonstrates the benefits from trade. These, and a few others, are the mainstays of "hands on" activities of the high school economics course.

The "Golden Oldies" may be giving way to new activities from the Internet. The Internet is providing alternatives to the standard simulations available to high school economics teachers. An advantage of the Internet is that it offers real-time opportunities for new learning activities. The explosion of stock market simulations around the nation provides the most obvious example. Other simulations involve finding federal budget allocations, managing a business, and conducting national monetary policy.

Also, the Internet offers several teaching activities to improve instruction in personal finance and money management—planning personal budgets, using credit, and engaging in savings and investing activities. Recently, there has been an expansion of various types of financial calculators made available on the World Wide Web. These provide convenient number crunching power for class projects and research assignments.

Now Topping the Charts: Hubs, Authorities, Content Sites, and Activities

Computer scientists of the Clever Project (*Scientific American* 1999) observe how difficult it is to find accurate information on the Internet.

> ... the Web has evolved into a global mess of previously unimagined proportions. Web pages can be written in any language, dialect or style, by individuals with any background, education, culture, interest and motivation. Each page might range from a few characters to a few hundred thousand, containing truth, falsehood, wisdom, propaganda or sheer nonsense.

The members of the Clever Project, while working to develop an improved search engine, have divided websites into two categories. Hubs (or gateways) are websites developed by people or organizations that provide extensive collections of hyperlinks to content websites in particular fields or specialties. Content sites are the websites that actually provide the content information. (These latter sites are called authorities by the Clever Project; we, however, reserve the "authority" label for those sites judged best at providing information that is comprehensive, accurate, reliable, and timely. In this article, hub and content site categories are used as a means to organize the Internet sites that we think hold the most promise for teaching economics. The emphasis is on the hubs and content sites that are recognized authorities in their respective fields or specialties.)

In addition, we have added a category of Internet sites that offer teaching and learning activities for immediate classroom use. These are well established, self-contained activities designed to allow the Internet to be used in an engaging and effective way by students as well as teachers.

Hubs for Economic Education

We have decided to limit ourselves to two sorts of hubs for economic education. The first set focuses directly on teaching and learning economics at the K-12 level. We have selected the two gateway websites— EcEdWeb and the National Council on Economic Education—as the authorities in this category.

The second set of hubs consists of those that offer hyperlinks to vast sets of information. This information is clearly organized, so that teachers and qualified students can locate the data and analysis they are seeking. In this category we have included Resources for Economists on the Internet by Bill Goffe and Econlinks by Scott Simkins.

ECEDWEB

EcEdWeb (ecedweb.unomaha.edu) is the most widely recognized website for teaching economics. EcEdWeb is developed and maintained by Kim Sosin, Professor of Economics at University of Nebraska-Omaha. On this site are links to a wealth of educational resources for economics teachers from K-12 to the college/university level. It offers several useful categories of information including general data and information regarding economics, and sites for K-12 teaching and college teaching. It is also the home of the Missouri Valley Economics Association (MVEA) and the National Association of Economic Educators (NAEE) Home Page.

One set of links focuses on economic data and information. Other hyperlinks are contained under the following categories:

- General Economics Sites
- Economy-wide, Macro Data, and Employment
- International Data
- Government Budgets and Debt
- Money, Currencies, and Finance
- Stocks, Mutual Funds, Company Information
- Personal Finance
- Population and Places
- Government and Politics
- Environmental Economic Information
- Economic Journals, Economists Directories, Working Papers
- A Variety of Opinions about Economic Issues

A second set of links at EcEdWeb is titled "Economic Resources for Teachers." It highlights curriculum materials, web teaching ideas, and several useful websites. Most useful to teachers are the extensive links to curriculum materials. Included here are lessons that teachers can use right away. Other links are descriptions of larger sets of materials (teacher guides, lesson plans, activities) that can be ordered for a small fee. Ordering information is provided.

ECONOMICSAMERICA: THE NATIONAL COUNCIL ON ECONOMIC EDUCATION

The National Council on Economic Education is a nonprofit partnership of leaders in education, business, and labor. The mission of the NCEE is "to help all students develop economic ways of thinking and problem solving that they can use in their lives as consumers, savers, members of the workforce, responsible citizens, and effective participants in the global economy." Founded in 1949, NCEE is the main source of professional development materials for teachers in K-12 economic education.

NCEE is the lead organization of a nationwide network of state councils and more than 260 university-based centers known as EconomicsAmerica. Several state councils and centers maintain their own websites that often contain valuable information about state academic standards, workshops for teachers, teaching awards programs, and curriculum materials.

NCEE publishes and distributes books, teaching strategies, and resources for classroom use. It offers numerous opportunities for U.S. teachers interested in economic education. Moreover, it has an extensive international program, which features training programs on the transition economies and opportunities to participate in study tours.

NCEE maintains two related websites. EconomicsAmerica (www.economicsamerica.org) describes the overall NCEE approach. This site features the Voluntary National Content Standards in Economics, a list of curriculum materials, and links to university and college based centers for economic education and state councils on economic education.

The other NCEE web page (www.nationalcouncil.org) has information on economic literacy, national economics teaching awards, NCEE's annual conference, an update on current programs, and a link to EconEdLink. NCEE in partnership with MCI Worldcom maintains the EconEdLink website, which features resources for teachers and students, including NetNewsline, CyberTeach, and EconomicsMinute.

A Gateway to Internet Resources for Economists

Bill Goffe of the Department of Economics and International Business, University of Southern Mississippi, is the developer and editor of Resources for Economists on the Internet (rfe.wustl.edu). This website, sponsored by the American Economic Association, serves as a gateway to more than 900 resources on the Internet of interest to professional economists in academia, business, and government. It is a must visit site for teachers who are interested in the wide array of data and analysis readily available to professional economists. More than 20,000 visits to this extensive and rich hub are recorded in a typical month.

In selecting these authoritative resources, the editor exercises professional judgment. The items selected either offer a substantial amount of information or are specialized to a particular field of economics. Here are some of the categories of information:

- News Media
- Conferences
- Organizations and Associations
- Consulting and Forecasting
- Other Internet Guides
- Data
- General Interest
- Teaching Resources

ECONLINKS

Econlinks (www.ncat.edu/~simkinss/econlinks.html) is a gateway developed by Scott Simkins, Department of Economics at North Carolina A & T University. Econlinks is designed to provide easy access to basic economic and financial information on the Internet. It is aimed at college students enrolled in introductory economics or business courses, but it is a great place for K-12 teachers to visit. It contains links to numerous sites—many of which are appropriate for high school students.

Here are some of the categories of information:

- Current news

- Business news

- Financial market information

- Economic analysis and forecasts

- Economic data

- Federal Reserve Banks

- Business magazines

- U.S. Government agencies and websites

- Government publications

- International resources

- Policy institutes (think tanks)

- Student resources

- Teacher resources

Using Hubs and Economic Content Websites

Two types of websites called hubs (or gateways) and content sites have been discussed above. Hubs are intended to serve as entry points that provide hyperlinks to actual economic information. This economic information is displayed on other websites, which are called content sites. In the process of searching (surfing) the Internet, it may take many mouse clicks on many hyperlinks to arrive at the economic information being sought. Good hubs and content websites are able to facilitate the search process. They play roles analogous to those of reference librarians who direct their clients to the sections of the library where the information is most likely to be located.

Good content sites should be designed to help the client find specific information quickly and effectively. The information may be arranged alphabetically, as it is on the Country Listing web page of the CIA's World Factbook site. Alternatively, the U.S. Census Bureau's website arranges topics by the following categories: people, business, geography, news, and special topics. Many content sites permit a client to type in a term and submit it as a query. These mini-search facilities then transport the user to the exact location of the information being sought.

Once the user navigates to the desired economic information, the question arises as to the quality of that data. Evaluation of the quality of information on the Internet requires the same research skills as judging data in other forms. Criteria such as accuracy, reliability, objectivity, and timeliness must be considered. Because there are no professional librarians to decide which information may be published on the Internet, the individual researcher bears a much heavier burden of evaluation.

One approach to reduce the cost of evaluating information from the Internet is to rely on recognized authorities. In the context of the Internet, authorities have become the hub and content websites that are provided by recognized organizations including government agencies, educational institutions, news media, reputable non-profit organizations, and established business firms. Below are examples of economics content websites provided by recognized organizations of each of these types.

> *Economic Content Websites*
> Government Agency:
>   U.S. Census Bureau: www.census.gov
>   Income and Poverty statistics
> Educational Institution:
>   Ohio State University: Financial Data Finder: www.cob.ohio-state. edu/dept/fin/
>   osudata.htm
>   Links to financial information
> News media:
>   Cable News Network-Financial (CNNfn): www.cnnfn.com
>   Current industry information
> Non-profit:
>   Environmental Defense Fund: www.edf.org
>   Economic benefits of recycling
> Business firm:
>   Deutsche Bank Securities: www.yardeni.com
>   Charts of macroeconomic data

Your World, Your Country, Your Home Town

There are thousands of economic content websites on the Internet, and new sites are being launched daily. Teachers and their students are interested in discovering, locating, and using the Internet to obtain specific information for their curricular and research projects. But how is this knowledge organized? Economists often organize information and data into formal categories, such as those that follow:

- Microeconomics

- Macroeconomics

- History of Economic Thought

- Mathematical Methods

- Monetary Economics

- International Economics

- Financial Economics

- Public Economics

- Health, Education, and Welfare

- Labor Economics

- Industrial Organization

- Economic History

- Economic Development

- Economic Systems

- Resource Economics

- Urban and Regional Economics

Unlike professional economists, K-12 teachers and students are not usually familiar with these traditional categories. Fortunately, the Internet facilitates access to information by using a variety of "natural" and intuitive approaches. As an example, let us consider a search for knowledge that proceeds from the broad perspective of the whole world, then to a specific country, down to the state level, and finally to the narrow perspective of a particular community. We will examine several economic variables from the international, national, state, and local perspectives. All data will be located on the Internet, and displayed in Table 1.

Table 1. Economic Information: International, National, State, and Local (mid-1999)

	Population	Income	Labor Force
World	5,819,555 bill	$5,180 per capita	n.a.
United States	272,989,299	$36,399 per capita	136,297,000
Wisconsin	5,223,500	$41,215per capita	2,950,800
Portage County	64,752	$38,551per capita	37,200

Our general approach is to use a popular gateway or hub to locate specific content websites, and then use the alphabetical, categorical, or look-up facility to obtain the required information. For international data, The World Bank provides such a gateway at www.worldbank.org. By selecting Data from the list of categories on The World Bank homepage, we gain access to the data tables that provide the most recent information on population and income.

For the United States and Wisconsin, recent population and income data may be found on the U.S. Census Bureau website at www.census.gov. Labor force information may be found on the Bureau of Labor Statistics site at www.bls.gov.

It is important for economics students to develop the knowledge and skill to locate information on many variables by using these techniques.

Teaching Activities on the Internet

Here are some examples of teaching activities to demonstrate to students how they can use the Internet to locate a variety of economic, demographic, and business-related information. These activities can help students develop Internet searching skills in addition to specific content information. Students should document the "path" by which they obtained the content "answer." The path consists of a series of web page names or URLs that provided the hyperlinks by which the answer was obtained.

Activity #1: Locating Economic Information on the Internet

Student Name: _____

For each of the items below, provide the answer to the question and the "path" (series of URLs that you used to locate this answer.

Note: This is a 3-column question and answer table. Enough space should be given to each answer to realistically allow the student to fill in the series of paths in the third column. This may require a full page.

Question	Answer	"Path"

1. Current population of the U.S.

2. Gross Domestic Product (GDP) for the U.S.
   for 2nd Quarter of 1999.

3. Per capita GDP for the U.S.

4. Unemployment rate for the U.S. for August 1999.

5. U.S. inflation rate for 1998.

6. Unemployment rate for Wisconsin in July 1999.

7. What is the average snowfall in Wisconsin?
   (Hint: Badger may know this.)

8. How many Japanese Yen can you get for one French Franc?

Each time that an activity of this type is assigned, the dates should be changed to reflect the most recent information released by the respective government statistical agencies. Most questions are based on national macroeconomic data, but some state and local information should be required. International information should be part of these activities. Current answers to all these questions may be obtained by e-mailing the authors at lweiser@uwsp.edu or mschug@uwm.edu.

Four sets of activities for exploring economic related information on the Internet were developed for high achieving sixth-grade students, and these are available on the World Wide Web at www.uwsp.edu/acad/dbecon/ACCOUNT/MCKNIGHT/CDKwebpg/cdkpg1.htm.

Two well-established web-based teaching activities are described below. These provide teachers and their students with immediate simulations that have engaged students in economic transactions, analysis, and policy.

SMG2000

There are numerous stock trading games from which to select. Many offer great services at competitive prices. The Stock Market Game (SMG2000.org) is perhaps the most established. SMG2000 is operated by the Securities Industry Foundation for Economic Education. It offers teachers and students an opportunity to play the Stock Market Game, which is a ten-week simulation in which students may invest a hypothetical $100,000. The electronic game allows students to buy and sell securities on all major stock exchanges. Students learn to understand the stock market, the costs and benefits involved in decision making, the sources and uses of capital, and other related economic concepts. Accompanying curriculum materials are available from the National Council on Economic Education.

THE MINT

Northwestern Mutual Life Insurance (themint.org) has set up a highly interactive website for middle and high school students as well as teachers and parents. It includes many engaging sections including:

▪ Saving and Investing: How to be a millionaire by saving and investing wisely; includes a financial calculator of how much you need to save and when you need to start.

▪ Government: Focuses on spending decisions of government, including a visit to the U.S. National Debt Clock.

▪ Spending: Take a quiz to learn whether you are a spender or saver.

▪ Making a budget: Explains the importance of budgeting and allows students to create their own budget.

■ Learning and Earning: Learn about the financial rewards of completing school.

■ Quizzes and Games: Learn where to invest $1,000, the magic of compounding and complete the renting vs. buying calculator, or play the Real World Credit Card Game

■ Your Role in the Economy: How does the economy affect your spending habits?

The Future of Teaching with the Internet

The Internet has become the primary provider of current economic information. For many teachers, it has significantly changed the way their economics courses are organized and presented. Access to historical and contemporary data has become very convenient compared to the prior methods of tedious library research. Now, a few clicks of a computer mouse bring to the screen a myriad of charts and graphs of prices, output levels, incomes, and labor force information. As economists are well aware, it is extremely risky to predict the future. However, there are some clear trends developing that may provide some help in forecasting the impact of Internet technology on teaching methods.

Good teachers have always tried to demonstrate to their students the important connections between classroom activity and the "real world" of work, family, and civic responsibility. Now, many teachers are using the timely information on the Internet to demonstrate and dramatize those connections. In areas such as career exploration, financial transactions, political analysis, and economic growth, teachers can help their students experience and understand the relationships between academic principles and the contemporary world. This educational approach is so powerful that we believe it will become pervasive in K-12 education.

One concern of educators regarding the increased use of computers in schools has been that students will become more passive and isolated as they are spoonfed by their individual electronic teaching machines. This fear is especially troubling because we know that active learning and group participation are important ingredients in successful educational programs. Interestingly, the experience of most teachers is that using the Internet enhances active learning by encouraging students to explore World Wide Websites beyond those that are specifically assigned by the instructor. Internet investigations are driven by the student using his/her intelligence, experience, and imagination to acquire knowledge and build connections. We regard this type of learning as highly active.

With regard to isolation versus group participation, working with the World Wide Web and e-mail seems to facilitate communication between the student and instructor, and among students. Many students seem motivated by the process of creating web pages and sending e-mail messages. The existence of an audience seems to stimulate students to work creatively. Teachers can structure assignments so that students will share ideas, sources, and authorship with classmates, students at other schools, or even students in other countries. Students can "e-mail an expert" in business or government with questions or suggestions. This type of active participation and communication is an important advantage of using the Internet for teaching economics.

Convergence between traditional print textbooks and electronic web-based information is a rapidly developing trend in economic education. As discussed above, economics teachers rely on their textbooks, but data on recent economic performance becomes obsolete within two or three years of the date of publication. Textbook publishers are creating websites that provide links to current data, so that teachers and their students can take advantage of the most recent information.[1] Eventually, publishers' websites will be highly integrated with texts, so that economic principles and descriptions will be in conventional print textbooks, while current data and recent policy initiatives will be provided electronically. The print textbooks will have a much longer effective life, and the associated websites will be constantly updated.

Problems with Teaching on the Internet

Although the future of teaching with the Internet appears bright, there are several issues that need careful attention. Access to computing resources must be adequate. Teachers need good computers in their classrooms so that Internet information may be integrated with other course material. Good projectors are required so that students may view the Internet data, tables, and graphs in their classrooms. Students must have convenient access to computers and the Internet so that studying can be done and assignments can be completed.

The educational effectiveness of teaching economics on the Internet must be considered. Time spent using Internet resources means that less class time will be spent using traditional materials. Which content and activities will be replaced? Will learning be enhanced? Are there effective ways to evaluate the knowledge and skills that students will be acquiring by using the Internet?

There are some potentially negative aspects of teaching economics with Internet technology. Student cheating is often a concern at the seventh through twelfth grade levels. A student with ordinary computer skills can locate material published by on-line newspapers, magazines, and government reports. The student can simply highlight sections of those documents, mouse click on Edit and then Copy in his or her Internet browser program, and then Paste that section into the document he or she is preparing in a word-processing program. After reformatting the text, there is no trace of this plagiarism. Students have been able to "copy" materials in the past, but Internet technology makes this activity extremely convenient. In addition, Internet websites have been established to sell term papers to students, and deliver those papers over the Internet. Teachers must be alert for these problems, which have the potential to undermine our academic system.

A great deal of attention has been focused on the ready availability of pornography on the Internet. Although a very small percentage of World Wide Websites contain pornography, it is necessary to prevent students from viewing this inappropriate material. Careful supervision by teachers is one way to accomplish this mandate. Another approach is to use a software solution know as a filter. A filter is a computer program that prevents access to certain websites deemed inappropriate for students. Filters can be customized by the school staff to screen out specific content. Teachers may request an override of the filter to permit access to a website that is needed for a valid educational purpose.

Caution should be exercised regarding the placing of personal information on students or staff on the World Wide Web. Names, pictures, telephone numbers, and addresses can be used by legitimate businesses for marketing purposes, or by criminals to facilitate illegal activity.

Conclusion

We teach workshops and courses for teachers interested in economics. In these programs, we typically involve teachers in exploring how the Internet can be used for improving instruction. First-time users are simultaneously amazed and frustrated. They are amazed at the quantity, accuracy, and relevance of resources available for possible instruction. Many confess that they had no idea that so much information was available so conveniently. However, they are frustrated at how hard it can be at times to find the answer to what seems to be a simple question.

Because the Internet is a powerful and yet a confusing technology, we have tried to provide teachers with well-established and authoritative websites for teaching economics. We have introduced a system of how such sites might be used. For the teacher who simply wants to get started, we have offered some suggestions for explicit learning activities that students can start on immediately or sites that students can visit on their own to begin learning economics. Whatever way teachers choose, the time to begin is right now.

Note
1. Examples of publishers' websites that are closely linked to economics textbooks are: www.harcourtcollege.com/econ/ mankiw/ for N. Gregory Mankiw's *Economics*, published by Dryden; www.mhhe.com/economics/colander/ for David C. Colander, *Economics*, 3rd Edition, published by McGraw-Hill; and www.mhhe.com/economics/samuelson/ for Paul Samuelson and William Nordhaus, *Economics*, 16th Edition, also published by McGraw-Hill.

References
Clever Project, Members of. "Hypersearching the Web." *Scientific American* (June 1999), http://www.scientificamerican.com 1999/0699issue/0699currentissue.htm
Schug, M.C., Richard D. Western and L Enochs. "Why Do Social Studies Teachers Use Textbooks? The Answer May Lie in Economic Theory." *Social Education* 61, no. 2 (1997): 97-101.
Shaver, James P. "The Status of Social Studies Education: Impressions for Three NSF Studies." *Social Education* 43, no. 2 (1979): 150-53. Appendix I.

List of all World Wide Websites referred to in the article.
Resources for Economists on the Internet: rfe.wustl.edu
The World Bank: www.worldbank.org
College Days for Kids Activities: www.uwsp.edu/acad/dbecon/ACCOUNT/MCKNIGHT/CDKwebpg/cdkpg1.htm
National Budget Simulation: garnet.berkeley.edu:3333/budget/budget-1.html
N.G. Mankiw's Economics Textbook: www.harcourtcollege.com/econ/mankiw
David Colander's Economics Textbook: www.mhhe.com/economics/colander
Paul Samuelson and William Nordhaus's Economics Textbook: www.mhhe.com/economics/samuelson
Economics America (National Council on Economic Education): www.economicsamerica.org
Econlinks: a gateway developed by Scott Simkins: www.ncat.edu/~simkinss/econlinks.html
United States Bureau of the Census: www.census.gov
Ohio State University: Financial Data Finder: www.cob.ohio-state.edu/dept/fin/osudata.htm
Environmental Defense Fund: www.edf.org
Deutsche Bank Securities: www.yardeni.com
CNNfn (Cable News Network-Financial): www.cnnfn.com
U.S. Bureau of Labor Statistics: www.bls.gov
Wisconsin Council on Economic Education: www.uwsp.edu/WisEcon
The Mint: themint.org
The Stock Market Game: SMG2000.org

CHAPTER 10

GLOBAL EDUCATION

Bob Coulson
Bayside Middle School,
Victoria, British Columbia, Canada
&
Alma Vallisneri
Scuola Media Statale,
Arceto, Italia

We shall not cease from
exploration
And the end of all our
exploring
Will be to arrive where
we started
And know the place
for the first time.

T. S.*Eliot* Four Quartets

The above quotation from T. S. Eliot mirrors what should become an ideal of teaching. A teacher should strive to transform students into educational travelers, guiding them to an intellectual territory to explore, and encouraging and facilitating that exploration. In this way the students take on an active role in their own learning process.

Telecommunications is a tool that allows teachers and learners to enhance the exploration: to make contact with other intellectual travelers from differing cultures, to explore together and come to an understanding of their cultural similarities and differences, and to gain a perspective of our globe that relatively few have had the opportunity to achieve. This "cross-cultural understanding" is an important element in the acquisition of a global perspective, a major goal of global education (Hanvey 1976).

Acquiring a Global Perspective

A few years after having commanded the spaceship that transported the first humans to walk on the moon, Michael Collins (1974) described the development of his own global perspective. Other astronauts and cosmonauts have described similar awakenings of a global view of our planet. The World Commission on Environment and Development begins its report with a reflection on the experience of the astronauts:

> In the middle of the 20th century, we saw our planet from space for the first time. Historians may eventually find that this vision had greater impact on thought than did the Copernican revolution of the 16th century, which upset the human self-image by revealing that the Earth is not the center of the universe. From space, we see a small and fragile ball dominated not by human activity and edifice but by a pattern of clouds, oceans, greenery, and soils. Humanity's inability to fit its doings into that pattern is changing planetary systems, fundamentally. Many such changes are accompanied by life-threatening hazards. This new reality, from which there is no escape, must be recognized and managed.

The National Council for the Social Studies (1982, 36) defined global education in terms of the acquisition of a global perspective:

> Global education refers to efforts to cultivate in young people a perspective of the world that emphasizes the interconnections among cultures, species, and the planet.

The challenge for the educator is to foster the development of a global perspective in students, many of whom spend as much or more time in front of the television as they do at school. At the present, sending them to view the earth as it hangs in space is impractical. Travel, combined with action projects abroad, provides perhaps the next most opportune method of acquiring and enhancing a global perspective, especially in the areas of cross-cultural understanding, as described by Hanvey, Tye and Tye, Case, and others (Carkner 1995, i). Yet, as inexpensive as travel is becoming, it is still beyond the reach of most classroom situations. At best, a few representatives from a class can travel to foreign lands and move toward that all-important perspective. Their report back to the rest of the class, however, is not likely to cause a spread of their ideals, knowledge, and understanding. And so it falls to the classroom teacher to devise strategies for the incubation of a global perspective in the students in his or her charge—strategies that can be applied within students, school, and community.

What Is a Global Perspective?

Hanvey (1976, 163) defined a global perspective as being composed of five elements or dimensions:

1. Perspective Consciousness

2. State of the Planet Awareness

3. Cross-Cultural Awareness

4. Knowledge of Global Dynamics

5. Awareness of Human Choices

Barbara Tye and Kenneth Tye (1992) at New York State University offered their view of perspectives in global education, and again, it is the idea of being able to see life from someone else's point of view:

> The cultivation of cross-cultural understanding...includes development of the skill of perspective-taking—that is, being able to see life from someone else's point of view. Global perspectives are important at every grade level, in every curricular subject area, and for all children and adults.

Darling (1995) described how we acquire or aspire to "objective attitudes" when contemplating, approaching, or dealing with cultures different from our own. She saw this attitude as distancing ourselves from the life experience of the other culture. This "objectivity" is a cultural "zone of safety" that allows us to view but not feel, pretend to understand but not empathize. It is in this concept of empathy that cross-cultural understanding is cultivated (Hanvey 1984; Darling 1995).

Cross-Cultural Awareness

Cross-Cultural awareness is defined by Hanvey (1976, 164) as:

> Awareness of the diversity of ideas and practices to be found in human societies around the world, of how such ideas and practices compare, and including some limited recognition of how the ideas and practices of one's own society might be viewed from other vantage points.

This ability to place oneself inside the head of another culture and look back at one's own actions, motivations, and beliefs from the other cultural perspective is important to be able to negotiate fruitful agreements and undertakings regarding the myriad of problems that face our planet. It leads, almost naturally, to Hanvey's fifth dimension—the Awareness of Human Choices—as one needs to understand how another culture might arrive at decisions.

Case (1993, 318) accepted Hanvey's discussions on the dimensions of a global perspective as a starting point and expanded them to include two dimensions, substantive and perceptual. He described the substantive dimension as "knowledge of various features of the world and how it works." This substantive dimension, therefore, can be viewed as the international education component of global education, more of a physical, social, and cultural geography. It provides a foundation on which to build global perceptual understanding. Case's second dimension, the essence of his view of global education, and the one that accommodates Hanvey's five dimensions, is the perceptual one. This he describes as "an orientation of outlook." Further, it "involves nurturing perspectives that are empathic, free of stereotypes, not predicated on naive or simplistic assumptions, and not colored by prejudicial statements."

Global educators have animated discussions about what is the most important goal of their endeavors. Many believe that issues of development and appropriate technology in the so-called "developing nations" must be a top priority. Others point out that environmental issues must be at the forefront if humanity is to survive. Regardless of one's position, it must be accepted that, without the acquisition of a global perspective with resulting cross-cultural awareness, none of the goals of global education can be realized.

Using Telecommunications and the Internet to Promote a Global Perspective

It is now an accepted fact that we in the industrialized world live in the "Information Age" (Dyrli and Kinnaman 1995). This Information Age is the direct result of the rise of computer technology in many aspects of contemporary existence.

The Internet provides opportunities for students and teachers to garner information on almost any topic imaginable. It is a vast storehouse of information and resources for the global educator. But resources and information do not, in themselves, promote a global perspective.

The Internet must be viewed as a facilitator of global education rather than an end in itself. It is an important tool for facilitating the development of joint projects. Its speed, ease of use, and availability provide the ability to exchange communications daily regarding the scope and progress of projects, and to undertake common research as groups in far-flung regions of the globe can view identical sources and assess their usefulness quickly.

The informed educator is aware that there is a lot of garbage on the Internet. Anyone can establish a website. There exists little or no scrutiny of sites that purport to contain valid research on almost any topic imaginable. It is a good idea, therefore, to stick to sites that are established by academic institutions, government, or recognized foundations and organizations. A good rule of thumb is always "when in doubt, don't use it."

Telecommunications, Action Projects, and the Internet as Alternative Media

INTERNET TOOLS AND THE GLOBAL EDUCATOR

The Internet is actually made up of a number of services, all of which can be accessed on their own. The web is the latest implementation. Other services include electronic mail, newsgroups, Gopher, and file transfer protocol (FTP). All of these services can be of use to the global educator.

Electronic mail is a very useful teaching tool. From the point of view of an Italian English as a Second Language (ESL) teacher, it is important that students actually use the mother tongue of the culture they are communicating with to discuss issues that interest or concern them. Electronic mail can offer a "contextualized" practice with abundance of authentic language relevant to the students' studies. Moreover, e-mail allows us to communicate quickly over long distances and students can experience "intercultural communication," becoming aware of the existence of a global village of which we are citizens.

Language teachers will appreciate that e-mail is text based, requiring reading and writing. Some may argue that the writing in e-mail is too conversational and sloppy. Students soon find, however, that misunderstandings and miscommunication occur when poor grammar and spelling are in evidence. An ESL teacher or, for that matter, any teacher of a second language, will find e-mail a particularly effective method of using that language.

Newsgroups are essentially discussion forums on the Internet. An individual or school can access newsgroups by way of using a news reader program on their computer and requesting that their Internet provider forward a "feed" of required newsgroups. The user then joins the newsgroup and begins to take part in the discussions. Newsgroups come and go. There are many of interest to global educators.

Gopher is, regrettably, being replaced by the web. Before the World Wide Web was so popular, a lot of meaningful academic research was first made available via Gopher. Its great strength lay in its search engines and their ability to find any text items. Of course, it must be admitted that Gopher was never cluttered with commercial sites as the web is now.

File Transfer Protocol (FTP) is the set of rules the Internet uses to move files around from computer to computer. Most users see FTP only as a line in the address of the website that appears just before the file or program is downloaded to their computer. FTP is an Internet application, i.e., software program, that has been used by the authors to move students' work across the globe. For example, a group of students in various countries are coauthoring a report on hunger in an African country. One of the teachers has set up a computer in the school as an FTP server. The students, working at different times of the day due to their differing time zones, each can download the report to their computer, work on it for a period of time, and then upload the latest update back to the computer running the FTP software. Of course, the students working in the school hosting the FTP site simply sit at that computer to work on the file. FTP also is the process by which files find themselves on the WWW. The associated graphics, audio, and HTML files are transferred to a WWW server using FTP.

Getting and Staying Connected: Maintaining Electronic Mail Links

A number of sites have been created on the Internet for the purpose of establishing communications between classrooms. The Global Schoolhouse (www.gsh.org), a collaboration between the Global Schoolnet Foundation and Microsoft, and Learning Circles (www.att.comeducation/lcguide/p.intro/a.intro.html) are two sites that promote student exchanges over the Internet.

A very well-established organization—and the one the author uses almost exclusively—is KidLINK (www.kidlink.org), a diverse network of educators who sponsor projects and maintain e-mail lists for students and their instructors. From the very useful, and somewhat quiet, Kidleader list, to the chaotic Kidscafe, KidLINK provides an invaluable resource, all the more remarkable in light of the fact that it is maintained almost exclusively by volunteer educators. It is important to note, however, that KidLINK rigidly enforces its focus of twelve- to fifteen-year-olds and their teachers. As of this writing, KidLINK operates in fifteen languages, including Russian and Japanese. KidLINK boasts that 110,000 children have used its facilities and its related projects. In fact, this number is probably very conservative, as many—the authors included—use the facilities of the KidLINK lists to establish connections, and then maintain those connections over the years without necessarily making further connections with the organization.

Any teacher wishing to embark on e-mail exchanges and joint projects, regardless of their applicability to global education, must be aware that, like any important endeavor in education, maintaining e-mail contacts requires work. Most on-line educators can quote many examples of contacts that faded away, no matter how much effort was invested in maintaining them. When a productive relationship is established on the Internet, it is a valuable and important global education resource. Care must be taken to stay on top of communication, stay organized, and not let other pressing demands hinder the dialog.

Joint Action Projects Promote Cross-Cultural Understanding

Action projects, along the lines suggested by Ashford (1995, 27), become joint action projects with students in classrooms in other parts of the world. These transglobal groups of students make up an action team. The process of collaborating over the Internet with students in other cultures enables students to "share perspectives, ideas, with other students from around the world."

As well as giving students a focus for their energies, action projects serve as a vehicle to "empower" students and to alleviate the despair that can be acquired as a result of contemplating seemingly insurmountable problems or learning of painful occurrences of inhumanity and suffering. Students are paired or grouped into global action teams that formulate and/or undertake an action project.

Using electronic mail and the World Wide Web, students and their teachers can embark on joint action projects around one or more global education themes. They can inquire and promote international development in one country, region, area, or community, through the auspices of UNICEF (www.unicef.org), its companion site for elementary students, "Children First" (www.childrenfirst.org), or via Brown University's Hungerweb (www.brown.edu/Departments/World_Hunger_Program). Students can study campaigns and programs that are currently underway and become involved, or use them as a model for their own joint campaigns.

Educators and students focusing on the State of the Planet can begin their research using sites such as the World Resources Institute Environmental Education Project (www.wri.org/wri/enved) or The Amazing Environmental Organization Web Directory (www.webdirectory.com). Those focusing on Human Rights are advised to begin their research at the University of Minnesota's excellent Human Rights Library (www1.umn.edu/humanrts). FishNet is a global ecology project cosponsored by the Shedd Acquarium of Chicago and the Nature Conservancy in an effort to protect an endangered coral reef in the Dominican Republic (fishnet.org).

Victoria and Arceto: A Developing Relationship

In October 1996, in response to a posting on the KidLeader e-mail list of the KidLINK organization, a grade eight class at Bayside Middle School in Victoria, British Columbia, teamed with a class at Scuola Media Statale in Arceto, Italy. The class in Arceto had previously used the KidCafe electronic mail list service of KidLINK. They had found this service quite difficult to use, however, and, as a result, had posted an invitation on the KidLeader mailing list.

The two groups exchanged introductions over the Internet, guided by the principles outlined by the KidLINK organization. The initial goals of the teachers undertaking the communication were more international and linguistic, rather than global. The teacher at Bayside Middle School intended on using the exchange as a tool for expanding and enriching the grade eight social studies curriculum, particularly focusing on the Italian Renaissance. For her part, the Italian teacher's responsibility was English instruction. Any exchange in English, regardless of the theme or content, was intrinsically valuable.

As the exchange progressed throughout the school year, it became increasingly clear that something special was occurring. Many of the students paired over electronic mail were becoming very good friends, exchanging home addresses in order to carry on their exchange away from the eyes of their instructors. Long discussions took place between the students, comparing the cultures of early adolescents in the two countries.

The highlight of the project, as far as these writers are concerned, occurred during a discussion between two students revolving around each one's course of studies. A Canadian student mentioned an exercise that had been recently completed regarding medieval castles and queried her Italian partner on whether or not he knew anything about castles, and if there were any in the vicinity. The response can be paraphrased as, "Of course. We have a castle in the middle of our town. Don't you? Doesn't everyone?" This exchange, including the response back to Italy that, no, we do not really have any true castles, nor do we know of any place within a thousand kilometers or so that does, caused quite a stir in both classrooms. A joint project was developed where the Italian class went on field trips to their castle to study and map it so as to describe it to their Canadian partners. For their part, the students at Bayside Middle School began a large sketch of the castle from the descriptions in preparation for actually constructing a model. The Italian students become so enthralled with their project and resulting newfound appreciation for their own culture, they constructed a website to be viewed by all. This process is described by their teacher:

> At this point a project was born. Students in Brentwood Bay e-mailed lists of questions, and the students in Arceto realized that, to answer them, they would have to carry on a research. They were quite ignorant about the origins and history of their castle, even if they had studied the Middle Ages in history. So, the exploration of the historical background of Arceto started. What is most interesting is that the stimulus to it had come from very far.

The students and staff working on the project decided that the final product would have to be in hypertext (HTML). The teachers involved in this project were the history teacher, the English teacher, and the computer teacher. The "Contornual Algorithm Strategy," created by Nazareno Taddei, an expert in communication and education, was adopted as a guiding strategy. This methodology, adapted to school needs by Luciano Tagliavini, the computer teacher, was created to make audiovisual material of any kind, but it has proved to be most effective for making hypertexts. The scheme that was followed while planning the hypertext with the students was the following:

Teacher
  Objective:
    Concerning the subject
    Concerning the kind of learning to be activated
    Concerning the formative learning
  Logical Flow Chart:
    Analysis of the precise subject in its connection with the kind of learning
  Psychological Flow Chart:
    Analysis of the psychological situation of students
  Pedagogical Flow Chart:
    Choice of the method (deductive/inductive)and teaching style
  Expressive Flow Chart:
    Choice of the communicative means (conceptual/contornual)

Student
  Objective:
    What do I want to communicate by my hypertext?
  Logical Flow Chart:
    Analysis of the content of the chosen communication
  Psychological Flow Chart:
    Analysis of the potential readers of the hypertext
  Pedagogical Flow Chart:
    Choice of the style of the hypertext
  Expressive Flow Chart:
    Choice of the features of the hypertextual structure

Operative Hints:

- Fix a clear object.

- Fix the communicative content of the hypertext.

- Plan the steps of the activity.

- Identify the data banks.

- Decide the working modalities:

- Parallel modality=everybody carries out a different task that is part of the whole work.

- Modality=working together at the same task.

- Keep a record of the work done.

- Provide an evaluation tool.

- Find readers-revisers of the final product.

Although it can be rightly stated that this exchange was not global education, the two groups did begin a process of appreciating their own cultures and becoming increasingly aware of the differences in each other's cultures.

This year the two educators, after a year's break, have linked their classes again, with more of a global objective. Ideas are being explored for one or more joint environmental projects that would be truly global in nature. These joint action projects will move the exchange firmly into the area of global education.

There are many valuable sites on the Internet to use as research in international and global education. These sites offer a great deal of valuable information on conditions in developing countries and environmental problems worldwide. As long as one is aware of the plethora of misinformation on the Internet, and sticks to credible sites whose credentials are known, one will find much that is useful in the classroom. Yet unless this information is used in a meaningful way to advance the cause of one or more of the themes of global education, the exercise simply becomes one more of many on the students' road to completion of his or her course of studies.

Joint action projects, initiated and maintained over the Internet by two or more educators in far-flung locations, are a meaningful, inexpensive way to advance the cause of humanity and the planet we live in. Through the Internet, students discuss firsthand the issues that are under study, devise strategies to deal with these issues, and implement these strategies as an action plan. Relationships, begun via electronic mail, have the potential to develop into long-term partnerships between the citizens of countries thousands of kilometers apart.

References

Ashford, Mary-Wynne. "Youth Actions for the Planet." In *Thinking Globally about Social Studies Education,* 75-90. Vancouver: Centre for the Study of Curriculum and Instruction, Faculty of Education, University of British Columbia, 1995.

Case, Roland. "Key Elements of a Global Perspective." *Social Education* 57, no. 6 (1993): 318-25.

Collins, Michael. *Carrying the Fire: An Astronaut's Journeys.* New York: Farrar, Straus and Giroux, 1974.

Darling, Linda. "Empathy and the Possibilities for a Global Perspective." In *Thinking Globally about Social Studies Education*, 35-50. Vancouver: Centre for the Study of Curriculum and Instruction, Faculty of Education, University of British Columbia, 1995.

Dyrli, Odvard E., and Daniel E. Kinnaman. "Connecting Classrooms: School Is More Than a Place." *Technology & Learning* 16, no. 3 (1995): 82-88.

Dyrli, Odvard E., and Daniel E. Kinnaman. "Integrating Technology Into Your Classroom Curriculum." *Technology & Learning* 14, no. 5 (1995): 38-44.

Hanvey, Robert G. "An Attainable Global Perspective." *Theory into Practice* 21, no. 3 (1976): 162-67.

National Council for the Social Studies. "Position Statement on Global Education." *Social Education* 46 (1982): 136-38.

CHAPTER 11

GLOBAL ISSUES

Gregory A. Levitt
University of New Orleans

"Children around the world are getting involved in the issues
that affect them and their future well-being. Kids these days are
concerned about several issues from the health of the planet to
economic issues but they are especially concerned about their
welfare and what will become of their future."

David Pine, Executive Director of the
Foundation for the Future of Youth

The purpose of this chapter is to introduce methods of teaching about global issues in K-12 classrooms and provide information about using the Internet to better understand the world. In the first section, "Instructional Approaches," we look at ten approaches that can be useful for teaching global issues. The second section, "Student Global Internet Projects and Programs," provides twenty websites that offer information, teaching resources, and projects to help classes get involved in solving global issues and problems. The third section, "Global Issues Websites," outlines five areas of global issues and provides websites that K-12 students and teachers can use to research and learn more about global issues. The fourth section "General Policy Websites for Global Issues," provides a list of twenty websites that deal with overall policy towards global issues.

While all of the topics listed in this chapter are global issues and problems, some are more controversial than others. It is important for students to seek information from all sides of each issue and evaluate all evidence for accuracy or bias. The following ten instructional approaches to teaching global issues and problems open up many possibilities for effective class consideration of these topics.

I. Instructional Approaches

As we enter the twenty-first century, teachers cannot ignore the need to inform their students about pressing global issues. However, information alone is insufficient to meet educational societal needs. Teachers must also help students develop the knowledge and skills necessary to actively participate in helping solve important global issues and problems. Each of the following ten methods or approaches can help to get K-12 students involved in addressing global issues.

1. THE PROJECT APPROACH

This is an in-depth study of a topic undertaken by a class, a group of students, or an individual student. With your students, search for a local (global) issue and help your students devise a project(s) to work on for a one to two week period. One helpful site is that of The Learning Space (www.learningspace.org), which is produced by a group of teachers in the state of Washington committed to the use of technology in the improvement of student learning. Their site includes links to global connections projects allowing you to join other global classroom projects or create your own.

2. PROBLEM BASED INQUIRY INSTRUCTION

This method begins with a question or problem and follows the scientific method of inquiry. Helpful sites include the Webquest Pages site for web-based lessons using the Inquiry model (edweb.sdsu.edu/webquest/webquest.html). Also, the World Wide Web Constructivist Project Design Guide is a LiveText Guide to initiate experienced educators and novices into designing constructivist, cooperative learning projects around the World Wide Web (www.ilt.columbia.edu/k12/livetext/curricula/general/webcurr.html).

3. INTERDISCIPLINARY ISSUE-CENTERED INSTRUCTION

This method combines curriculum areas in English and Social Studies or Science which have common threads in the already established school curriculum. Many advocates of interdisciplinary approaches consider that this process will be more beneficial if only a few thematic conceptual units are utilized per school year. Two useful sites for this kind of instruction are: Water and Our Global Environment (Interdisciplinary eighth grade unit) at www.stark.k12.oh.us/Docs/units/1996/water.mr/ and K-12 Interdisciplinary Lesson and Unit Plans at www.stark.k12.oh.us/Docs/units/.

4. DISCUSSION

The purpose of a discussion is to solicit and involve the student in content transmittal. Discussions promote understanding and clarification of concepts, ideas, and feelings. With the Internet, students can have electronic discussions, via e-mail, with other people around the world. One helpful site is: EnviroLink Forum at www.envirolink.org/express/, which attempts to stimulate an exchange of information and ideas within the environmental community.

5. SIMULATIONS ARE ROLE PLAYS INVOLVING REAL LIFE SCENARIOS

Simulations attempt to approximate reality as closely as possible. Unlike games where there are winners and losers, simulations are simply role plays. They are effective both in skill development, and in helping students gain insights and understandings of things they would not otherwise get a chance to experience. The model United Nations is a good example (www.un.org/Pubs/CyberSchoolBus/munda/munmore.htm) In this simulation of the United Nations system, students assume the roles of ambassadors to the United Nations and debate the current issues on the UN's agenda. Through diplomacy and negotiation, Model UN students seek ways for the world community to deal with complex global concerns such as the environment, economic development, refugees, AIDS, conflict resolution, disarmament and human rights.

6. PANEL DISCUSSION

A panel discussion consists of the discussion of an issue or topic by more than one person, often under the guidance of a leader or chairman. In this type of exercise, participants clarify and evaluate their own feelings and opinions in relation to specific issues or topics being discussed and develop an awareness of the feelings, opinions, and rationales of others. One program that promotes panel discussions is the Great Decisions Program at www.fpa.org/program.html. The Foreign Policy Association developed the program in 1954 to engage large numbers of people in active discussion of foreign policy alternatives and to equip citizens to take action and make responsible decisions in the area of international affairs. Teachers can join this program or use its resource guide to set up panel discussions with local leaders in their classrooms.

7. RESOURCE PERSON/GUEST SPEAKER

As in most classroom activities, the success or failure of a classroom visit by a resource person is usually determined in the process of planning the appearance. The key to success is for the teacher to share information and ideas with the guest speaker. For a checklist of suggested preliminary procedures for having a classroom visitation by a resource person, see http://ss.uno.edu/SS/New/ResPerson.html. One interesting use of resource persons is that provided by Classroom Connect's Quest Series quest.classroom.com/market/aqmarket.asp. These programs allow students to use e-mail to contact and interview academic specialists in various areas during the projects, so that top experts can serve as resource persons for the students.

8. CASE STUDIES

The case study method of teaching is a widely used educational technique in learning situations, such as professional training. You could select a local company or industry to assign students a case study or select one, such as pollution in the Rio Grande, from the Trade and Environment Database (TED) at www.american.edu/projects/mandala/TED/TED.HTM. TED has a unique inventory of cases of trade and environment, and is a good starting point for research and discussion of trade and environment topics. You can search TED, participate in TED conferences, and even undertake your own TED case studies.

9. DEBATES

In debates, participants adopt a solution or approach to a specific situation and attempt to persuade others that their solution or approach is the proper one. The method of debate can be an effective device for encouraging participants to clearly and logically form arguments based upon evidence, and to develop a sense of efficacy in their ability to change policy or sway public opinion. One useful approach is that of McGraw-Hill's "Taking Sides," which requires students to synthesize everything they have learned and to present a coherent, well-researched, well-supported position before classmates and instructor (see www.cybsol.com/usingtakingsides/guide/method4.html).

10. MOCK TRIALS

Mock Trials are classroom recreations of actual or imaginary trials. Every attempt should be made to create an actual courtroom setting in the classroom. See, for example, the Center for Civic Values' National Mock Trial Competition (www.civicvalues.org/mock_trial.htm), which provides an intensive, hands-on experience in law and public policy, set in the context of the American judicial system. Each state develops a hypothetical case about issues of significant current interest. Teams of high school attorneys and witnesses spend several months preparing and then presenting the case to judges and juries of lawyers and community members at regional and state competitions.

Regardless of the teaching methods utilized in the classroom, there are always things that students can do to help solve global issues and problems. For example, you can educate your students about global issues, encourage students to talk to other people about global issues and problems, and write letters or send e-mail to senators, representatives, and government officials. Below is a listing and description of links related to various global issues and problems.

II. Student Global Internet Projects and Programs

The sites listed below are intended to educate and inspire students and interest them in global issues. They will be useful for teachers looking for appropriate ideas and programs, or for presentations of an issue that can provoke good discussions.

1. UNICEF's Voices of Youth: www.unicef.org/voy/
   Voices of Youth has been developed as part of UNICEF's 50th Anniversary celebration. Through Voices of Youth, you can take part in an electronic discussion about the future as we face the 21st century. This site includes "The Meeting Place," where students can share ideas about important world issues; "The Learning Place," where students will find activities to do and problems to solve; and "The Teachers' Place," where teachers (and others) can discuss human rights education and global issues, including the Rights of the Child.

2. International Youth Foundation (IYF): www.iyfnet.org
   Founded in 1990, the International Youth Foundation (IYF) is an independent, international, nongovernmental organization dedicated to the development of children and youth throughout the world.

3. Kids Can Make A Difference (KIDS): www.kids.maine.org/prog.htm
   KIDS is an educational program for middle and high school students, which focuses on the root causes of hunger and poverty, as well as possible solutions, and how students can help. The major goal is to stimulate students to take some definite follow-up actions as they begin to realize that one person can make a difference. This site contains a Teacher Guide, Hunger Quiz, Kids Newsletter, Kids Speak, Hunger Facts and some ideas in What Kids Can Do.

4. Youth Net: www.youth.net
   Youth Net desires to help educators and students turn their ideas from a local project into a global project. There are no fees to place your K-12 project on Youth Net, which allows schools to avoid the expenses of placing their server on-line or having a commercial site host their projects.

5. World Game Institute's What Can You Do?: www.worldgame.org/recall/whatdoenv.html
   The World Game Institute is a 27-year old, non-profit research and education organization whose mission is to supply the perspective and information needed to solve the critical problems facing global society of the twenty-first century.

6. Young Environmental Activist: www.globalresponse.org/yea/
   Young Environmental Activist helps sponsor student activism to protect the planet.

7. Global Learning and Observations to Benefit the Environment (GLOBE):
   www.student.wau.nl/~arnold/globe.html
   GLOBE is a worldwide network of students, teachers, and scientists working together to study and understand the global environment. Students and teachers from more than 7,000 schools in more than 80 countries work with research scientists to learn more about the planet.

8. Youth in Action Network: www.mightymedia.com/login.htm
   Youth in Action Network is an interactive on-line service for youth, educators, organization members, and classrooms who want to learn about, and participate in, positive social action and service projects. Issues examined include topics such as the environment, human rights, and more.

9. The United Nations Cyberschoolbus: www.un.org/Pubs/CyberSchoolBus/homepage/
   Cyberschoolbus was created in 1996 as the on-line education component of the Global Teaching and Learning Project, which aims to promote education about international issues and the United Nations. The Project produces teaching materials and activities designed for primary, intermediate, and secondary school levels and for training teachers.

10. One Day Foundation: www.oneday.org/we-are.htm
    One Day was founded in January 1994 by a group of committed high school students seeking to assist in the settlement of personal, national, and international differences.

11. Global Change Game: www.gcg.mb.ca/
    Global Change Game, which is played on a colorful hand-painted world map the size of a basketball court, explores the major global problems of our time.

12. Choices for the 21st Century Education Project: www.choices.edu/index.html
    Contains publications for students that include multiple perspectives on important global issues.

13. The "One World, Our World" School Assembly Program: www.1wow.org
    This is a special multimedia program that promotes peaceful conflict resolution with a global perspective and cross-cultural appreciation in support of Federal Title IV requirements.

14. U.S. Department of State's Geographic Learning: geography.state.gov/htmls/statehome.html
    This State Department site is useful for teaching geography and foreign affairs. It demonstrates how geography can help us better understand the forces that shape foreign affairs.

15. EarthALERT!: www.smcoe.k12.ca.us/besd/fes/pkelly/EA!.html
    EarthALERT! is a collaborative Internet project. This site helps students to search designated links to various sites on the World Wide Web, and then create web pages that will discuss the alarming issues faced by the world.

16. The Global Youth Program: stanleyfdn.org/citpro/GlobalEd/youth/default.html
    This site describes the educational activities of the Global Youth programs, whose projects address interdependence, human values and culture, the environment, peace, and change.

17. Facing the Future: People and the Planet: www.facingthefuture.org
    This non-profit site is dedicated to increasing awareness about the problems associated with world population growth and its economic, environmental and social effects.

18. National Institute of Environmental Health Sciences Kids' Pages: www.niehs.nih.gov/kids/home.htm
    The National Institute of Environmental Health Sciences (NIEHS) is the organization within the National Institutes of Health (NIH) that studies the effects of the environment (everything around us!) on human health.

19. Earthwatch Global Classroom: www.earthwatch.org/ed/home.html
    Earthwatch Institute is an international nonprofit organization whose mission is to promote sustainable conservation of the earth's natural resources and cultural heritage by creating partnerships between scientists, educators, and the general public.

20. EnviroLink Network: www.envirolink.org
    EnviroLink Network is a grassroots on-line environment community that unites hundreds of organizations and volunteers around the world with millions of people in more than 150 countries.

III. Global Issues Websites

This section is divided into five areas: (1) Environmental concerns, (2) Basic human needs, (3) Economic Concerns, (4) International Conflicts and Peace Efforts, and (5) General Policy Websites. In each section there is a listing of websites that offer information and analyses. We begin with environmental concerns.

1. ENVIRONMENTAL CONCERNS

Our natural environment affects most aspects of our existence. Below are seven environmental concerns: global warming, ozone depletion, deforestation, acid rain, desertification, pollution/toxic waste, and population. Each topic includes a list of websites with short description.

A. Global Warming

1. Global Warming: Focus on the Future: www.enviroweb.org/edf
Focus on the Future is the official web version of the exhibit "Global Warming: Understanding the Forecast," which has been touring the U.S. and has been on display at the Smithsonian Institute.

2. Public Utilities Commission of Ohio (PUCO): www.puc.state.oh.us/consumer/gcc/index.html
PUCO has been actively engaged in global climate change issues since 1994, and its site serves as a clearinghouse of information about global climate change. Its links explain the science and chronology of global climate change.

3. Our Planet Magazine: www.ourplanet.com
This is the magazine of the United Nations Environment Programme.

4. The Earth Times: www.earthtimes.org
The leading international newspaper on the environment and sustainable development, and such interrelated concerns as population, conflict-resolution, governance, and human rights.

B. Ozone Depletion

Friends of the Earth: www.foe.co.uk/index.html
This nonprofit organization pursues a number of campaigns to protect Earth and its living creatures.Its site has links to many important environmental sites, covering such broad topics as ozone depletion, soil erosion, and biodiversity.

C. Deforestation

1. Rainforest Action Network: www.ran.org/ran/intro.html
Rainforest Action Network works to protect the Earth's rainforests and support the rights of their inhabitants through education, grassroots organizing, and non-violent direct action. The site includes a section for kids called Kids Corner, which offers excellent suggestions to get students involved in civic action projects.

2. Deforestation: Causes and Solutions: www.davison.k12.mi.us/academic/global/deforest.htm
Deforestation is a major global problem with serious consequences for the world's climate, biodiversity, and atmosphere. It also threatens the cultural and physical survival of indigenous peoples. This site, hosted by Davison Schools in Michigan, focuses on the problem.

D. Acid Rain

1. Hot Links to Web Sites on Acid Rain: www.lakeheadu.ca/~garverwww/chem2610/acidrain.html

2. National Geographic Society: www.nationalgeographic.com
This site provides links to material related to the atmosphere, oceans, and other environmental topics.

E. Desertification

1. United Nations Environment Programme (UNEP): www.unep.ch
   This home page of UNEP offers links to sites dealing with critical topics of concern to students of global issues, such as desertification, migratory species, and the impact of trade on the environment.

2. United Nations Convention to Combat Desertification: www.iisd.ca/linkages/desert/desertsites.html
   This site offers selected Internet resources on desertification.

F. Pollution/Toxic Waste

1. National Oceanic and Atmospheric Administration (NOAA): www.noaa.gov
   NOAA warns of dangerous weather, charts the seas and skies, guides the use and protection of ocean and coastal resources, and conducts research. This site offers many links to research materials and to other web resources.

2. Toxic Waste River Rafting Game: www.niehs.nih.gov/kids/jvtoxic.htm
   Keeping the water supply clean and pure (and drinkable!) is very important. Take a tube ride down a "toxic waste" river in this site presented by the National Institute of Environmental Health Sciences, and see how long you can avoid the hazards!

G. Population

1. Six Billion Human Beings!: www.popexpo.net/eMain.html
   This site offers a unique on-line interactive experience that allows students to examine the mechanisms of population growth, see how the world population has increased in your lifetime, and discover other interesting demographic facts.

2. WWW Virtual Library: Demography and Population Studies: coombs.anu.edu.au/ResFacilities/DemographyPage.html
   This site keeps track of leading information facilities of value and/or significance to researchers in the field of demography. It contains important links to information about global poverty and hunger.

3. Population Reference Bureau (PRB): www.prb.org/prb/index.html
   On this site, PRB provides timely, objective information on U.S. and international population trends.

4. Overpopulation FAQ/Site Map: www.carnell.com/population/overpopfaq.html
   This website presents information on overpopulation.

H. Teacher/Student Resources on the Environment

1. Environmental Education Link: eelink.net
   This site offers links to environmental education resources on the Internet.

2. Green Teacher: www.web.ca/~greentea
   This magazine by and for educators aims to enhance environmental and global education across the curriculum at all grade levels.

3. KEY Knowledge of the Environment for Youth: www.key.ca/index.html
The Key Foundation offers students and teachers current information and teacher resources about the environment.

4. World Resources Institute's Environmental Education Project: www.wri.org/wri/enved
This environmental education project was initiated in 1992, based on the premise that educators play a key role in creating a sustainable future. Its four areas of focus are: developing high-quality educational materials; disseminating these materials through educational networks and teacher training workshops; working with educational organizations in other countries; and partnering with U.S. educational organizations to promote environmental education.

5. Fishnet: fishnet.org/
Fishnet is an organization that is devoted to using technology to help students and teachers look at global problems such as choral reef damage. This site is intended to be a repository for teachers to find and place environmentally oriented technology projects.

2. BASIC HUMAN NEEDS

Every human being is entitled to certain basic rights. Some basic human needs commonly addressed by the United Nations are listed below.

A. Health Care

World Health Organization: www.who.int
The home page of the World Health Organization provides a wealth of statistical and analytical information about health and the environment in the developing world.

B. AIDS

The 10 Most Pressing Issues Involving Children and Youth in a World of AIDS: www.fxb.org/kids/top_10_issues.htm
This resource site has leads and links for further information.

C. Women

1. Women's International Net: www.geocities.com/Wellesley/3321
Women's International Net (WIN) is an electronic magazine devoted to three purposes: furthering knowledge of women's issues worldwide; bringing together women from all over the world for dialogue and greater mutual understanding; and tapping new sources of talent in writing and enabling women from different countries to express their views and situations.

2. Global Gender Sites: pubweb.ucdavis.edu/documents/ggi/resources.html
This site is presented by the Gender and Global Issues Program (GGI) at the University of California, Davis.

D. Human Rights

1. Human Rights Web: www.hrweb.org/
This site offers the history of the human rights movement, text on seminal figures, landmark legal and political documents, and ideas on how individuals can get involved in helping to protect human rights around the world.

2. InterAction Advocacy Program: www.interaction.org/advocacy/index.html
InterAction is an advocate for international relief, refugee and development programs that save lives and help poor people help themselves.

3. Human Rights Library: www1.umn.edu/humanrts/index.html
The University of Minnesota has an extensive list of resources and links with access to the vast database of the Centre for Human Rights in Geneva.

4. Amnesty International: www.amnesty.org/
The Amnesty International site is regularly updated, and provides cutting-edge information on human rights around the world.

E. Education/ Nutrition

The State of the World's Children; Focus on Malnutrition: www.unicef.org/sowc98/approach.htm
This UNICEF site deals with the fight against malnutrition, showing how actions "as diverse as improving women's access to education, fortifying staple foods with essential nutrients, enhancing the spread of practical information and increasing government social-sector spending have all led to improved nutrition in a number of countries."

F. Sanitation/Safe Water
Sanitation involves the disposal of human wastes and the purifying of water so that diseases are prevented.

International Water and Sanitation Centre: www.irc.nl/
This site focuses on assisting people in developing states to get access to safe drinking water.

G. Shelter
Today, nearly 50 million people live as refugees or are internally displaced within their own country. Approximately 1 billion people do not have adequate shelter and 100 million people have no shelter at all.

World Shelter Project: www.daedalusproject.com/project.html
The Daedalus organization created the World Shelter Project to help alleviate two of the world's intractable and growing, population-related problems: those associated with the disposal of municipal solid waste, and the vast homeless population of the world for whom there is a critical shortage of adequate shelter and low-cost housing.

3. ECONOMIC CONCERNS
The economy of the country we live in determines much about our lifestyle. How easy is it to buy food? Is housing affordable? Are long-term loans common among our citizens? The following four topics deal with major economic concerns.

A. International Debt
This is one of the world's most serious economic problems, because growing debt payments leave few resources for investment in infrastructure, machinery, technology, or education.

Global Debt and Third World Development: www.mtholyoke.edu/acad/intrel/globdebt.htm
This site examines the debt burden of developing countries.

B. Poverty

World Game: www.worldgame.org/recall/poverty.html
This site of the World Game Institute deals with critical problems. According to the World Bank, more than 1 billion people in the world live in conditions of extreme poverty. They are either malnourished (600-800 million people) or the victims of famine (16-20 million), refugees (17 million), homeless or with inadequate shelter (1.1 billion); they have no health care (1 billion); their homes and neighborhoods have little or no sanitation or clean water supplies (1.7 billion); they are usually illiterate (1 billion) and have no access to education or educational opportunities; they have no energy supplies; they are often unemployed or under-employed (20% to 30% of population in developing countries); and, because they are most often powerless, they have the fewest human rights.

C. Energy

At the beginning of the twenty-first century, two to five billion people will depend on fuelwood for heating water and cooking food. But due to rapid deforestation, most of these people will live in wood-deficit areas.

To examine the question why access to abundant, clean supplies of energy is important to the world, see www.worldgame.org/recall/energy.html

For information about sustainable energy and development, the site of Solstice—the Internet information service of the Center for Renewable Energy and Sustainable Technology (CREST)—is worth a visit at solstice.crest.org/index.shtml.

4. INTERNATIONAL CONFLICTS AND CONFLICT RESOLUTION

A. Conflicts

1. Armed Conflicts Report: www.ploughshares.ca/content/ACR/ACR99.html
   This report lists and explains world conflicts, and also provides conflict summaries for countries and world regions.

2. DefenseLINK: www.defenselink.mil
   This is the official website of the Department of Defense and the starting point for finding U.S. military information on-line. The information systems BosniaLINK and GulfLINK can also be found here. The search function can be used to investigate such issues as land mines.

3. Federation of American Scientists (FAS): www.fas.org
   The Federation of American Scientists is engaged in analysis and advocacy on science, technology and public policy for global security. A privately-funded non-profit policy organization whose Board of Sponsors includes over 55 American Nobel Laureates, it provides a variety of resources of value to students of global issues.

4. ISN International Relations and Security Network: www.isn.ethz.ch
   ISN is a one-stop information service in the fields of international relations and security. Among the services offered are: an annotated links library, a limited area search tool (ISN LASE), a selection of resources on current world affairs, and specialized fact databases. ISN also develops educational modules in the fields mentioned and acts as a platform for networking, dialogue, and cooperation within the international security community.

5. ConflictNet: www.igc.org/igc/conflictnet/
Examines global issues and conflicts with particular concern for the Third World.

B. Peace Efforts

1. United States Institute of Peace: www.usip.org
The United States Institute of Peace is an independent, nonpartisan federal institution created and funded by Congress to strengthen the nation's capacity to promote the peaceful resolution of international conflict. Click on Highlights, Publications, Events, Research Areas, and Library and Links.

2. International Peace Academy (IPA): www.ipacademy.org
IPA is an independent, non-partisan, international organization dedicated to promoting the peaceful settlement of armed conflicts between and within states.

3. Project Ploughshares: www.ploughshares.ca
Since its founding in 1976, Project Ploughshares has promoted the concept of "common security": that security is the product of mutuality, not competition; that peace must be nurtured rather than guarded; that stability requires the reduction of threat and elevation of trust; and that sustainability depends on participatory decision-making rather than on exclusion and control.

4. PeaceNet: www.igc.org/igc/peacenet
The PeaceNet site supports action for positive social change in the areas of peace, social and economic justice, human rights, and the struggle against racism.

5. Carnegie Endowment for International Peace: www.ceip.org
As a tax-exempt nonprofit organization, the Endowment conducts programs of research, discussion, publication, and education in international affairs and U.S. foreign policy.

5. GENERAL POLICY WEBSITES FOR GLOBAL ISSUES

1. Policy.com: www.policy.com
Policy.com is a comprehensive public policy resource. Drawing from its network of policy influentials, Policy.com showcases leading research, opinions and events shaping public policy on dozens of issues including education, technology, and healthcare. Policy.com is non-partisan and free to users.

2. Great Decisions Program: www.fpa.org/program.html
"Great Decisions" is the largest nonpartisan study, discussion, and action program in the United States on contemporary foreign policy issues. The program is presented through the Foreign Policy Association, and the American Association of University Women.

3. United States Information Agency (USIA): www.usia.gov/usis.html
The USIA is an independent foreign affairs agency within the executive branch of the U.S. government. USIA explains and supports American foreign policy and promotes U.S. national interests through a wide range of overseas information programs. The agency promotes mutual understanding between the United States and other nations by conducting educational and cultural activities.

4. World Wide Web Virtual Library: International Affairs Resources: www.etown.edu/vl
   This section of the WWW Virtual Library presents over 1,400 annotated links in a range of international affairs topics. Sites are chosen because of long-term value, favoring those with cost-free, high-quality information and analysis on-line.

5. The Henry L. Stimson Center: www.stimson.org
   The Henry L. Stimson Center is an independent, nonprofit, public policy institute committed to finding and promoting innovative solutions to the security challenges confronting the United States and other nations in the twenty-first century.

6. International Institute for Sustainable Development (IISD): iisd1.iisd.ca
   The International Institute for Sustainable Development (IISD) seeks to promote sustainable development in decision-making internationally and within Canada.

7. The North-South Institute: www.nsi-ins.ca/info.html
   The Institute's research supports global efforts to strengthen international development cooperation, improve governance in developing countries, enhance gender and social responsibility in globalizing markets, and prevent ethnic and other conflict.

8. U.S. Agency for International Development: www.info.usaid.gov
   The United States Agency for International Development (USAID) is the independent government agency that provides economic development and humanitarian assistance to advance U.S. economic and political interests overseas. Issues such as democracy, population and health, economic growth, and development are covered on this website.

9. World Bank: www.worldbank.org
   The mission of the World Bank is to promote development by means that include building capacity and forging partnerships in the public and private sectors in developing countries. This website also contains links to other important global financial organizations.

10. Center for Teaching International Relations (CTIR): www.ctironline.com
    CTIR is a division of the University of Denver's Graduate School of International Studies. It provides teachers with the instruction and the materials they need to increase global awareness among their students.

Global problems may seem huge and unsolvable to most students. It is easy for students to think that nothing they can do will help, but they can make a difference. The information and projects listed in this chapter will, I hope, stimulate the interest of students in global issues and help them to develop the skills necessary to work in their communities to address these concerns and problems. Perhaps the best strategy for using the information is to select a project to work on and let students explore the wonders of the Internet and attempt to find solutions to major problems.

CHAPTER 12

ART-BASED RESOURCES

David B. Williams
College of Fine Arts at Illinois State University

History and social studies are the stories of everything that has happened—the study of the arts is part of the study of history. Music, visual arts, dance, theater, crafts, writing, and other arts are both artifacts of and a means by which to study a culture.

Douglas Selwyn (*Arts and Humanities in the Social Studies* 1995)

Resources from the arts can be found aplenty on the Internet and the World Wide Web (WWW). These resources can be integrated into stories that portray historical, social, cultural, and ethnological events. The arts not only serve, as Selwyn suggested, as a unique vantage point to study a culture; they carry the critical affective and aesthetic messages that are so important to truly experiencing an enriched telling of the stories of people, society, and history.

A Story: Migrant Workers and the Depression

An example will help to illustrate the power of using arts materials from the web for social studies classroom activities and for telling stories about people and events. If you were preparing a unit on migrant workers and the period of the Great Depression of the 1930s, you could search the Internet for materials from art, photography, painting, music, and theater to help build a story around this topic.

Figure 1 on the following page illustrates what you might find on the Internet from such a search, and presents a collage of windows open in a web browser from a variety of websites related to migrant workers and the Depression. (Links to all the sites illustrated in this chapter are listed at the end of the chapter.) These sites portray how integral artistic expression was to the lives of the people of this time. In the upper right-hand corner, a Library of Congress website, titled "Voices from the Dust Bowl," has a powerful photo essay of Depression-era migrant workers. There is a link from this site to jazz music of the period. There also appears another Library of Congress site devoted to theater projects funded under the New Deal and productions performed in traveling theater groups across the country during the Depression, some directed by such well-known directors and actors as Orson Welles.

In the upper left-hand corner, the Internet search reveals an Edward Hopper painting from the Museum of Modern Art in New York City. This painting portrays the stark contrast of the railroad, a key migrant mode of transportation during this time, and the large Gothic architecture of a home of the well-to-do of that period. Many websites can be found devoted to Jimmie Rodgers, whose music gained him the distinction as the "Blue Yodeler" and the "Singing Brakeman" because of the appeal of his ballads and yodeling in the 1920s and 1930s. The window in the lower left-hand

Figure 1: Migrant Workers and the Depression

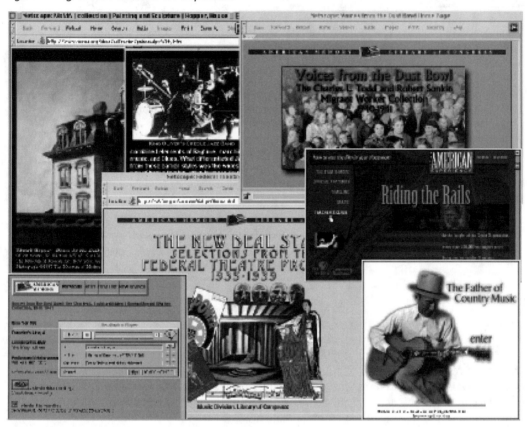

corner shows a RealAudio clip of the tune "A Traveler's Line," performed by Mary Sullivan. Such sites demonstrate the variety of arts materials that can help you build a story about American people and workers during this time.

The collage of websites portrayed in Figure 1 provides a springboard of ideas that could be used in a variety of classroom settings from elementary through high school. Middle school students, for example, could be encouraged to make comparisons between architectural styles of the wealthy (e.g., the Gothic architecture from the Edward Hopper painting) and those of poorer socioeconomic groups (e.g., shanties of migrant workers), present and past. Social studies teachers might analyze the song lyrics of a musician like Jimmie Rodgers and compare them with present-day lyrics from folk music. And high school classes could study and compare films that depict migrant workers, not only from the United States but from other countries and cultures, as well.

To make effective use of Internet arts resources, however, it helps to understand the technical nuts-and-bolts behind the graphics, sounds, and video used on the Internet.

Graphics, Sounds, and Video Behind the Web Stories

The web is a multimedia experience. To be multimedia it must use at least three forms of digital expression, some combination of text and fonts, graphics, sounds, animation, or video. We briefly examine the different forms in which graphics, sound, and video are created, stored or uploaded, and retrieved or downloaded over the web.

GENERAL DIGITAL MEDIA CONSIDERATIONS

All materials designed for the web are computer platform independent. This means that any computer connected to the Internet should be able to access and use these materials. There are commonly agreed upon universal formats for the digital media used on web pages: GIF and JPEG for graphics; AU, WAV, AIFF, and RA for sounds; and AVI, MPEG, and QuickTime (MOV) for video. All web files have a common two- or three-letter extension (e.g., photo.jpg, music.ra, or movie.avi) that must be attached to the end of the file name; this extension tells the web browser the type of media that must be displayed or played.

When creating media for the web, smaller file sizes are better. The bigger the file, the longer it takes to download over a modem or Internet connection. Digital sounds, video, and even graphics can result in very large file sizes. Each minute of digital music, for example, can consume ten megabytes of file space! When creating digital media for the web, one must balance issues of resolution (how good it looks or sounds) against the file size. The goal is to create the best looking or sounding media in the smallest file size possible. As we discuss each of the three basic media types, graphics, sound, and video, we discuss issues of resolution and file compression.

GRAPHICS

The quality or resolution of computer graphics depends on two factors: how many dots per inch (dpi) are used to make up the graphic and how many colors are used for each of those dots. A computer screen usually has a resolution of around 72-two dots per inch, so web graphics do not need to be any more precise than that. The number of colors can range from 1-bit (2 colors, black and white), to 8-bit (256 colors), to 16-bit (thousands of colors), to 24-bit (millions of colors). For most web graphics, 8- and 16-bit color sizes are the more common.

The two types of graphic formats used on the Internet are GIF and JPEG files. The extensions are .gif and .jpg. GIF images can have no more than 8-bit or 256 colors. This format is used for the colored line art and clip art you see on the Internet: the icons, the borders, the banners, and the like. The banners for the Voices from the Dust Bowl and The New Deal Stage web pages in Figure 1 are both GIF images. There is also a special form of GIF called "animated GIF" that can be used to animate artwork.

JPEG images can have millions of colors (24-bit color). This format is used for photographs on the net. With photos, you need a rich array of colors. The photo in Figure 1 of Edward Hopper's "House by the Railroad" is a JPEG image. Both JPEG and GIF formats perform special types of compression of the graphic information in a photo or clip art. The JPEG or GIF form of a graphic is always smaller than the original graphic. GIF is optimized for clip art with only a few numbers of colors; JPEG is optimized for photos with lots of colors. If you make a GIF and a JPEG of the same photo, you will find that the GIF file is larger in size than the JPEG, because JPEG is especially designed for photo compression.

SOUNDS AND MUSIC

The quality or resolution of computer sounds and music created for the web depends on two factors: how many samples of sound the computer records or plays within a second, and how precise a number is used to store each sample of sound. The sampling rate might be something like 22,000 samples per second. The sampling rate is referred to in kiloHertz or kHz. Common sampling rates are 11 kHz, 22 kHz, or 44 kHz. The precision of the samples is 8-bit or 16-bit, similar to the 256 or thousands of colors used with graphics. The "Traveler's Line" sound file shown in Figure 1 was recorded at 22 kHz with 16-bit sound samples. Web music recordings are typically 22 kHz with 8-bit or 16-bit sound samples.

The earliest universal sound format for sound files was the AU format. AU files have a very low resolution of 11 kHz with 8-bit samples—not very good for music. WAV and AIFF files are common to Windows and Macintosh computers, respectively. Most web browsers will recognize both formats. WAV and AIFF formats permit very high resolution (up to 44 kHz and 16-bit samples), but the file sizes are very large. The WAV version of the "Traveler's Line" is 4.8 megabytes in size. The RealAudio format (shown in Figure 1) is a proprietary sound format designed for Internet radio broadcasts; it provides significant compression of the sound file and keeps a high degree of music fidelity. The RealAudio, or RA, file version of "Traveler's Line" is a very small 200 kilobytes in size.

VIDEO

When considering issues of resolution for video, all of the factors for sound and graphics are also important. After all, a video is just a series of still graphic images with music and voice added. Most digital video is recorded with a graphic resolution of 72 dpi and 16-bit color, and an audio resolution of 22 kHz and 8- or 16-bit sound samples.

The new factors that must be considered with video are frame rate and frame size. Most videos that you see on television and in the movies have a frame rate of 24 to 30 frames per second (fps). Computers can capture video frames from 1 to 30 fps, depending on how fast the computer is and whether it has any special hardware to assist in the video capture. Capturing video and audio at 30 fps creates very large movie files! Many digital videos on the web are captured at around 10 to 12 fps. Frame size refers to how big the image is for the movie. Size can range from 160 x 120 dots, or pixels, up to a full-screen size of 640 x 480 pixels. Many web videos are 160 x 120 in size for this reason.

Three common video formats found on the web are Microsoft's Video for Windows (AVI) format, Apple Computer's QuickTime format (MOV), and an industry standard format, MPEG. MPEG is the digital video format used in DVD video discs. Figure 4, the Getty Museum's Forum of Trajan site, has several examples of QuickTime video, including what is known as QuickTime VR. QuickTime VR creates a Virtual Reality video that lets you walk through an environment—in this case, the Forum of Trajan in ancient Rome. The African Music and Dance Ensemble site in Figure 5 contains several QuickTime videos of dancing and drumming.

Ask the Internet to Find Arts Resources

How do you find arts resources for your stories on the web? Ask the Internet! Locate primary websites that specialize in the various arts topics (e.g., music, art, theatre, photography, film). Some sites are devoted to tracking and evaluating web links related to a particular topic. Several of these sites are listed at the end of this chapter. Excellent examples include the Indiana University "Worldwide Internet Music Resources" site; the Johns Hopkins University "Folk Music Index"; "The Artist's View of World History and Western Civilization" with links to resources all over the web, codified by historical locations, events, and dates; the "American Folklife Center" site sponsored by the Library of Congress; the complete works of William Shakespeare site maintained by Jeremy Hylton at MIT; and the Metropolitan Museum of Art's "World Wide Arts Resources" website. These are but a few to whet your appetite! A second strategy is to use keywords with the search engines on the web. Brehm's chapter in this publication provides excellent guidance for this strategy, as well as advice on compliance with "fair use" guidelines for presenting materials from websites in class (p. 14).

Four Examples of Web Stories Using Arts Resources

Having examined some of the technical issues related to finding arts materials on the web, you will find that additional illustrations of these resources will help in using them to create stories for social studies classroom activities.

RAILROAD WEB STORY

High school and middle school U.S. history teachers might want to explore the development of the railroad and its impact on the migration of the West and industrial development in this country. Figure 2 is a collage of websites related to a story about railroading in the United States. This variegated, exciting mix of arts sites portrays the folklore as well as the technology of the rapid expansion of railroading. In the upper left-hand corner is another Edward Hopper picture called "Railroad Sunset," from Carol Gerten's Virtual Art Museum. In the upper right-hand corner is an advertisement for the Sante Fe railroad's "Super Chief" passenger train from Chicago to Los Angeles. This ad is formatted as a JPEG file for downloading from the Internet. Below that is a page from the Rounder records site promoting its two-album CD disc of Classic Railroad Songs with both a WAV and a RealAudio version of the music for you to listen to. Notice the file size difference between the WAV and RA versions!

In the lower right-hand corner is a wonderful page on the MultiEducator virtual history site, featuring vintage photos of early steam engines. The thumbnail images are GIF graphic files; when you click on any thumbnail, a large-sized JPEG version of the image is displayed. Much more contemporary is the Art Crimes site in the top center of the collage, which features train art, murals, and graffiti painted on box cars from all over the world. And in the lower left is a page that presents the story behind Buster Keaton's famous silent movie, *The General* (1927). *The General* is based on a true story from the Civil War in which Union spies tried to capture a Confederate train in Georgia and use it to destroy all the bridges back to Chattanooga, Tennessee. Colored GIF images of movie posters highlight the story. Going beyond just railroading in the United States, history teachers could have their students study the interesting parallels between the development of the railroad and the development of the Internet, and similarities in the impact each has had on society.

Figure 2: Railroad Web Story

Figure 3: Children's Stories of the World Through Art and the Web

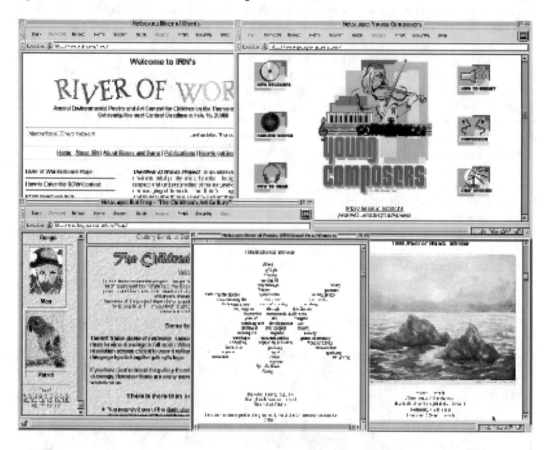

CHILDREN'S STORIES OF THE WORLD THROUGH ART AND THE WEB

Elementary teachers might collaborate with art and music teachers in their schools to promote social studies goals through creative arts activities (i.e., global understandings of people and cultures). Figure 3 shows three sites that feature children's creative work from around the world. Websites like these are ideal for teaching customs and culture through the eyes of children. At the bottom left of the collage is the Children's Art Gallery, run by Iwo Gajda of Oslo, Norway. Here you will find creative art projects from children, literally from all over the world.

In the upper-left corner of Figure 3, we see a window open to the River of Words, Children's Environmental Poetry and Art Contest. The contest was sponsored by the International Rivers Network. The River of Words page of its site provides many exhibits of both poetry and art from children around the globe related to river conservation, such as those in the lower center and the right-hand corner of the figure. Most of the graphics from the art exhibits are saved as JPEG images. In the upper right-hand corner of Figure 3, you see a website devoted to music compositions by young composers worldwide. These files are in MIDI format, a special music format that requires a MIDI music device installed in your computer to play back the composition.

TRAJAN FORUM WEB STORY

High school history teachers can take advantage of objects of art, and architectural drawing and modeling, to help add realism to the study of ancient cultures—bringing museums and exhibits into the classroom. The Getty Foundation has a number of rich and exciting web projects that are most appropriate for social studies and history study. The one featured in Figure 4 is a virtual reality site drawn from an exhibit on display in 1998 at the J. Paul Getty Museum, titled "Beyond Beauty: Antiquities as Evidence." The on-line exhibit uses QuickTime virtual reality, or VR, videos to let you and your students walk through a computer reconstruction of the Forum built by Emperor Trajan in Rome around AD 98.

As you walk through the on-line exhibit, you see photographs of actual antiquities from the Getty exhibit as well as computer VR models that show you what it was really like to visit these incredible structures. The window in the lower left corner of Figure 4 is a statue of Trajan himself. The site includes a QuickTime VR movie that looks inside the Basilica as it may have appeared many, many years ago. You can select VR movies that let you walk through the courtyard as well as the library of the forum. Other QuickTime videos tell the story of how these simulations were created.

On the right side of the collage is the website of Synaulia, a music ensemble that specializes in the music and instruments of ancient Rome. This site again illustrates the depth of material available to help you provide a deeper and richer view of topics in social studies. Comparisons of musical instruments and performing groups popular today provide wonderful connections to the past.

Figure 4: Trajan Forum Web Story

Figure 5: African Culture Web Story

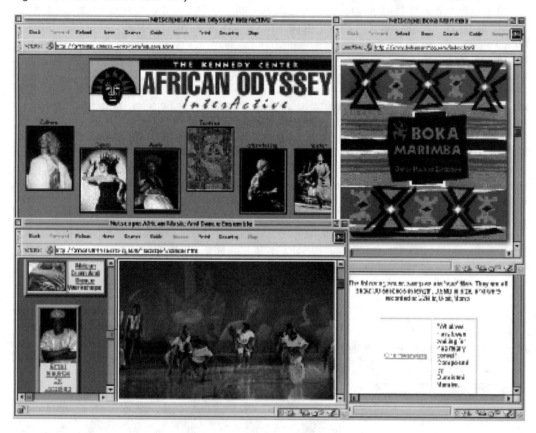

AFRICAN CULTURE WEB STORY

Social studies teachers at all levels are looking for new ways to integrate multicultural content into classroom activities. The arts provide a rich resource toward this goal. Figure 5 shows a collage of windows from various sites related to Africa. In the upper left-hand corner is an interactive site devoted to the arts and culture of Africa and the Kennedy Center's African Odyssey Festival. The image that creates the banner for this site is a GIF image.

Below this window is a site dedicated to the African Music and Dance. This site is rich in QuickTime videos, GIF and JPEG images, and digital audio files. In the upper right-hand corner, the window shows the website of the Boka Marimba ensemble, a group from Portland, Oregon, that specializes in the music of Zimbabwe. The site includes a link to a WAV sound file of one of its compositions, "Chemwanyiera." Notice that the sound was recorded at 22 kHz, 8-bit, mono. Most of the images on the site are GIF graphics.

Tips for Creating Your Own Web Art and Music

One thing we have not discussed is how you and your students can create these images yourselves. In the interest of space, a brief mention of the common software and hardware tools will suffice.

GRAPHICS

The major industry software program for editing digital graphics is Adobe Photoshop for both Macintosh and Windows computers. It is available in a scaled-down, less expensive version as PhotoDeluxe. Two popular shareware programs for graphics editing are GraphicConverter (Mac) and

LViewPro (Win). All of these applications handle JPEG and GIF file formats and their conversion from other popular formats, such as PICT and BMP.

There are a few items of hardware that are critical. For capturing graphics for web pages, you need an inexpensive color scanner. Your students can take live action snapshots with an inexpensive digital camera. An inkjet color printer is also essential for printing out graphics and web pages. Each of these items can be purchased for $200 or less.

AUDIO

For capturing and editing digital audio and music, you have several software options. You can make digital recordings from compact audio discs, from tape recordings, and even live recordings. Key audio editing software applications are SoundForge XP (Win) and PeakLE or SoundEdit 16 (Mac). For shareware alternatives, consider SoundEffects (Mac) and CoolEdit or GoldWave (Win). Mac and Windows computers also have a simple digital recorder usually provided free with the software operating system.

For hardware, the Mac comes equipped with what you need to capture digital audio in any of the forms noted above. Most Windows computers come with a sound card that has the ability to play back and capture digital audio from a CD disc, a microphone, or a tape recorder plugged into the microphone input.

VIDEO

Video is more complex, both in terms of software and hardware. The need to capture 15 to 30 frames per second of both graphic and audio really pushes the capabilities of a computer. Many Macintosh computers come with video capture hardware built into the computer. You can purchase inexpensive video capture hardware for a Windows machine ($150 or less). With the video capture hardware usually comes a low-end video capture and editing software application of some sort. The professional video editing software package is Adobe Premiere. Less expensive programs, such as Videowave for Windows, are quite suitable for classroom projects.

MULTIMEDIA COMPUTER WORKSTATION

What type of computer workstation do you need to do some of the basic multimedia work described above? Without choosing between Macintosh and Windows computers, here are a few considerations for a multimedia computer system. The computer workstation needed for creating multimedia must be more powerful than the computers you use to play multimedia and search the web. Here's a brief guide for a computer for browsing Internet sites and a computer for multimedia development:

- Basic multimedia browsing computer: Macintosh PowerPC or Windows Pentium computer with 32 mb of RAM and 500 mb hard drive; 8-bit VGA color and monitor; CD-ROM drive and sound card; and 56k modem.

- Basic multimedia development computer: 200 mHz or better Macintosh PowerPC or Windows Pentium computer with 64 mb of RAM and 2 gb hard drive; 16-bit SVGA color and monitor; CD-ROM drive and sound card with digital audio capture; low-resolution digital camera and flatbed scanner; Zip drive; and 56k or better Internet connection.

Let us elaborate on these guidelines. Faster is better. Choose the fastest computer processor available: 300 megaHertz processing speeds or greater will give you the needed speed when dealing with digital audio and video. The more memory, the better. Capturing and editing digital audio and video takes up lots of computer storage space. The voluminous hard drives that come with present-day computer systems, usually several gigabytes or larger, are more than adequate. You want at least 32 megabytes of random-access memory, but 64 megabytes is more comfortable. To extend your storage further, and to make it easy to store the work of several student groups, as well as your own, consider one of the larger, superfloppy formats like Iomega Zip disks.

The faster the Internet connection, the better. If your school is directly connected to the Internet through Ethernet or DSL technologies, you have excellent Internet "bandwidth," meaning you can download lots of sounds, graphics, and movies. If you need a modem to connect to the Internet, then 56K modem speed will give you adequate Internet bandwidth for the multimedia sites suggested in this article. Anything slower than this, like 28.8 modem speed, will be noticeably slow in downloading movies and large sound files. The graphics and text, and RealAudio sounds, should download in an acceptable.

What about multimedia peripherals for developing multimedia in your classroom? The computer should have a sound card with the ability to digitize audio and a CD-ROM or DVD-ROM drive (most computers these days do). You will want an inexpensive color ink-jet printer and a low-end color scanner. Some nice additions beyond this are a low-end digital camera, a MIDI music synthesizer and keyboard, a digital video capture card, and a VCR; and a CD-ROM drive that reads and writes (or "burns") CD-ROM disks. The CD-ROM burner is a convenient way to save and store your work.

The End of the Story

As you have seen, a wonderful world of history and culture exists on the World Wide Web, and can be viewed and appreciated through the eye and ear of artists, musicians, poets, movie directors, photographers, and composers. You can weave all of these forms of artistic expression into stories that make up social studies activities in your classroom. Enjoy!

Links from the Web Examples
Below is a list of URLs for websites either noted in this chapter or likely to be of interest to readers. The web is a living document, so please realize that these links may change. The links shown here are to the primary home page of the site and not necessarily to the specific pages illustrated above.

Migrant Workers
    Library of Congress, American Memory Project, and Others: lcweb.loc.gov
    The Jimmie Rodgers Official Website: www.jimmierodgers.com/welcome.html
    The Museum of Modern Art: www.moma.org

Railroading in America
    Artists View of History: history.evansville.net
    The Multimedia History Company: www.multied.com, www.rrhistorical.com
    Art Crimes: www.graffiti.org
    Rounder Records: www.rounder.com
    CGFA Virtual Art Museum: www.bibl.u-szeged.hu/cgfa
    The Greatest Films: www.filmsite.org

Children's International Art Work
    Children's Art Gallery: redfrog.norconnect.no/~cag
    River of Words: www.irn.org/row/
    Young Composers: www.youngcomposers.com

The Forum of Trajan
    ArtsEdNet and the Getty Center: artsednet.getty.edu
    Amiata Records-Synaulia: www.amiatamedia.com/ita/series/ma/pages/ar1396i.htm
    Synaulia: www.domenicaifori.it/synaulia.htm

African Culture
    Kennedy Center African Odyssey Interactive: artsedge.kennedy-center.org/odyssey.html
    Boka Marimba: www.bokamarimba.com
    Guggenheim African Art Collection: artnetweb.com/guggenheim/africa
    African Music And Dance Ensemble: cnmat.cnmat.berkeley.edu/~ladzekpo/

Internet Research Sites for the Arts and Others
    ARTSEDGE: The National Arts and Education Information Network: artsedge.kennedy-center.org
    Gallery Guide On-line: www.gallery-guide.com
    Metropolitan Museum of Art World Wide Arts Resources: world-arts-resources.com
    Johns Hopkins University Folk Music Index: MiltonsWeb.mse.jhu.edu:8001/research/folkindex
    Worldwide Internet Music Resources: www.music.indiana.edu/music_resources
    Bluegrass World: www.bluegrassworld.com
    Greatest Films: www.filmsite.org
    Artists in the White House: arts.endow.gov/Archive/Features9/ArtistsWH.html

American Folklife Center Home Page: lcweb.loc.gov/folklife/afc.html
Dave Williams Arts Internet & Teaching Links: www.orat.ilstu.edu/~dwilliam/docs/wkLinks
Shakespeare: the-tech.mit.edu/Shakespeare/works.html
Worldmusic: www.worldmusic.org
Dejanews: www.dejanews.com
AltaVista: www.altavista.com
Spider's Apprentice: www.monash.com/spidap.html

Additional Resources

Barrett, Janet R., Claire W. McCoy, and Kari K. Veblen. *Social Way of Knowing: Music in the Interdisciplinary Curriculum.* New York: Schirmer Books, 1997.

Selwyn, Douglas. *Arts and Humanities in the Social Studies.* Washington, D.C.: National Council for the Social Studies, 1995.

Stull, Andrew T., and John D. Spiak. *Art on the Internet: A Student's Guide.* Upper Saddle River, N.J.: Prentice-Hall, 1999.

CHAPTER 13

MULTICULTURALISM AND THE INTERNET

Deborah A. Byrnes
College of Education at Utah State University
&
Grace Huerta
College of Education at Utah State University

As the United States becomes increasingly diverse, the citizenry must be equipped with the knowledge, skills, and values necessary to understand and deal with the inevitable, substantive differences among groups and individuals in the population (Vogt 1997). Multicultural education is a reform movement designed to address this need and to change how educators teach and students learn about diverse cultures. Multicultural education theorists (Banks 1994; Garcia 1995; Grant and Tate 1995) prescribe changes in both the curricula and instructional practices of the nation's public schools. Research studies support such prescriptions by indicating that educational experiences can influence students' beliefs, attitudes, and values regarding diversity (Byrnes and Kiger 1996; Pate 1995; Vogt 1997). Teachers, given appropriate skills and resources, can and do make a difference. Fortunately, with the development and continued growth of the Internet, quality multicultural education resources are much more accessible to teachers. Internet resources can assist both in-service and preservice teachers in the implementation of social studies standards published by National Council for the Social Studies (NCSS) and individual states that point to the need for a greater understanding and acceptance of diversity.

The purpose of this chapter is to assist teachers in using the Internet to help meet multicultural education goals. Through the sharing of vignettes and exemplary websites, we want teachers to see how the Internet can provide easy access to materials and instructional practices that will help them to prepare children to function successfully in modern diverse societies. Attention is focused specifically on how the Internet can be used by teachers to help students view concepts, issues, and themes from the perspectives of diverse groups of people, as well as how it can be used to help students accept and respect diversity and develop a sense of political efficacy.

We share vignettes of seven elementary, middle school, and high school teachers who are using the Internet for the above purposes. The vignettes are organized within the context of five categories of sites: (1) comprehensive multicultural sites, (2) specific theme sites, (3) cross-cultural connections with keypals, (4) collaborative projects, and (5) sharing oneself with the world. For each category we include additional websites that could be used to promote multicultural goals. We chose these categories because they incorporate characteristics of educational practices that are supported by the research on improving actions, attitudes, and beliefs related to diversity. Specifically, research supports practices whose outcomes include (a) increased self-esteem; (b) greater cognitive sophistication and reasoning ability; (c) increased empathy; (d) meaningful, equal-status, cooperative interactions with diverse groups; and (e) a commitment to and understanding of constitutional principles of fairness and justice (Byrnes and Kiger 1996; Pate 1995; Vogt 1997).

Comprehensive Multicultural Sites

It is always helpful to have several strong comprehensive websites bookmarked for those times when you want to see what is broadly available in the area of multicultural education. The websites listed at the end of this vignette provide teachers with a plethora of resources. Although such sites might seem overwhelming and time consuming to search, there are some real "gold mines" to be found by the teacher who knows how to focus his or her searches.

VIGNETTE #1

Grade: Middle School
Standards: Time, Continuity, and Change; Individuals, Groups, and Institutions
Website: "Rhino Seekers Multicultural Link": cc.usu.edu/~graceh/rhino.htm.

This site, created by Grace Huerta and Christina Hum at Utah State University, is especially oriented for middle school and secondary school teachers. Because the site is divided into a number of content areas, educators can explore interdisciplinary approaches to multicultural social studies instruction. A special effort has been made to include sites that address multiple historical perspectives, something that many textbooks fail to do.

Barbara Martinez, after a surfing expedition of "The Rhino Seekers Multicultural Education Link," located some excellent material she could use for her middle school westward-expansion unit. She decided to expand her unit by presenting a "Buffalo Soldier Perspective," using materials from the Internet (e.g., www.library.yale.edu/jobs/buflink.htm). During the Indian Wars of 1866 to 1891, 10,000 African Americans constituted 10 percent of the U.S. Army and 20 percent of the cavalry. Known as "Buffalo Soldiers," they battled for the western territories and, simultaneously, endured prejudice from their officers and citizens. Through Internet research, role playing, and diary writing, Martinez's students develop an understanding of what it was like to be a Buffalo Soldier.

Martinez assesses her students' abilities to think critically about the contributions of minorities to western expansion through reflective writing and discussion. In addition, she engages her students in dialogue about the conflicts that have arisen when pitting one minority group against another. Students conclude the unit with presentations and reenactments of the daily life experiences of the Buffalo Soldiers.

Additional High-Quality Comprehensive Sites
Multicultural Pavilion: curry.edschool.Virginia.EDU/go/multicultural/home.html
Hall of Multiculturalism: www.tenet.edu/academia/multi.html
Specific Theme Sites—Theme sites are excellent tools for helping students and teachers broaden their understanding of people and events in their country and the world and to recognize that they should consider a variety of perspectives in analyzing any given event, historical period, or person. Such sites can quickly help teachers become aware of materials and perspectives that were not part of their own education.

VIGNETTE #2

Grade: Early Elementary
Standards: Culture; Individual Development and Identity; Individuals, Groups, and Institutions
Website: "Making Multicultural Connections Through Trade Books": www.mcps.k12.md.us/
curriculum/socialstd/MBD/Books_Begin.html

Montgomery County Public Schools (MCPS) in Maryland developed this multicultural database site to assist elementary teachers in selecting books that broaden and enrich the perspectives of students in their district. Searches can be conducted by cultural group, grade, or theme. Most of the books listed on the site are written and/or illustrated by members of the cultural group.

Sarah Fontaine uses this site to help her quickly and easily add a multicultural perspective to her curriculum. Fontaine has long taught a unit on grandparents in her second-grade classroom. In the past she used Mercer Meyer's book *Just Grandma and Me* as the literature base of her unit. As she has become more aware of how her classroom needs to reflect the diversity in her students' lives and community, she has begun to seek out multicultural books and materials for her classroom. A quick stop at "Making Multicultural Connections Through Trade Books" gives her an annotated list of well-known, multicultural children's books around the theme of grandparents. From this list, she chooses five books representing grandparents in different cultures: *Abuela* (Hispanic), *Knots on a Counting Rope* (Native American), *Something from Nothing* (Jewish), *Grandfather's Journey* (Japanese American), and *Picking Peas for Parents* (African American). After a brief teacher introduction to all of the books, students select which book they want to learn more about. Cooperative groups are formed based on book preferences, and Fontaine instructs each group to find a creative way to share the story with others in the class (e.g., story cards, role plays, posters, murals, and dioramas). After the groups present all of the book projects, the students share similarities and differences among the grandparents in the books. For enrichment purposes, a student who wants the additional challenge rates his or her book on a 5-star scale and writes several sentences to support his or her rating. After a final edit, these reviews are easily posted at the Internet book store, Amazon.com (www.amazon.com) for others to read.

VIGNETTE #3
Grade: Middle School
Standards: Culture; Time, Continuity, and Change
Website: What Did You Do in the War, Grandma?: www.stg.brown.edu/projects/WWII_Women

Judi Scott and Linda Wood developed this site, which includes excellent oral histories of women during World War II written by high school English honors students at South Kingstown High in Rhode Island. The site was funded by a variety of agencies and is managed by Brown University.

By visiting the website "What Did You Do in the War, Grandma?", Michael Larkin's ninth-grade U.S. history class learns about World War II from the perspectives of women who took part in the war effort. By exploring on-line, oral history articles, narratives, and resource links, this site provides another perspective of historical events.

Students form cooperative learning groups and learn about how the war resulted in a tremendous shortage of labor. Not only was there a great demand for labor to build weapons and equipment, men left civilian employment for military service in large numbers. As a result, women rushed to fill the jobs. The narratives provide great insight into the nature of those jobs and society's response, both positive and negative, to women's changing roles in the United States.

Following the site visit, Larkin leads the class in discussion. He poses questions such as, "Was it patriotism and propaganda that made women find war jobs?" "Or was it money, independence, and pride in learning new skills that motivated them?" Larkin suggests various writing prompts that address how the war influenced changing roles of women in society and in what ways society has been comfortable and uncomfortable about those gender-role changes today.

Students are also able to use the oral history story data posted here as models for their own oral history projects. Unique to the narratives available at this site, these oral histories were collected by students for students. Employing an interdisciplinary approach, in this case, U.S. history and language arts, Larkin uses this site, links, and search engines to guide students through the process of conducting their own oral history research relevant to other topics, such as the Great Depression, the Vietnam War, and the civil rights and women's movements.

VIGNETTE #4

Grade: High School

Standards: Time, Continuity, and Change; Power, Authority, and Governance;
Individuals, Groups, and Institutions

Website: Exploring African American Issues on the Web: www.kn.pacbell.com/wired/BHM/
AfroAm.html

This "Blue Web'n" site (an award given by Pacific Bell to excellent educational sites), created by Tom March, is excellent for middle school or high school teachers. Study topics include the civil rights movement, racism, hate crimes, prominent historical figures, and the arts, as well as an optional videoconferencing link.

Sean Baker asks his seniors to analyze and critique historical and contemporary issues relevant to the African American experience. As students begin their studies in African American history, Baker introduces three different resources offered at March's site. In cooperative teams, the students are responsible for finding out what the following resource links have to offer: "Black History Hotlist," "Sampling African America," and "Black History Treasure Hunt." This activity helps students acquire knowledge and develop basic research skills.

Baker then focuses the students' attention on one particular issue, the "Tuskegee Tragedy." Following Baker's introductory lecture on the subject, students study on-line articles about the Tuskegee Study and other related issues. Using interactive discussions with historians available at this website, students analyze the similarities and differences between issues such as the AIDS medical trials conducted by the Center for Disease Control and the Tuskegee Study. Students are invited to role play historical scenarios, examine video references, and study historical and contemporary documents, such as President Bill Clinton's "Letter of Apology to Tuskegee Victims."

Finally, in cooperative group presentations, Baker's students compare and contrast the events surrounding the Tuskegee Syphilis Study with other health issues influencing disempowered groups in the United States today (e.g., prison inmate medical research, immigrant health-care access).

A Sampling of Other Exciting Multicultural Theme Sites
Every Month Is Black History Month: socialstudies.com/feb/blackhistory.html
Asian American and Asian Studies: www.askasia.org/for_educators/fe_frame.htm
The Holocaust: remember.org
Multicultural Celebrations: teacherlink.ed.usu.edu/TLresources/longterm/Byrnes/intro.html
Diversity of Western America: www.pbs.org/weta/thewest

Cross-Cultural Connections with Keypals

Keypals can be used as a tool to help students develop greater understanding of others by providing opportunities for children and adolescents to interact with people who live and think quite differently from themselves. Keypals is an electronic version of penpals. E-mail, the Internet, or video-conferencing technology is used to exchange thoughts, feelings, and information. Keypals might live in the same city or thousands of miles away in a different country. There is a real advantage to having keypals who are close enough to visit because that allows for exciting in-person, follow-up connections to be made.

Some teachers have chosen adult keypals for their classrooms. Adults (e.g., history buffs, graduate students, senior citizens, preservice teachers) can serve as "telementors" on a particular multicultural topic, or in some cases they may be willing to role play or impersonate a well-known historical figure or book character.

Keypal arrangements should include clear commitments and time frames so that students are not disappointed by keypals who do not follow through. For the teacher who has only one Internet line available, students can write their messages in a word-processing program, then copy to a disk, and the messages of many students can be sent together as an attachment to the keypal location.

VIGNETTE #5
Grade: Elementary
Standards: Culture; People, Places, and Environments
Website: Heineman Keypals: www.reedbooks.com.au/heinemann/global/keypalt.html

Rigby Heineman provides a helpful resource for teachers looking for keypals within and outside of the U.S.A. They have a great guide to appropriate "netiquette" (Internet etiquette) for keypals.

Brian Park, a teacher of rural students in Iowa, uses keypals to help his students learn more about communities of the United States, practice their inquiry skills, use writing for authentic purposes, and develop relationships with people from different cultural and geographical backgrounds. Using "Heineman Keypals," Mr. Park made the following request:

> Third-grade teacher looking for a class of approximately twenty-five students in a
> different region of the U.S. that wants to do a joint social studies project. Our rural
> school is located in the Midwest (but don't tell your students that, yet).

A third-grade teacher, Teresa Redder, in Phoenix responds that her class may be interested in a joint keypal project. After trading phone numbers, the teachers contact each other to talk about their common curriculum goals and time frames. It is decided that their students will study each other's communities using an inquiry process.

The study begins by having students formulate some general questions that will help them get to know the other team: "What is your school like?" "What do kids do in their free time?" These questions are sent via e-mail to the other school, with a prearranged due date for answers. The receiving class must answer the questions without revealing where their school is located.

Using information from their first contact with the other school, students formulate additional questions that will help them to pinpoint the state and region in which the other school is located: What is your climate like? What are the major products of your state? What types of land and water forms are present? These questions are sent back and forth until both teams have guessed the other school's location.

Each classroom team then puts together a small shoe box of artifacts that best communicates to the other school information about what is important in its community (e.g., a miniature rubber chicken, a recipe, a class picture, an empty bottle of sunscreen). The students select each item with care, and record a rationale.

The other classroom students, upon receiving the box, write small-group papers hypothesizing why certain artifacts have been included and what they mean. These papers are then exchanged by traditional mail or sent as e-mail attachments to the other class. Keypals respond to and return each other's papers. Follow-up discussions by Park and Redder focus on what they learned and thought about each other's communities, examining commonalities as well as areas of difference.

Other Helpful Keypal Sites
Classroom Exchange: www.epals.com
Intercultural E-Mail Classroom Connections: www.stolaf.edu/network/iecc

Collaborative Projects

Collaborative projects on the Internet involve students at different schools working together on a common subject to collect information, share information, or to solve problems. To meet multicultural goals, collaborative projects should involve students from different backgrounds and cultures working together cooperatively. Projects might include community surveys (e.g., comparing rural and urban communities), oral histories (e.g., students locating Holocaust survivors in their own communities and recording their stories), service-learning (e.g., creating a web page for a nonprofit organization), or intergenerational interviews (e.g., collecting information on family traditions). Harris (1998) suggested that collaborating with five to ten classrooms can be advantageous because you get greater diversity of perspective and if one class has technical problems, your project can still continue. Newcomers to collaborative Internet projects are encouraged to join an up-and-running project to get experience prior to putting out their own call for project participants.

Brown, Cummins, Figueroa, and Sayers (1998) stated that, for collaborative projects to truly support multicultural goals, the language in which the project is conducted and the subject selected for research must be chosen with care. The project should not favor groups of students who are already more privileged. When students bring different languages to the experiences, for example, Spanish and English, teachers should consider the benefits of conducting some aspects of the project in Spanish and some in English. Bilingual students or community members could assist with translations as needed. Topics should be chosen that have the potential to showcase the contributions and knowledge of all participants.

VIGNETTE #6
Grade: Upper Elementary
Standards: Civic Ideals and Practices; Individual Development and Identity
Website: Youth in Action Network: www.mightymedia.com

The "Youth in Action Network" was created by Mighty Media and Associates. The Action Network brings together a diverse group of students, teachers, and activists to identify contemporary social and environmental conflicts, research and communicate about possible solutions, and design strategies to confront problems.

Eliza Harati wants to use the upcoming Martin Luther King Day holiday as an opportunity to inspire her students to be actively engaged in creating a better world for all people. She does so by registering her class with the "Kindness and Justice Challenge" (www.kjchallenge.org), a Youth in Action collaborative project site designed to develop a national tradition of collecting and posting acts of kindness and justice during the ten days prior to Martin Luther King Day. Once registered, Harati receives free lesson plans from the project sponsors.

She begins her project by having students study the contributions of Martin Luther King, Jr., and by having them look for examples of caring and justice in their own worlds. Children share examples from newspapers, television shows, and personal observations. Ten days before Martin Luther King, Jr. Day, Harati challenges her students to put into action what they had been studying. Each day students in her class are asked to share acts of kindness and justice that they had personally engaged in and to post these on the Internet. The number of acts that are posted nationwide can be reviewed on an up-to-the-minute basis. Students also respond to grade-level-appropriate dilemmas that are posted on a daily basis at the Internet site. The most impressive responses to difficult dilemmas nationwide are later posted in the National Kindness and Justice Hall of Fame for students to read. As a concluding activity and assessment, each student in Ms. Harati's class selects the act he or she felt was his or her personal best and shares why.

Additional Collaborative Project Sites
Kid Projects: www.kidlink.org/KIDPROJ/index.html
Social Action Projects: www.iearn.org/iearn
Global SchoolNet's Internet Projects Registry: www.gsn.org/pr/index.cfm

Sharing Oneself with the World
Research tells us that children and adolescents who have high self-esteem are less likely to hold prejudices (Pate 1995). Classroom environments and activities that promote positive self-esteem are one way educators can work to reduce prejudice and increase tolerance. Internet sites that give children a voice through safe, supervised chat lines and provide opportunities for publication of children's work can contribute to children's feeling of success and positive worth.

VIGNETTE #7
Grade: High School
Standards: Individual Development and Identity; Culture
Website: Amigos (in Spanish and English): www.kn.pacbell.com/wired/bluewebn/fr_History.html

This is a "Blue Web'n" site developed by Carmen Guanipa and Linda Woods Hyman. This website is designed to be of particular interest to ethnically diverse middle school and high school students, parents, and teachers.

Eleventh-grade psychology teacher Jeannine Chan uses the Amigos web page to present a multicultural approach to self-esteem building. This site is especially helpful to Latino/bilingual adolescents, as lessons also appear in Spanish. Chan has her students follow the site's self-guided activities that emphasize three areas: confidence building, mental and physical well-being, and the improvement of cross-cultural communication skills.

Prior to visiting the Amigos site, Chan brainstorms with her students, posing questions such as, "What is self esteem?" "What are some indicators of a low and high self-esteem?" "How can a person improve his or her self-esteem?" After the students have shared possible examples aloud, Chan asks class members to compile their own personal list of self-esteem indicators. Students then visit the "Ask Carmen" section of the Amigos site. Chan invites students to compare their list of characteristics with those researched by Dr. Carmen Guanipa and the staff of the Counseling and School Psychology Program at San Diego State University. Students, in addition, can send general questions to Dr. Guanipa and her staff. Next, Chan has the students read and discuss articles about self-esteem building, which are posted at the site. Cooperative learning groups then report their findings to the class.

Tapping into the "Information" section of the Amigo website, Chan encourages the groups to conduct their own research projects using Amigo's links to topics such as diversity, culture shock, drugs and alcohol, healthy living, mental health, and interpersonal relationships. Students must define the terms, give examples of how these issues can influence one's self-esteem, and share strategies that can help their peers pursue a positive life-style.

Finally, Chan wraps up the unit by having the class read the Amigo site's "Multicultural Stories." She evaluates their knowledge of the issues presented by having the students write their own personal narratives regarding self-esteem and/or cross-cultural experiences. Students may choose to post their essays to the Amigos "Multicultural Stories" web page.

Sharing Place for Young Children
Kids Space: www.kids-space.org

The Internet provides interesting new tools and resources for promoting multicultural goals. Children and adolescents can become more cognitively sophisticated as they (and their teachers) use the Internet to gain diverse perspectives and to learn about past and present inequities in our society. They can gain confidence and self-esteem through sharing their own work with a worldwide audience and also through having the contributions of their own culture recognized. Students can develop empathy and understanding as they read about and relate to others who are different from themselves. And they can grow in acceptance and tolerance as they work together with others on collaborative projects. Although the Internet allows students to gain perspective and interact with a broader range of people, it cannot replace face-to-face communication. Electronic relationships are not enough. We must also provide opportunities for children and adolescents to work and play together with the full richness of communication only available in real time in real life.

References

Banks, James. *Multiethnic Education*. Boston: Allyn & Bacon, 1994.

Brown, K., J. Cummins, E. Figueroa, and D. Sayers. "Global Learning Networks: Gaining Perspective on Our Lives with Distance." In *Beyond Heroes and Holidays*, edited by E. Lee, D. Menkart, and M. Okazawa-Rey. Washington, D.C.: Network of Educators on the Americas, 1998.

Byrnes, D. A., and G. Kiger, ed. *Common Bonds: Anti-Bias Teaching in a Diverse Society* 2d ed. Wheaton, Md.: Association for Childhood Education International, 1996.

Garcia, E. "Educating Mexican-American Students: Past Treatment and Recent Developments in Theory, Research, Policy and Practice." In *Handbook of Research on Multicultural Education*, edited by James Banks and C. McGee Banks. New York: Macmillan, 1995.

Grant, C., and W. Tate. "Multicultural Education through the Lenses of the Multicultural Education Research Literature." In *Handbook of Research on Multicultural Education*, edited by James Banks and C. McGee Banks. New York: Macmillan, 1995.

Harris, J. *Design Tools for the Internet-Supported Classroom*. Alexandria, Va.: Association for Supervision and Curriculum Development, 1998.

Pate, G. S. *Prejudice Reduction and the Findings of Research*. ERIC Document Reproduction Service ED 383 803, 1995.

Vogt, W. P. *Tolerance and Education: Learning to Live with Diversity and Difference*. Thousand Oaks, Calif.: Sage. 1997.

CHAPTER 14

TEACHER EDUCATION

D. Mark Meyers
Rowan University

Technology has become a mainstay of American education. It is mentioned daily in numerous newspaper stories, television reports, and in a myriad of other media outlets. Today, most television commercials end with an address for a web page. Even though it appears that virtually everyone in society can see the relevance for the Internet in education, it is far more difficult for all constituent groups in education to reach agreement on its usage. Would it not be great if someone could just walk in and tell all teachers, "Do this and your classroom will be an Internet wonder!" As all teachers can tell you, however, each classroom is a unique environment with its own constraints and possibilities. This requires a shift in view of teaching and teacher education. As Poole (1995, 406) suggested, "Education must, therefore, continue to broaden its definition of what constitutes a successful student, for no two graduates will be equally or identically shaped by what goes on in schools."

The school must no longer be looked upon as a factory, producing identically prepared students. Instead, each student must be presented with the opportunity for personalizing his or her instructional goals (Powell, Farrar, and Cohen 1985). This chapter discusses a three-step approach—modeling, practice, and use—to ensure that technology and the Internet can assist in such personalized goal setting within teacher education.

In many ways, what we ask teachers to do with technology, especially the Internet, requires them to rethink their instructional assumptions. Some standard bearers in the schools demonstrate the uses of technology, but these teachers alone cannot change the view of an entire profession. Teachers in the classroom often believe the students know more about computers than they do. As Chris Dede has noted,

> One of the mistakes we made in implementing educational technology was focusing first on students, rather than teachers, because when the computers on the students' desks are mysterious devices to teachers, it's unreasonable to expect effective integration into the curriculum. (O'Neil 1995, 7)

Unless teachers are confident of their ability to use the computer, they tend to shy away from its use. Instead, they choose something they know they can handle; confronted by innovation, they may choose noninvolvement (Ellen 1987). Exposing preservice teachers to technology increases their motivation to use technology and also increases the likelihood that they will use technology in their classroom (Williams and Matthew 1995). If preservice teachers develop confidence that they can control and use technology, they can then provide the same service to their students. There it will "trickle down" into the teaching practices of the schools (Johnson and Harlow, 1993, 361). Teachers are not convinced by good ideas alone. Instead, it takes good ideas that have worked for someone else. Teachers will borrow successful ideas, not merely use ones they read about that might be good. These changes will involve the development of communities in which students and teachers investigate areas of interest and information is exchanged freely between school, university, and community.

Modeling

Student teachers must see explicit examples of ideas that can be effective when they are in their own classroom. Teacher education programs can provide demonstrations of such visions. The level at which these demonstrations are presented is not as important as is the fact that they are presented. As Larry Cuban indicated, this also provides a means of communication, because a shared experience is a necessary first step to open communication. As Cuban (1992, 9) puts it,

> Teaching in professional schools, to undergraduates, and to sixth graders binds our occupation together because in acting as teachers, we model professional behavior; we exhibit our views of knowledge and learning; we advertise our ideas, how we reason, and how we struggle with moral choices whether we intend to or not.

Modeling of Internet use must provide the student with the ability to access different forms of technology. Most teacher educators would readily agree that it would be a disservice to teachers to provide education in only a single methodology of classroom instruction. However, this idea becomes amplified when the methodology involves technology. Teacher educators must provide multiple perspectives for their students when modeling technological uses. Without multiple representations, students are able to perform well on measures of "factual knowledge," but these same students suffer in terms of knowledge transfer for later use (Jacobson and Spiro 1993). Teachers must be cognitively flexible and, therefore, must be taught in a cognitively flexible manner. An example from another profession can serve as an exemplar. Spiro (1988) and his colleagues (Spiro, Vispoel, Schmitz, Samarapungauan, and Boerger 1987) demonstrated that doctors taught in a linear progression had trouble recognizing diagnoses in ambiguous situations presented in medical practice. While serving as students, these doctors could recite information successfully for grades, but when placed in a "real-life" setting, or ecologically valid setting (Neisser 1976), the same students failed to make a proper diagnosis. The same could be said for teachers in the classroom, especially preservice teachers. If a teacher is asked to develop a paragraph of explanation about a classroom situation, most could do so with no problem. However, many teachers might have a problem with developing the same responses if placed in a "real" setting. Teachers may know how to recognize the use of such knowledge themselves, but lack the ability to provide students with the same opportunity (Spiro, Feltovich, Jacobson, and Coulson 1992). The modeling, therefore, provides the teachers-in-training with the ability to develop skills, both technological and nontechnological, as well as the ability to recognize the moments to use them.

An example of this modeling can be seen in a methods classroom. A variety of information must be presented to the students in such a course. The teacher can present such information using presentational software, e-mail, Internet materials, handouts, and text readings. This variety of materials models for students the connection between technology and the course materials. The students can "see" the material from a variety of perspectives, allowing each student to construct meanings in his or her own area of cognitive strength. For example, every history teacher presents students with primary source documents to review. In most cases, the amount of primary source materials available locally is limited in scope and content. However, the Internet provides ready access to many. Additionally, many students believe that any primary source document is fact—the way that it happened. The students see history as if it was a video playing out before them. This erroneous view can be corrected through an assignment. Students can be given a general assignment; for instance, find letters written home by soldiers of both armies during the war and compare the soldiers' views of the conflict. There is not a single website that answers this question. Students will find multiple answers. A sample list follows:

Letters from an Iowa Soldier in the U. S. Civil War: www.civilwarletters.com/home.html

Letters from a soldier from New York: home.pacbell.net/dunton/SSDletters.html

Letters from a Confederate general: www.he.net/~brumley/hillrev.htm

Letters from the Civil War site: www.geocities.com/Pentagon/7914

As students proceed through the assignment, they discover that contradictory information exists from both sides. This leads to a terrific class discussion on the constraints and possibilities of primary source materials. As has often been found in education, the quest for knowledge can be more important than the results of the quest. Students in this instance learn more by what they have been doing, rather than what they have found specifically.

Practice

The modeling of technological uses in the classroom is only a first step. If one were to leave the process at this point, a number of false assumptions made by the trainees could come into play in their own classrooms. For example, when watching the activity described, a novice could easily fail to recognize the time invested in the activity by the teacher, because of the ease in which the material was presented. The novice must be provided with an opportunity for guided practice, which will accomplish two things: (1) provide an opportunity for the acquisition of advanced knowledge only available in an active environment and (2) provide an opportunity for guided practice so that the student sees all that goes into technological uses, within the safety net provided by the instructor.

For example, students creating HyperStudio stacks for a lesson presentation for the first time might not realize the amount of time needed to create a quality presentation. They see the instructor's stacks during class presentations, but when they create their own, they are shocked by the time required. Some novices require an hour per minute of presentation—ten hours for a ten-minute presentation. The instructor needs to provide assistance, to ensure that this time does not get ridiculously long. By answering questions and providing general support, the instructor provides a safety net for the students. One such project that the teacher can help students with is the preparation of HyperStudio stacks for display on the Internet.

PUTTING HYPERSTUDIO ONTO THE INTERNET

The process of putting a HyperStudio stack on the Internet is quite simple. The biggest problem is to ensure that you provide your students with web browsers that have either the HyperStudio plug-in software or access to it. The latest version of the plug-in can be found at www.hyperstudio.com. Once you have created a HyperStudio stack, you must save it with the suffix ".stk," which is needed to inform the browser of the type of program used. After you have saved the stack, you must go to the menu bar and select "export web page." This extra function will create an HTML document that allows the browser to read the stack correctly. The stack can now be used by anyone with a connection to the Internet.

A SAMPLE LESSON

In many social studies classrooms, students are assigned to research an important question in history. In this case, students research the decision to drop the atomic bomb. Each student in the class is assigned to a group of six members. Each group is given a particular role. These roles are U.S. Government, U.S. Civilians, U.S. Soldiers, Manhattan Project Scientists, and Japanese Civilians. In each case, the students are to use the materials garnered at a series of websites in order to develop an argument for or against the dropping of the bomb, from the perspective of the group to which they have been assigned. The websites that can be used include the following: Gene Dannen's site, www.dannen.com/decision/index.html; the Last Act site, lastact.webjump.com; and the ABC News series, Century, abcnews.go.com/century/tvseries/abomb.html.

Once students have completed their research, each group member must develop a HyperStudio presentation. The mission of the presentation is to use materials from the sites, and others, to persuade others of the validity of their position. This persuasion can take the form of primary source readings, video, sound items, or pictures. All information must be documented, and each stack must conclude with a bibliography card.

Once the student stacks are completed, they must submit them on a disk in order to be placed on the class website. This allows students to access the stacks of other group members. At this point, students must visit the class website and review the stacks of their other group members. The group members will then communicate with their partners via e-mail with any suggestions they have about the group's stacks. From these communications, the group will then develop a group presentation on the topic, made up of materials garnered from the individual presentations. The group stack is then presented to the rest of the class. After the presentations, the class discusses the types of presentations made by each group, the methods of persuasion attempted, and their comparative effectiveness. Additionally, the completed group stacks will also be made available via the Internet. Students must follow up with a journal assignment to review the presentations of the other groups outside of class. During this reflection exercise, students review their own attempts at persuasion and list lessons learned from the sessions in their class journal.

The time allotted for such an assignment depends on the meeting times of the course. However, class time is needed at the beginning of the lesson and for the final presentations. The time needed for research and preparation of the individual stacks is usually two weeks, with the group stacks usually taking an additional week. This assignment has been attempted only with weekly meeting courses, but could be readily adapted to a class that meets a few times a week. An important component of this assignment is the need for the teacher to be available for problem solving and general pep talks. Students in this situation are attempting something new, and will be "pushing the envelope" of their knowledge. They will need the instructor to provide some sort of safety net.

Vygotsky (1934) referred to such a safety net as the "zone of proximal development." Ideally, students would stretch their abilities by working in areas they could not have reached alone. However, Vygotsky's ideas have been interpreted differently in many U.S. classrooms. "English speaking scholars interpret the concept more narrowly than Vygotsky intended" (Moll and Whitmore 1993, 19). The social aspect of the zone of proximal development is what has been missing in many classrooms. Students are being challenged, but individually, in a competitive environment, which runs contrary to the ideas of Vygotsky. Instead, students should be assessed on what they can do in collaboration, rather than what they can accomplish in isolation. This leads to a pattern of study that "lags behind the children's development, so we characterized the history of the child, failing to capture the ongoing process or to provide future development" (Griffin, Belyaeva, Soldatova, and Velikhov-Hamburg Collective 1993, 124). Strommen (1993) found that more correct answers came out of cooperative environments than competitive environments and that the only effective strategies for problem solving were located in cooperative environments. These cooperative environments can be created in a variety of settings; however, technology provides an effective means of establishing such a setting via e-mail. Students can be assigned to complete comparison activities using e-mail with a partner. The power that e-mail provides such an activity is the diversity of combinations that can be created for these activities. For example, students in social studies methods courses can share e-mail messages with students in other subject-area methods courses, such as English, and can compare reactions to a given piece of literature. Besides different subject areas, e-mails can be shared with students in other schools, regions, or even levels of learning. Currently, a group of undergraduate methods students is sharing e-mails with graduate students at a school in another part of the country. The messages sent between the two groups provide methods students with a chance to interact with professionals who differ from them in a number of ways: graduate versus undergraduate, English versus social studies, experienced teachers versus novice teachers, and all of this between teachers in different regions with different problems associated with teaching in that region. The interactions provided by e-mail allow student teachers to be exposed to material that would be outside the reach of a typical methodology classroom. Teachers in training can listen to a professor tell them "what it is like in the field," but if they get information from other sources that reinforce the professor's views, the lessons are more than doubly learned. Some of the students involved have indicated that they would like to do something similar during their student teaching experience.

Use

Providing prospective teachers with models of professional behavior and opportunities to practice such models are only the beginning of the creation of an individual teacher's style. Only through practice will that teacher's style become apparent. This practice must be in as many opportunities as possible, in as many different settings as possible, and must provide connections from the methods classroom to the practical setting. The methods of technology used by a cooperating teacher in the field will have an impact on the use of technology by a preservice teacher (Meyers 1996). In these practical settings, preservice teachers will be able to see the connections between the use of technology they have seen in their methods courses and the "real classroom." Only through this direct practical connection to the theory of the methods course will novice teachers be able to see that technology is not something of importance only to the university.

When student teachers are in the field, they will be exposed to many teachers who will both be exemplars and nonexemplars of technology uses in the classroom. It is vital that student teachers practice the appropriate reflective activities that will allow them to sort these experiences into their appropriate roles in their own teaching model. Instead of seeing students as absorbing the introduction of an official curriculum or teaching plan, teachers must help students to see the meaning of the new information. The meaning will form a link between information and understanding (Caine and Caine 1995). This link will assist in metacognitive activities that students will be able to perform. Research into thinking systems has provided a view that we have to focus simultaneously on general metacognitive processes of problem solving and organized knowledge structures, which provide the conceptual tools for thinking (Johnson 1993). One such tool available for the classroom exists in the form of journals. Journals can provide students with the ability to recognize what they know and what they do not know. Journals also provide teachers with similar information so that teaching strategies can be tailored to benefit specific—and identified—areas of need (Bagely and Gallenberger 1992).

Following the work of J. Doyle Casteel at the University of Florida, I have developed a method of journal writing for my methods students that I have found to be highly effective. It is important for preservice teachers to see their own development over time, as well as the connection of previous materials to their current situations and vice versa. The journal takes the form of a roughly three-page per week format (Students should understand that "a page" serves as a guideline, not a limit to personal expression.) On the first page, students describe what they have learned during the week—in their own words and voice, not those of another teacher. On the second page, the students react to the learnings of the week. They are encouraged to communicate their fears, concerns, criticisms, and questions. Performing this activity will also enable the student to identify those things that they believe would be done differently if they were in the classroom of another teacher, especially their own classroom. The third page is left blank each week, until the last week of the semester, or the field experience. On this final reflection page, students are instructed to return to their entries for the previous weeks, both major examples of learning and initial reflections. Their final reflection will allow them to identify those areas of learning that might have been implicit during the early portions of the experience as well as connect those ideas raised at various times during the experience to those of other portions or even to those ideas raised in other methods courses. This final reflection provides students with a clear view of their own development during a time when they will have changed the most professionally. Hopefully, it will introduce students to a practice of reflection that will stay with them as they enter the profession. Through the development of metacognitive processes, students accept accountability for their actions, another step in academic attachment (Wehlage, Rutter, Smith, Lesio, and Fernandez 1989). When students become attached to their own developing skills, they can begin to develop their own model of teaching.

The development of students' metacognitive opportunities must be accompanied by the development of discourse. Students must have opportunities to develop academic discourse, that is, both linguistic and cultural knowledge about what it means to be a member of a particular community, for instance, a classroom, in order to achieve academic competence (Gutierre 1995). Students must use discourse in school; however, school discourse is qualitatively different from everyday discourse because "words are not only used as a means of communication, but as an object of study as well" (Moll and Whitmore 1993, 20). This is especially important for methods teachers when they are in the field. They will be exposed to communication in various forms, both helpful and hurtful, and they will need guidance in how to filter this information. The journal, discussed previously, provides a clear view of the students' thought processes during a field experience. This can provide an abundance of information that can be used during an exit interview. However, this can often be too late, especially regarding technology uses.

During methods courses, student teachers are exposed to varied uses of technology. During their practical experience, these same uses might be ignored, amplified, attacked, or fall anywhere along a continuum between amplified and attacked. It is vital that student teachers be provided with a means of communication during these practical experiences in which they can discuss concerns, especially with other students involved in their own field experience. Because many students are alone in school buildings for their experiences, the methods teacher must provide connections within the class/school by providing assignments that allow for/require interactions between students. For example, students currently in field placements must develop a list of problems in the field experience they did not anticipate, with the intended audience being students entering the experience the following year. This list is then sent to another member of the class, who in turn reacts to it. Students receive one e-mail (another student's list) and send two e-mails (their list and a reaction to another) while copying the instructor. Students are also required to interact with two other students, as they cannot receive a list from the same person to whom they sent a list. This provides the students with a feeling that they are not alone in a practicum experience. It also provides the instructor with a valuable "problems" list.

Students can also interact with a larger audience of preservice teachers by participating in a preservice teacher listserv, for example, PRESTO from Mississippi State University. Methods students can be required to join the listserv and provide a portfolio of messages that they have sent and received that provides clear evidence of materials and ideas they have garnered. Participation in this list must be forced initially; student teachers tend to find other uses for their time during the course of the semester. However, once introduced to the types of materials that can be garnered from participation in such a list, the student will hopefully develop a habit that he or she practices when he or she enters the profession. Again, the interaction with the listserv is a microcosm of the method being discussed: in the listserv the students are provided with a model, the opportunity to practice, and finally a chance to use the material. The students are then presented with a means of connecting their own vision of themselves as teachers with the material presented in their methods courses.

I had a student ask me, "Can't we just teach history and forget all this other stuff?" It would be great if it were that simple. In today's ever-changing world of standards and assessments, more and more emphasis is placed on technology. With Y2K on everyone's mind, it is as if the Internet were the flavor of the month. With politicians seeing the Internet as a sure-fire attention-and-vote-getter, it is more important than ever for teacher education to take it seriously. But when all is said and done, if it becomes a matter of money thrown at technology, in a form of lip service, success will be doubtful. If teacher education really wants to present technology and the Internet to preservice teachers successfully, it requires modeling, practice, and use. Then and only then, can we all focus on all this technology as a part of "just teaching history."

Websites for Teacher Education

listproc@Ra.MsState.edu: The preservice teacher listserv.

www.cssjournal.com/journal: Computers in the Social Studies. A website for a terrific electronic journal.

www.pacificnet.net/~mandel: Teachers helping teachers. A website with information for teachers, by teachers.

www.teachers.net: The teachers' website. an on-line gathering place full of valuable information.

discoveryschool.com/schrockguide: Schrock's Guide. One of the best sites available for teachers. Constantly updated!

www.execpc.com/~dboals: History/Social Studies site for K-12 Teachers. Terrific resources of material for methods classes.

www.nde.state.ne.us/SS/ss.html: Social Studies Educational Resources. From the State of Nebraska, contains valuable connections to materials.

education.indiana.edu/~socialst: Social studies sources from Indiana University.

score.rims.k12.ca.us/: SCORE. Materials for the social studies.

www.loc.gov: Library of Congress. A great resource for primary documents; includes great teacher materials.

bob.ucsc.edu/civil-war-letters/home.html: Letters from an Iowa Soldier in the U. S. Civil War.

home.pacbell.net/dunton/SSDletters.html: Letters from a soldier from New York.

www.he.net/~brumley/hillrev.htm: Letters from a Confederate general.

www.geocities.com/Pentagon/7914: Letters from the Civil War site.

www.hyperstudio.com: HyperStudio site. Available for upgrading plug-ins.

References

Bagely, T., and C. Gallenberger. "Assessing Students' Dispositions: Using Journals to Improve Students' Performance." *The Mathematics Teacher* 85 (1992): 660-63.

Caine, R. N., and G. Caine. "Reinventing Schools through Brain-based Learning." *Educational Leadership* 52, no. 7 (1995): 43-47.

Cuban, L. "Managing Dilemmas While Building Professional Communities." *Educational Researcher* 21, no. 1 (1992): 4-11.

Ellen, P. S. "The Impact of Self-Efficacy and Performance Satisfaction on Resistance to Change." *Dissertation Abstracts International* 48 (1987; University Microfilms No. 87-24, 826).

Griffin, P., A. Belyaeva, G. Soldatova, and the Velikhov-Hamburg Collective. "Creating and Reconstructing Contexts for Educational Interactions, Including a Computer Program." In *Contexts for Learning: Sociocultural Dynamics in Children's Development*, edited by E. A. Forman, N. Minick, and C. A. Stone, 1,120-52. New York: Oxford University Press, 1993.

Gutierre, K. D. "Unpacking Academic Discourse." *Discourse Processes* 19, no. 1 (1995): 21-37.

Jacobson, M. J., and R. J. Spiro. *Hypertext Learning Environments, Cognitive Flexibility, and the Transfer of Complex Knowledge: An Empirical Investigation.* Urbana, Ill.: Center for the Study of Reading, 1993. (ERIC Document Reproduction Service ED 355 508).

Johnson, L., and S. Harlow. "Modeling Instructional Change Using Interactive Multimedia in Teacher Training." In *Technology and Teacher Education Annual*, edited by D. Carey, 361-62. Charlottesville, Va.: Association for the Advancement of Computing in Education, 1993. (ERIC document reproduction service ED 355 937).

Johnson, R. T. "Context for Research on Technology and Teacher Education." In *Approaches to Research on Teacher Education and Technology*, edited by C. D. Maddox and M. D. Waggoner, 23-34. Charlottesville, Va.: Association for the Advancement of Computing in Education, 1993.

Meyers, D. M. "Responses of Social Studies Preservice Teachers to a Presentational Software Package: Using the Computer to Contextualize and Recontextualize Academic Content." Ph.D. diss., University of Florida, 1996.

Moll, L. C., and K. F. Whitmore, K .F. "Vygotsky in Classroom Practice: Moving from Individual Transmission to Social Interaction." In *Contexts for Learning: Sociocultural Dynamics in Children's Development*, edited by E. A. Forman, N. Minick, and C. A. Stone, 19-42. New York: Oxford University Press, 1993.

Neisser, U. *Cognition and Reality*. San Francisco: W.H. Freeman and Company, 1976.

O'Neil, J. "On Technology and Schools: A Conversation with Chris Dede." *Educational Leadership* 53, no. 2 (1995): 6-12.

Poole, B. J. *Education for an Information Age: Teaching in the Computerized Classroom.* Madison, Wis.: Brown and Benchmark, 1995.

Powell, A. G, E. Farrar, and D. K. Cohen. *The Shopping Mall High School.* Boston: Houghton-Mifflin, 1985.

Resnick, L. B. *Education and Learning to Think.* Washington, D.C.: National Academy Press, 1987.

Spiro, R. J. *Cognitive Flexibility Theory: Advanced Knowledge Acquisition in Ill-Structured Domains.* Champaign, Ill.: Center for the Study of Reading, 1988. (ERIC Document reproduction service number 302-821).

Spiro, R. J., P. J. Feltovich, M. J. Jacobson, and R. L. Coulson. "Cognitive Flexibility, Constructivism, and Hypertext: Random Access Instruction for Advanced Knowledge Acquisition in Ill-Structured Domains." In *Constructivism and the Technology of Instruction: A Conversation*, edited by T. M. Duffy and D. H. Jonassen, 57-75. Hillsdale, N.J.: Lawrence Erlbaum, 1992.

Spiro, R. J.,W. Vispoel, J. Schmitz, A. Samarapungauan, and A. Boerger. "Knowledge Acquisition for Application: Cognitive Flexibility and the Transfer in Complex Context Domains." In *Executive Control Processes*, edited by B. C. Britton, 177-200. Hillsdale, N.J.: Lawrence Erlbaum Associates, 1987.

Strommen, E. "Does Yours Eat Leaves? Cooperative Learning in an Educational Software Task." *Journal of Computing in Childhood Education* 4, no. 1 (1993): 45-55.

Vygotsky, L. *Thought and Language.* Translated and edited by E. Hanfmann & G. Vakar. Cambridge: Massachusetts Institute for Technology, 1934, translated in 1962.

Wehlage, G. G., R. A. Rutter, G. A. Smith, N. Lesio, and R. R. Fernandez. *Reducing the Risks: Schools as Community of Support.* New York: Palmer Press, 1989.

Williams, N. L., and K. I. Matthew. "Preservice Teachers' Navigation through Hypercard Stacks: Responses to the Stages of Writing Development." *Journal of Computing in Childhood Education* 6, no. 1 (1995): 25-41.

CHAPTER 15

PROBLEM-BASED LEARNING

Anthony W. Lorsbach
College of Education at Utah State University
&
Fred Basolo, Jr.
College of Education at Utah State University

When we were in school, we did not have the opportunity to act as a city planner, environmentalist, attorney, public health official, or a business owner, much less a concerned citizen. Today, however, more and more students have the opportunity not only to play these roles but to actually learn about their world from these divergent perspectives through problem-based learning (PBL). PBL, sometimes called project-based learning, "is an instructional method that uses real world problems as a context for students to learn critical thinking and problem-solving skills, and acquire knowledge of the essential concepts of the course" (Center for Teaching Effectiveness 1997). PBL has proven so effective in recent years that it is the dominant instructional strategy in medical schools around the world (Wilkerson and Gijselaers 1996). The advent of the Internet significantly elevates the potential of the PBL curriculum in providing engaging and worthwhile learning experiences.

Though initially developed for medical education, PBL can address many areas of education. For example, Scheurman and Newmann (1998, 24) discussed three criteria for authentic intellectual achievement in social studies developed by the Center on Organization and Restructuring Schools. Briefly, these criteria are (1) Construction of knowledge that "lead[s] students to synthesizing, generalizing, hypothesizing, and arriving at conclusions that produce new understandings for them"; (2) Disciplined inquiry in which students engage "in extended conversational exchanges with teacher and peers in a way that builds shared understanding" and "address ideas central to the discipline with enough thoroughness so that conceptual relationships can be explored and complex understandings produced"; and (3) Value beyond school that "helps students make connections between disciplinary content and either public problems or personal experiences." We believe PBL is an excellent teaching-learning method to develop these intellectual achievements for students in the social studies classroom. Research into problem-based learning curricula shows that PBL has great potential. For example, Hughes (1995, 432) reported that PBL "can enhance the transfer of concepts to new problems, can heighten intrinsic interest in the subject matter, and can strengthen self-directed study skills."

Margetson (1994) has discussed PBL as a solution to the constant call for educational reform.

> Problem-focused education takes this further. It embodies critical thinking in educative learning rather than importing it as an additional perspective. In doing so it opens the curriculum, not by assuming that a move must be made from disciplinarity to interdisciplinarity, but by considering whatever is needed in tackling problems. This leaves open the question of whether what is learned is helpfully regarded as "disciplinary" or "interdisciplinary" or not. Problem-focused education seeks understanding of appropriate depth in response to the problems in question...The structure and process of problem-based learning is open and encourages self-directed learning and group work systematically in an increasingly coherent experience of educative learning.

Although there is no one way to implement PBL, Moursund (1998) described nine characteristics of PBL using information technology:

1. It is learner-centered, providing students with some choice of content and sources.

2. It has authentic content and purpose that is real-world, complex, and contradictory.

3. It is challenging in that the PBL takes time, resources, discovery, and higher-order skills.

4. The result of PBL is a product, presentation, or performance.

5. PBL results in collaboration, be it among several students, classes, or remotely.

6. There is incremental and continual improvement as the work proceeds.

7. It involves teacher facilitation as a guide, mentor, resource, and learner.

8. It has explicit goals.

9. It is constructivist in nature.

The last point, while seemingly simple, can provide a very helpful perspective to the teacher concerned with implementing PBL and warrants some discussion on its own before we consider PBL in relation to the Internet.

Constructivism as a Referent for Problem-Based Learning

Constructivism is a word used frequently by educators of late to describe a theoretical rationale for research and teaching. Many current reform efforts in education are associated with the notion of constructivism. But what exactly is constructivism, and how can it be useful to the practicing teacher in implementing PBL?

Constructivism is an epistemology, a theory of knowledge used to explain how we know what we know. A constructivist epistemology is useful to teachers if used as a referent, that is, as a way to make sense of what they see, think, and do. The constructivist epistemology asserts that the only tools available to a knower are the senses. It is only through seeing, hearing, touching, smelling, and tasting that an individual interacts with the environment. With these messages from his or her senses, the individual builds a picture of the world. Therefore, constructivism asserts that knowledge resides in individuals; that knowledge cannot be transferred intact from the brain of a teacher to the brains of students. The student tries to make sense of new knowledge by trying to fit it with his or her experience. Consequently, words are not containers whose meanings are encapsulated in each word itself; words gain meaning through an individual's construction of knowledge. We can communicate with another person because the meaning of our words is compatible with the meaning others give the same words. Communication is an important act to constructivist teachers—one that is key to implementing PBL successfully.

With constructivism as a referent, teachers often use problem solving as a learning strategy. To learn, a person's existing conceptions of the world must be unreliable, unviable, and problematic. When our conceptions of the world are problematic, we try to make sense out of the situation based on what we already know (i.e., we use prior knowledge to make sense of the data our senses perceive). Other persons are part of our experiential world; thus, others are important for making meaning.

"Others" are so important to constructivists that cooperative learning is a primary teaching strategy. It allows individuals to test the fit of their experiential world with a community of others because others help to constrain our thinking. The interactions with others cause perturbations, and, by resolving the perturbations, individuals make adaptations to fit their new experiential world. The cooperative nature of problem-based learning complements this model of learning.

From a constructivist perspective, learning is not the search for truth. It is a process that assists us in making sense of our world. Using a constructivist perspective, teaching the social sciences becomes more like the social science that scientists do—it is an active, social process of making sense of experiences. Indeed, actively engaging students (we have all heard the call for "hands-on, minds-on") is the goal of most education reform. It is an admirable goal, and using constructivism as a referent to implement PBL provides curriculum framework for reaching that goal.

Learners need time to experience, reflect on their experiences in relation to what they already know, and resolve any problems that arise. Accordingly, learners need time to clarify, elaborate, describe, compare, negotiate, and reach consensus on what specific experiences mean to them. This learning process must occur within an individual; however, the person's inner voice can be supplemented through discussions with others.

Therefore, an important part of a constructivist curriculum should be the negotiation of meaning. Students must be given opportunities to make sense of what is learned by negotiating meaning, comparing what is known to new experiences, and resolving discrepancies between what is known and what seems to be implied by new experience. Ideally, the resolution of discrepancies enables an individual to reach an equilibrium, with no remaining curiosity about an experience in relation to what is known. Negotiation also can occur between individuals in a classroom. The process involves discussion and attentive listening, making sense of the points of view; it is then possible to discuss similarities and differences between the theories of peers within a group. Justifying one position over another and selecting those theories that are viable can lead to consensus that is understood by those within a peer group.

The Internet as a Medium for Problem-Based Learning

To summarize, constructivism is a model of knowing in which individuals construct a picture of their world, learning is problematic and adaptive, and communication with others is vital to constrain thinking. PBL is an instructional method that is learner-centered and real-world, and involves collaboration. PBL is certainly an excellent example of constructivist teaching and learning, but can these lofty ideals and goals actually be carried out in classrooms with limited resources? The answer, of course, is yes—with access to the Internet.

The Internet can be a perfect medium for constructivist-based PBL because it can provide real-world problems requiring collaboration with classmates, or peers from around the world. Using the Internet can give teachers access to real-world problems to make students' understanding of the world problematic, be it from ignorance or prejudice. For example, the International Education and Resource Network (I*EARN, see below for URL) provides students with opportunities to collaborate with others from around the world to offer solutions to problems such as the lack of clean water in Nicaragua, the exploitation of child labor, racism, and poverty. Using the Internet as a teaching medium allows students to gain understanding of other points of view (from a constructivist perspective, this constrains thinking and permits negotiation of meaning). As students develop solutions to problems, they learn of the world's complexity and that, for example, developers and conservationists alike have valid points to consider. The Internet provides students with greater access to the knowledge and opinions of experts as they begin to formulate solutions. Finally, the Internet is the perfect means to communicate to others the product or presentation of the PBL—parents, administrators, concerned citizens, teachers, and students from around the world can bear witness to the meaningful learning demonstrated by students. By making students' results public, they, in turn, become teachers to others—which we believe is another opportunity for students to learn from the experience.

How the Internet Enhances Problem-Based Learning

As students take more ownership of their learning in the form of its direction and construction, an impartial enabler becomes necessary. The Internet does more than act as a resource of information. The Internet provides students with an exciting, creative, and engaging way to obtain, analyze, and deliver information. Most students are attracted to the Internet because it allows them the chance to take charge as they gather information, to be creative as they construct web pages, and to receive recognition as they communicate their own ideas. Teachers appreciate this electronic medium because it is fast and less messy than the traditional chalk-and-paper routine. Problems may be presented to students on a teacher-created web page. Besides presenting the problem statement, this page may include links to real and or teacher-created pages that provide additional information. The page may also have a message board, which would allow them to post questions or information that all members of the class could access.

PBL is an excellent way to reinforce process skills, which include observing, classifying, measuring, predicting, inferring, identifying and controlling variables, formulating and testing hypothesis, interpreting data, experimenting, constructing models, and communicating. A PBL experience allows students not just to learn about social science but to conduct social science research. Students have the freedom to make a shrewd guess, develop their own fertile hypothesis, and take courageous leaps to tentative conclusions (Bruner 1960).

One of the challenges in PBL is choosing an appropriate topic. The topic should be one that evokes a high student interest level, has real-life implications, and can be easily explored by students. One such topic used by Fred Basolo is called "Cosmic Collisions," which instructors of the Summer Adventures program developed in 1997. The program was developed by the Illinois Mathematics and Science Academy and conducted on the campus of Illinois State University. The PBL components and student results may be seen at www.imsa.edu/team/spi/SADVI. The same topic was used again the next summer in the SIMaST (Students Integrating Mathematics, Science and Technology) program, a part of the Center for Mathematics, Science and Technology at Illinois State University (www.ilstu.edu/depts/cemast/Basolo.html/index.htm). Students eagerly embraced the "Cosmic Collision" PBL because they know that it is possible for objects in space to have an impact on earth, that many books and movies exist about the topic, and that such an event could directly affect their quality of life.

Once you choose a topic, the first step is to engage the students. The engagement will identify the real-life need for the PBL investigation and build excitement and motivation within the students. Engaging the students is best done by someone with expertise and interest in the topic. We teachers know that students will be more receptive to information if it comes from professionals in that field. In the example of "Cosmic Collisions," Carl Wenning, astronomer and director of the Illinois State University planetarium, presented the problem to the students and asked for their help in evaluating the risk associated with Near Earth Objects (NEOs) colliding with the earth. At this time the tasks of the students should be clearly outlined:

- Assess the likelihood of an impact.

- Assess the risks associated with such an impact.

- If necessary and possible, propose a plan for minimizing the effects of an asteroid impact.

- Make recommendations about the need, if any, for further research on the identification and tracking of NEOs and/or plans for minimizing the risks associated with NEOs.

- Prepare a final presentation of your findings and publish it on the World Wide Web.

The next step is for the teacher to provide students with assistance in performing their tasks. This step is crucial because teachers must do this without directing or interjecting. The teacher must now get out of the way and let the students take control of the problem. Students should be encouraged to use past knowledge to determine the directions taken. This is the most valuable part of the experience for the students, because now they construct their own knowledge and take ownership and pride in learning. At this point in PBL, the teacher should help students determine what they still need to discover. A good way to uncover this is by having periodic discussions with the students in which they form two lists. On one list, they write what they now know, and on the other, they list what they still need to know. Such a discussion allows students to reflect on what they know, share information, and decide for themselves what is important to know. The teacher may also help the students by providing them with resources that they may choose to use. An example of teacher-provided resources may include informational articles, on-line resources, letters from organizations, principles of risk assessment, search engines, and web page creation. When students work in small groups on PBL, they encounter different successes and frustrations so it is a good idea for them to submit periodic status reports to the teacher. Teachers review the reports and offer some assistance if needed.

PBL is complete when all the initial tasks have been accomplished. Students should share their PBL experience with others (e.g., place their pages on the web so that classmates and parents may see them on-line). The assessment of the student's PBL experience should reflect the product of the group as well as the individual student's performance. The evaluation should assess the extent to which each task was completed and the extent to which each individual contributed.

Internet Resources for PBL Instruction

We hope that, after this brief introduction, you will be interested in learning more about PBL as a method of instruction and how to implement PBL by using the Internet. If so, we encourage you to take advantage of the following resources.

▪ The Southwest Educational Development Laboratory: www.sedl.org
Includes information on PBL, some of which refers to postsecondary use of PBL, although many resources are pertinent to all grade levels. Here PBL is defined and a PBL approach to lesson planning is described; links to other PBL sites are also available.

▪ Center for Problem-Based Learning, Illinois Math and Science Academy: www.imsa.edu/team/cpbl
Was established to encourage PBL research, information exchange, teacher training, and curriculum development. The site defines and describes what PBL looks like in the classroom and provides examples. Teachers from all grade levels will find this site valuable. Links to other PBL resources are available.

How has PBL been used in the classroom? We hope the following examples begin to illustrate for you the power of using PBL in the classroom.

▪ Exploring The Earth (ETE): cotf.edu/ETE/etehome.html
Provides teachers with tools for students to become environmentally aware and to acquire the values and attitudes necessary for sustainable development. Toward this end, the ETE modules encourage collaborative groups of students to conduct research in environmental areas and to generate products that demonstrate understanding. Resources are provided to address global issues through the use of satellite images, and to create classrooms featuring active-learning approaches, assessment through exhibitions, teamwork, students taking responsibility for their own learning, and awareness of the dynamics of both physical/biological and socioeconomic variables. ETE emphasizes problem-based learning (PBL) and collaborative learning groups for student-directed inquiry into Earth systems education. The emphasis in this model is for students to take responsibility—and a more active role in the learning process. And as in real-life situations, the goal is not in answering questions correctly, but in figuring out the right question to ask.

■ The Center for Problem-Based Learning (CPBL) at the Illinois Science and Math Academy: www.imsa.edu/team/cpbl.html
Has several examples of integrated problems available on-line. One particular example, The Buffalo Commons Project, provides helpful guidelines to the teacher for whom PBL is new. Students are members of a Buffalo Commons Commission to advise the president and Congress on the establishment of a Buffalo Commons somewhere in the Great Plains. This problem is most appropriate for middle and high school students.

The CPBL also offers detailed guidelines, including assessments, on SuperLand: How safe is it? This project, suitable for middle and high school students and adaptable to other geographic areas, asks students to determine whether a theme park should be constructed in southern Illinois. Another problem is Transforming Garbage into Gold. This problem about waste and recycling is structured for use in many locations (urban, suburban, and rural) and adaptable to many grade levels.

■ The International Education and Resource Network (I*EARN): www.igc.apc.org/iearn
An international nonprofit organization which sponsors collaboration between students and teachers on social and environmental projects on an international scale. Participants designed many structured projects, including the following in social studies:

> First Byte Project
> Cultural Bridges with China
> Faces of War
> Teddy Bear Project
> First/Indigenous Peoples
> The Holocaust/Genocide Project
> Inside View, An Urban Student Newsletter
> Kids Can Elementary/Middle School Newsletter
> Child Labour Project
> Eradication of Poverty
> World Religions Project
> One Day in the Life Cross-Cultural Comparison
> Clean Water for Nicaragua
> Recovery/Substance Abuse
> Peace Project
> World Millennium Project
> E-Mail as Reconciliation Tool in Communities in Conflict
> International Foods and Cultural Patterns
> Schools De-Mining Schools (with United Nations)
> BikeAbout, A Mediterranean Exploration by Bicycle
> Hidden Histories, A WWW-based Project
> Folk Costumes around the World
> Racing Against Racism

I*EARN also allows students and teachers to design their own projects and seek partners throughout the world. Projects for all grade levels are available here.

References

Bruner, J. *The Process of Education*. Cambridge, Mass.: Harvard University Press, 1960.

Center for Teaching Effectiveness "What Is Problem-Based Learning?" *Newsletter* of the Center for Teaching Effectiveness, January 1995. Dover: University of Delaware, 1997. (www.udel.edu/pbl/cte/jan95-what.html).

Hughes, A. S. "Toward a More Thoughtful Professional Education for Social Studies Teachers: Can Problem-based Learning Contribute?" *Journal* 25, no. 4 (1995): 431-45.

Margetson, D. "Current Educational Reform and the Significance of PBL." *Studies in Higher Education* 19, no 1 (1994): 5-19.

Moursund, D. "Project-based Learning in an Information-Technology Environment." *Learning and Leading with Technology* 25 (1998): 8, 4.

Scheurman, Geoffrey, and Fred M. Newmann. "Authentic Intellectual Work in Social Studies: Putting Performance before Pedagogy." *Social Education* 62, no. 1 (1998): 23-25.

Wilkerson, L., and W. H. Gijselaers, eds. *Bringing Problem-Based Learning to Higher Education: Theory and Practice*. San Francisco: Jossey-Bass, 1996.

CHAPTER 16

CITIZENSHIP PROJECTS

John W. Saye
Auburn University
&
John D. Hoge
University of Georgia

Organizational barriers to thoughtful social studies instruction have long been recognized by teachers and researchers (e.g., Cuban 1984; Goodlad 1984). The barriers include restricted preparation time, the fifty-minute class period, dry, coverage-oriented textbooks, large numbers of students, standardized testing, and limited media resources. Despite these barriers, social studies teachers are persistently urged to do more to cultivate higher-order thinking skills on a variety of citizenship issues (Newmann 1991; Rossi 1995).

The growing classroom presence of the Internet both complicates and makes more urgent the goal of preparing rational citizens (Risinger 1997). Information Age citizens must make reasoned judgments in an exploding, ungoverned universe of information. The extremely open learning environment of the Internet creates new challenges for managing content and offering high quality instruction (Braun 1997; Singleton and Giese 1998). The reliability and adequacy of information varies widely in the unregulated universe of websites. Unlike more traditional learning environments, there is no linear or linking narrative to give form to the content. Students may follow highly idiosyncratic paths and become distracted, disorganized, or confused. To help counteract these characteristics, teachers must help learners acquire sophisticated skills for synthesizing and making meaning in the Internet information environment.

Using the Internet in a school setting poses significant time management problems as well. Access to websites can be slow. Heavily used sites may not always be available on demand. The lack of linear paths and the lack of discrimination in search engines can make the Internet an inefficient tool for accomplishing many traditional learning objectives.

Despite such drawbacks to its use, the growing presence of the Internet obliges social studies teachers to address the challenge of producing reflective consumers of the public issues information offered there. Doing so requires that we find ways to manage the information glut so that Internet information resources advance rather than impede civic thinking and participation goals.

The Internet can help teachers overcome traditional organizational barriers to thoughtfulness if we sharply focus its use around the goal of civic competence. In this chapter we focus on a central theme taken from the tenth strand of the NCSS Standards, *Expectations of Excellence: Curriculum Standards for Social Studies* (1994). The tenth stands deals with Civic Ideals and Practices. The theme on which we will focus is: How can we best ensure that all citizens have an equal voice in decisions about our society? This focus on a fundamental idea in our field—and on evaluating the quality of arguments about this idea—provides a framework for organizing a high-quality Internet-Based Citizenship Inquiry Project (IBCIP). This chapter offers three examples of IBCIPs and further demonstrates how Internet resources can be used to speed and otherwise facilitate social studies teachers' work toward achieving higher-order thinking on citizenship issues.

Organizing Instruction for Internet Use

To tap the Internet's potential as an instructional partner, teachers need a management strategy that incorporates this technology into the classroom. Adding an IBCIP offers teachers an efficient approach to achieving higher-order thinking about citizenship issues. As the chapter examples illustrate, carefully designed IBCIPs use the expertise available on the Internet to facilitate independent student learning. More self-regulated learning frees more of the teacher's time for teacher-mediated small group discussions. Such meetings give teachers deeper insight into students' thinking so that misconceptions can be clarified and deeper reasoning encouraged (Saye, in press).

IBCIPs can be successfully implemented in a classroom that has access to only one Internet-connected computer. Effective IBCIP integration does not require every student to be on-line every moment. A productive IBCIP may be created with one Internet-connected computer, a second less powerful computer for production work, and a focused set of other audiovisual and print resources. The availability of more Internet-connected computers allows more options in designing IBCIPs but may also complicate aspects of their management.

With careful planning, a teacher can organize IBCIPs with three-to-five small group teams that rotate through well-defined activities. To be productive, self-regulated learners, students must be clear about what is expected of them and how their performance will be assessed. Frequent feedback on progress must be provided. Given this organizational scheme and additional issue-specific supports (see examples below), teams can work independently with the Internet, commercial software, and collections of more traditional media, freeing the teacher to confer with students and conduct small-group discussions. At appropriate intervals, the teacher may schedule whole-class sessions for overviews, discussions, and presentations of final student products.

Preparation for Instruction

Use of Internet sources can accelerate and enrich IBCIP planning and preparation time. Commonly available news sites (e.g., www.usnewswire.com and www.wired.com/news) provide teachers with substantial current information on a variety of citizenship issues. Issue selection should match established curriculum goals and students' maturity. Teachers may easily tie their lessons to national social studies standards (e.g., www.ncss.org/standards/toc.html) and, in many cases, objectives based on their own state standards (e.g., admin.doe.k12.ga.us/gadoe/sla/qcccopy.nsf or see www.csun.edu/~hcedu013/res.html for a gateway to all SDEs). Collegial interaction on topics related to your IBCIPs is available from a variety of discussion groups and listservs such as The Instructional Technology Committee of the National Council for the Social Studies (www.ncss.org/links/listserv.html) and the Humanities & Social Sciences On-Line (h-net2.msu.edu/lists). A full list of social studies newsgroups is available from www.csun.edu/~hcedu013/newsgroups.html.

Once a teacher has developed a focused citizenship question, issue, or problem for investigation, workable boundaries must be established within the vast available Internet content. Perhaps the biggest organizational challenge facing teachers who seek to implement an IBCIP is the "unboundedness" of the Internet. Software is available to screen content that is inappropriate for an educational setting. The universe of remaining educational sites, however, is enormous. Strategies must be developed to limit the field of exploration so that students remain focused on the problem and class time is used efficiently (Caruso 1997).

Teachers may bound content in a number of ways. Software such as WebWhacker (www.ffg.com) or Web Buddy (www.dataviz.com) allows teachers to preselect sites and download them to school computers. Using these utilities, teachers may construct topical menus of sites that students access without being connected to the Internet. Not only does such a strategy allow teachers to channel student site choices, it guarantees that sites will be available during class meeting times. Downloaded sites may also expand the number of available workstations because students may conduct their explorations on off-line computers.

Use of an on-line, teacher-developed gateway to sites offers another, less restricted boundary strategy. Simple web construction tools such as Claris HomePage and Adobe PageMill make it easy for teachers to construct class home pages that feature sites they have selected for class investigations. Although not as tightly bounded as "whacked" sites, teacher-constructed websites also allow exemplary student work to be shared with audiences beyond the classroom.

As most of us have experienced, standard search engines often return trivial or otherwise inappropriate websites. A number of gateway sites can help teachers meet the challenge of locating high-quality teaching ideas and Internet resources for IBCIPs. For example, California State University-Northridge provides a social studies specific clearinghouse site (www.csun.edu/~vceed009/socialstudies. html), as well as a special page with many ideas for IBCIPs (www.csun.edu/~hcedu013/on-lineactivities.html). The SCORE site (score.rims.k12.ca.us) offers reviewed social studies resource sites as well as suggestions for conceptualizing problem-based learning and performance-based assessments. The Internet Scout Project, sponsored by the National Science Foundation, (www.scout.cs.wisc.edu/scout) provides daily and weekly updates of key sites for students, parents, and teachers at all levels.

Although the Internet offers rich primary source materials and time-saving planning resources, teachers must use organizational strategies that maximize this technology's potential for facilitating thoughtful classrooms (Hancock 1997; Windschitl 1998). IBCIPs offer an effective strategy for increasing students' engagement and reasoning on civic issues. The complex culminating activities of IBCIPs make optimal use of rich content while encouraging teamwork and creative, divergent thinking. IBCIPs allow teachers to overcome several longstanding organizational obstacles and do a better job of preparing citizens who are critical consumers of the information resources available on the Internet.

Elementary School IBCIP Example

Focus: What beliefs about good conduct and proper living can be drawn from the different religions in our society?

Task: Students develop religion-specific presentations, which they present on Parents' Night.

A. Begin this IBCIP by having a community member present an overview of his or her religion and share religion-based beliefs about good conduct and proper living. Ask this resource person to address areas such as charity, humility, nonviolence, prayer, respect for elders, and tolerance of other religions. If possible, videotape the presentation for later reference.

B. Debrief the experience by asking the students to identify similar religion-based beliefs that they have learned. Note similarities and differences. Use a KWL chart to identify what students know, want to know, and later will have learned about each major world religion and any other religion or ethical system represented in the classroom.

C. Assign the students into religion research groups. Each group should have the following members with their specific responsibilities:

Group Director: monitors/schedules the work of the group; acts as liaison with teacher; fills in for absent group members.

Data Recorder(s): keeps a record of all facts found and their sources.

Display Developer(s): develops electronic and/or print media needed to support presentation; works closely with presenter and writer/researcher.

Writer/Researcher: works with data recorders and display developers to create the report script.

Presenter(s): makes presentations; works with display developer.

Webmaster: does on-line searching, downloading, printing; works closely with writer/researcher and the data recorder.

D. Distribute a data retrieval chart to each group. The chart should include the following categories: names of major holidays; name(s) given to supreme beings, such as "God"; customs for worship; other customs; major religious ceremonies; origin of the religion; and beliefs regarding proper life conduct. As an example, show the class a completed data collection chart for a religion that has not been assigned to a group.

E. Start the groups on their research. Let one or two groups start with audiovisual and print resources, while the other groups begin to locate resources on the Internet. Use sources such as the following:

Internet resources for the study of religion, including pages on religious studies and comparative religion, Western, Eastern, and U.S. religions: www.academicinfo.net

Descriptions of sixty-three religions, faith groups, and ethical systems. Typical information for each entry includes a brief history, sacred texts, beliefs and practices, sects, and links to related sites: www.religioustolerance.org/var_rel.htm

F. Hold a conference with the groups as they move through the process of collecting their information and developing their presentations. Encourage comparisons among the religions, among the groups' research results, and among the presentations. Practice the presentations for Parents' Night.

ENRICHMENT ACTIVITIES

- Develop a web page that displays the results of the students' research.

- Conduct research on nations where the selected religions are dominant. Try to determine how the dominance of the religion has influenced daily life in these nations.

- Search for codes of ethical and moral conduct that are not based in a recognized religion.

Middle School IBCIP Example

Focus: Is it possible to have a homework policy that is supported by research conclusions, the administration, and a majority of parents, teachers, and students?

Task: Students develop a homework policy that they present to the members of the PTA/O at its next meeting at their middle school.

A. Begin by creating an artificial homework crisis. During the crisis, raise questions about parents' attitudes, students' homework loads, the school's policy (or lack of policy) on homework, and issues such as the weight of homework assignments in the gradebook. Focus on the issues of what should be included in a homework policy and who should make those decisions.

B. Divide students into interest groups, representing the views of educational researchers, school administrators, parents, teachers, and middle school students. Assign the following roles with their specific responsibilities:

Coordinator: monitors/schedules the work of the group; acts as liaison with teacher; fills in for absent group members.

Negotiator: takes part in all sessions needed to articulate actual policy; works with presenter and writer/researcher to shape their work.

Display Developer: develops electronic and/or print media needed to support presentation; works closely with presenter and writer/researcher.

Writer/Researcher: creates questionnaires, scripts, reports, and so forth.

Presenter: makes presentations; works with display developer and negotiator.

Webmaster: does on-line searching, downloading, printing; works closely with writer/researcher.

C. Distribute the following list of questions to help the groups clarify their potential positions, key issues, and concerns.
   ▮ What functions or purposes may homework serve?
   ▮ What criteria should be used to evaluate homework?
   ▮ What percentage of a student's grade should be based on homework?
   ▮ What homework practices are most used, most effective, and most disliked?
   ▮ What subjects tend to have the most homework, and how much time does each take?
   ▮ Who should check homework: parents, teachers, or students?
   ▮ What limits should be set on homework help?

D. Groups meet to develop a research plan and survey that may be given on paper, in a direct personal interview, via e-mail, or posted on appropriate listservs. Strategies for data collection, analysis, and presentation are developed. Potential websites and books to aid research are the following:
   ▮ The B. J. Pinchbeck's Homework Helper site has received more than 102 web awards and offers more than 450 links to information sources on the web: www.bjpinchbeck.com
   ▮ National Middle School Association serves as a voice for the educational and developmental needs of young adolescents: www.nmsa.org
   ▮ The following site provides the searchable ERIC data base of education documents and links to other Internet information sources: askeric.org
   ▮ This site presents listserves that discuss policy issues related to young children, K-12 school administration, middle level education, and parenting: ericps.crc.uiuc.edu/eece/listserv.html
   ▮ Cholden, H., J. Friedman, and E. Tiersky. *The Homework Handbook: Practical Advice You Can Use Tonight to Help Your Child Succeed Tomorrow.* NTC Contemporary Publishing Company, 1998, 224 pages. ISBN: 0809228815. Price: $12.95.
   ▮ Eisenberg, M. B., and R. E. Berkowitz. *Helping with Homework: A Parent's Guide to Information Problem-Solving.* Syracuse, N.Y.: ERIC Clearinghouse on Information & Technology, 1996, 182 pages. ISBN: 0937597422. Price: $20.00.

E. When results are in, the groups discuss their findings and draft individual homework policies. The policies must include a statement of the purposes of homework, and recommendations regarding the amount of daily homework, and the weight of homework in determining subject grades.

F. The groups negotiate a unified homework policy statement. The presenters and coordinators from each group work to develop the PTA/O presentation. The presentation is reviewed by all members of the class, other classes and teachers, and the principal. Adjustments to the policy statement and presentation are made as needed.

G. After hearing the PTA/O presentation, the PTA/O discusses and votes on the student recommendations.

ENRICHMENT ACTIVITIES

▌ Design a web page or slide show that describes the project.

▌ Conduct e-mail exchanges with other schools, students, or groups.

▌ Gather international views on homework using the Internet.

▌ Contact, via regular mail or e-mail, the authors of books and articles used in this project to seek their reaction to the new homework policy.

High School IBCIP Example

Focus: Do we need to reform our present system of financing campaigns?

Task: Posing as members of various interest groups, student teams use the Internet as a resource to design a campaign supporting their group's position on campaign finance reform.

A. Using a newsmagazine article or newspaper editorial, introduce some of the problems surrounding our present system of financing election campaigns. List the major issues and problems associated with the present system.

B. Tell the students that they will each be involved in designing an advertising campaign, which should include a television commercial, a direct mail flyer, a billboard, and a speech to be given before a congressional committee hearing on campaign finance reform. Students will use a multimedia presentation program to demonstrate their campaigns. Provide an example of a persuasive campaign on an issue such as gun control.

C. Each team will have five members. Assign the following roles with their specific responsibilities.

Project Coordinator: coordinates the efforts of group members to ensure that all elements of the project are completed on schedule; leads members in researching the topic and developing a campaign strategy; delivers the speech to Congress.

Script Writer: composes the commercial script; assists in developing a storyboard for the commercial if the group chooses not to do a live performance; acts in commercial if group chooses a live performance; assists in composing the flyer.

Speech Writer: composes the speech script; assists in composing the flyer; acts in commercial if group chooses a live performance.

Graphic Designer: designs the billboard and flyer; assists in developing a storyboard for the commercial if the group chooses not to do a live performance; acts in commercial if group chooses a live performance.

Technical Director: uses group's ideas to produce the final presentation; uses technology tools to assist with design tasks in producing the commercial, flyer, and billboard.

D. Assign the teams to the interest groups listed below and have them investigate their interest group's views on campaign finance reform. To guide the groups' investigations, give each group a data retrieval chart with the following headings: Description of my group; description of the problem; proposed solutions to the problem; my group's position; arguments for this position; opponents' arguments; responses to opponents' arguments.

- Democratic Party: www.democrats.org/party/positions
- Republican Party: www.rnc.org/search
- Television and Radio Broadcasters Associations: www.nab.org/Issues
- Common Cause: www.commoncause.org
- National Association of Manufacturers: www.nam.org
- AFL-CIO: www.aflcio.org/home.htm
- American Civil Liberties Union: www.aclu.org/congress/campaignfinance.html

Supply groups with the following list of government, news media, and policy institute sites to further extend their background research:

- Federal Election Commission: www.fec.gov/pages/citnlist.htm
- CNN AllPolitics: allpolitics.com
- C-Span: www.c-span.org/campfin.htm
- USA Today: www.usatoday.com/news
- Brookings Institute: www.brook.edu/gs/campaign/cfr_hp.htm
- Cato Institute: www.cato.org/testimony/ct-bs051497.html

E. Projects are judged on accuracy and thoroughness of information, identification of opposing arguments, creative defense of position, clarity of expression, and quality of final product. Following project presentations, individuals write an editorial defending their personal view on the issue.

References

Braun, Joseph A., Jr. "Past, Possibilities, and Potholes on the Information Superhighway." *Social Education* 61, no. 3 (1997): 149-53.

Caruso, C. "Before You Cite a Site." *Educational Leadership* 55, no. 3 (1997): 24-25.

Cuban, L. "Policy and Research Dilemmas in the Teaching of Reasoning: Unplanned Designs." *Review of Educational Research* 54, no. 4 (1984): 655-81.

Goodlad, J. I. *A Place Called School.* New York: McGraw-Hill Book Company, 1984.

Hancock, V. "Creating the Information Age School." *Educational Leadership* 55, no. 3 (1997): 60-63.

National Council for the Social Studies. *Expectations of Excellence: Curriculum Standards for Social Studies.* Washington, D.C.: NCSS, 1994.

Newmann, Fred M. "Higher Order Thinking in the Teaching of Social Studies: Connections between Theory and Practice." In *Informal Reasoning and Education*, edited by J. Voss, D. Perkins, and J. Segal. Hillsdale, N.J.: Erlbaum, 1991.

Risinger, C. Frederick. "Citizenship Education and the World Wide Web." *Social Education* 61, no. 4 (1997): 223-24.

Rossi, J. A. "In-Depth Study in an Issues-Oriented Social Studies Classroom." *Theory and Research in Social Education* 23, no. 2 (1995): 87-120.

Saye, John W. "Creating Time to Develop Student Thinking: Team-Teaching with Technology." *Social Education* 62, no.6 (1998):356-62.

Singelton, Laurel R., and James R. Giese. "American Memory: Using Library of Congress On-Line Resources to Enhance History Teaching." *Social Education* 62, no. 3 (1998): 142-44.

Windschitl, M. "The WWW and Classroom Research: What Path Should We Take?" *Educational Researcher* 27, no. 1 (1998): 28-33.

CHAPTER 17

CIVIC-MORAL DEVELOPMENT

Joseph A. Braun, Jr.
Department of Curriculum and Instruction
Illinois State University

At the conclusion of the movie *Mr. Holland's Opus*, the principal gives Mr. Holland a compass as a retirement gift. This gift symbolizes a metaphor she shared with him at the beginning of his career about the role a teacher plays: it illustrates that in addition to the role of teaching students information about "subjects," a teacher must also serve as a compass—a compass that provides moral guidance as students prepare to navigate their way through the world. Heightening that need for teachers to be a moral compass for students is the vast information and communication exchange known as the Internet. Mehlinger (1996) described how the teacher's role of information dispenser is shifting with all that is available on-line. A central point in this chapter is the idea that the role of teacher as a moral compass will become even more necessary as a result of the Internet. Before describing the specific affective aims and activities that social studies teachers can use in serving this role, some orientation to this role of moral compass seems warranted.

Scott (1991) identified three distinct affective aims, which will focus the discussion in this chapter: values, empathy, and moral development. Based on each of these aims, strategies for classroom use will be described in relation to using the Internet. Some strategies will be about the use of the Internet and what role it can play in our world—what teachers can do to address the affective influences and moral dilemmas the Internet brings to the human experience. Other strategies will focus on actual Internet sites the reader can visit, which relate to these affective aims. One of the leading proponents in the field of affective education, Merrill Harmin (1992), suggested a synthetic approach to the different aims, which incorporates a variety of strategies and WWW sites:

> Nor is the solution to discard our experience and search for yet another new method for tackling the old problems. As others have begun to suggest, there is much of value in both the traditional approaches and the new approaches to values education and moral educa-tion. Why not take the best elements of each, synthesize them, and improve from there?

The chapter concludes with an examination of the controversy surrounding the teaching of values as well as threats to values that the Internet itself seems to pose (Huffman 1994).

Affective Aims and the Social Studies Teacher as a Moral Compass

Just as compasses have points of orientation (N, S, E, W) for the user that provide a sense of where to head, reference points for social studies teachers regarding teaching values, empathy, and morals can be found in curriculum documents such as *Expectations of Excellence: Curriculum Standards for Social Studies* (National Council for the Social Studies Task Force 1994). The performance expectations for five of the ten thematic strands of the social studies standards offer explicit curriculum support for teaching affective aims: Individual Development and Identity (the study of individual development and identity); Individuals, Groups, and Institutions (the study of interactions among individuals, groups, and institutions); Science, Technology, and Society (the study of relationships among science, technology, and society); Global Connections (the study of global connections and interdependence); and Civic Ideals and Practices (the study of the ideals, principles, and practices of citizenship in a democratic republic; National Council for the Social Studies 1994).

Curricular goals and performance expectations that support affective education goals are important orientations for social studies teachers to establish, but social studies teachers should also consider other key points regarding their role as a moral compass providing guidance for students. While at one time advocates for the popular affective technique known as values clarification urged, in its theoretical approach, that teachers remain neutral regarding their values, one of the original developers of values clarification activities (Harmin 1988) has repudiated this position of neutrality. No longer is anyone urging teachers to remain neutral in the face of inappropriate material that can be encountered on-line. Of course, what constitutes inappropriate material might be open to different points of view, but essentially what is inappropriate for the school room can be succinctly characterized by two four-letter words: hate and smut.

Ultimately, the school law precept of *in loco parentis* (which means the teacher serves in place of the parents) should guide teachers in dealing with smut and hate found on the Internet. It seems simple: parents would not tolerate it in their home and neither should teachers tolerate it in schools. Yet sometimes teachers are stymied as to where to begin and what to do about these topics.

The following sections of this chapter describe teaching strategies that can promote learning for all three affective aims of social studies in relation to the Internet. The first affective aim (values) is well-suited for addressing the issues of hate and smut.

Values: Inculcating Versus Clarifying

The first affective aim deals with values that Shaver and Strong (1982, 17) defined as "standards and principles for judging worth." Part of the controversy about values education concerns the very nature of values themselves. Numerous groups have advocated a variety of lists of values, including this one from the Aspen Declaration—a coalition of character education advocates (Lickona 1998).

- Respect

- Responsibility

- Trustworthiness

- Caring

- Justice

- Citizenship

The National Council for the Social Studies has thirty-one beliefs and democratic values grouped into four broad categories (followed by examples selected as particularly appropriate to the Internet): (1) rights of the individual (liberty, security, privacy); (2) freedoms of the individual (thought, inquiry, expression); (3) responsibilities of the individual (honesty, compassion, respect for the rights of others); and (4) beliefs concerning societal conditions and governmental responsibilities (protection of individual rights and freedoms, working for the common good).

Because this chapter promotes a comprehensive approach to affective education, a comprehensive view regarding the teaching of values is appropriate. Thus, in the following discussion, both moral-social issues and matters of personal concern are considered values despite the fact that Turiel (1983) identified distinctions in the realm of social knowledge between morality and convention. Similarly, a comprehensive approach means that decisions about values can be made individually or as part of a group. Most importantly, researchers who have tried to measure the instructional effectiveness of values outcomes have also suggested a comprehensive approach. At this point, the evidence as to whether one particular approach is better than another in helping students attain particular values and attendant behaviors is inconclusive. (Lockwood 1978; Leming 1985).

Essentially, values education divides itself into two camps: those who would inculcate values versus those who would let students inquire into different choices and consequences (Metzger 1986). As the above suggests, what is advocated here is a combination of both. The following strategies illustrate both advocacy of what students should believe and how they should behave in ways essential for the common good (inculcating) followed by allowing them to reflect on and consider individual choices as they make decisions about how to conduct some aspects of their lives (clarifying).

Character Education

A currently popular approach to inculcating values has as its goal instilling a sense of good citizenship and represents a more traditional approach to values education (Kohn 1997). Often a list of rules for appropriate conduct is posted in prominent places. Students are exhorted (or rewarded) to follow these codes for the good of the school. An example of a set of rules regarding student behavior when using the Internet might include the following:

- Exit a site with improper language or photos immediately.

- Do not use improper language when exchanging e-mails.

- Never make arrangements to meet in person someone you know only over the Internet.

- Avoid all sites that your parents would not approve for your viewing.

- Realize the Internet is public; whatever you might publish there will be available to everyone.

- Do not download files or install software on school computers without permission.

- Evaluate the accuracy of content before you cite anything found on-line.

Teachers would still need to define what these rules mean, and make any appropriate additions. Additionally, they must make sure students comprehend the rules and monitor student compliance. Thus, fundamental to character education is a reliance on exhorting students to do the right thing and expecting them to do it. On the other hand, advocates of values clarification, as well as advocates associated with the other aims of empathy and moral development, would place a heavy emphasis on involving students in the process of developing the rules as well as expecting them to adhere to them.

One school district, endorsing character education as an element in its elementary social studies curriculum, uses the following approach to promote appropriate conduct when using the Internet. They offer students a license for going on-line. First, students receive instruction in skills such as conducting searches and Internet etiquette (Braun, Fernlund, and White 1998). They also study and become familiar with the "rules of the road" for going on-line, including writing an essay about why they should obey them, which the teacher can parallel to the rules young people study before they apply for a driver's license. Students take a written test and then show their on-line competence in using the Internet. They demonstrate their understanding of the "rules of the road," Internet etiquette in using e-mail, and conducting on-line searches. Once they qualify for a license, they receive a laminated card, including a photo taken by a digital camera. When on-line, the student displays the license via a clip attached to the computer station. If the student violates the "rules of the road" while on-line, the license can be revoked.

CLASSROOM STRATEGIES

While not foolproof, this approach is representative of the character education movement. In tracing its origins over several decades, one notes that the movement's original strategies were rather blatant, and single-mindedly patriotic; currently, character education combines different meanings and goals regarding what is character and how it can be developed in students (Kohn 1997). It can take many forms, ranging from conflict resolution programs to behaviorist use of rewards, such as field trips and special assemblies. Other classroom strategies that would foster the goals of character education might include the following:

- Writing articles for the local paper describing what students are learning about solving ethical problems related to the Internet.

- Organizing and holding workshops for parents and other teachers on responsible Internet use.

- Collecting a storybook on specific issues of responsible Internet use.

- Researching news stories about ethical and legal problems related to Internet technology and then discussing the stories in class.

Topics that could be explored that relate to the Internet and issues related to character eduction include the following:

- *Access to the Internet:* Issues of gender and socioeconomic differences that have an impact on access.

- *Theft of information:* Stealing the intellectual materials and rights of authors to the products of their work.

- *Theft or destruction of property:* Hacking into on-line services or using the Internet to spread viruses

- *Privacy:* Accessing private information about people, businesses, or organizations.

RESOURCES ON THE INTERNET

The following sites contain information and resources that specifically address character education:

www.character.org

This site includes eleven principles of character education and lists of resources including books, articles, and journals. Maintained by the Character Education Partnership, this is clearly the most useful site on the topic.

www.wiseskills.com

This site is a retailer of educational materials related to character education, but nonetheless is useful as a site of resources to purchase curriculum materials.

coe.sdsu.edu/NCIE/NCIE.html

This site provides resources, information, a forum, and a directory of current membership regarding issues-centered education, which aims to help teachers to create stronger linkages between students' lives and subjects, topics, and issues they study.

www.neiu.edu/~ccunning/chared

A professor of education maintains this robust site. The site uses "frames" as part of the web page interface, and the menus are self-explanatory. It includes pages addressing general information (and a link to a thorough history of the Internet), good ideas (different conceptions of what is character education), institutions (research and commercial), Internet resources, non-Internet resources, religious education, and a list of some leading character educators.

www.fac.org/publicat/cground/ch14_1.html
This site is a reproduction of the chapter "Character Education in the Public Schools," by Charles C. Haynes, from his book *Finding Common Ground.*

Values Clarification

A second strand of values education represents the other end of the spectrum from character education (Metzger 1986). Character education represents programs using various strategies designed to inculcate certain norms and expected behaviors; values clarification, on the other hand, represents a variety of strategies that lead students through a process of exploring and inquiring into their own values, ranging from moral issues to matters of personal taste. Proponents of values clarification set forth a theory that students go through seven subprocesses as values become more integrated with behavior (Simon, Howe, and Kirschenbaum 1972).

CLASSROOM ACTIVITIES

The following activities are modifications of activities originally developed for clarifying values in relation to computers over a decade ago (Taffee 1984; Braun, Fernlund, and White 1998). The teacher should adjust these activities to meet the particular needs and experiences of students. Based on student needs, expanding or eliminating suggested prompts is appropriate and encouraged. Responses to prompts represent students' values and beliefs. As mentioned previously, originally proponents of this approach urged a teacher to take a neutral approach to whatever values students might express, but that is now viewed as irresponsible; when appropriate, teachers should and must deal with issues that relate to the physical and psychological well-being of their students, regardless of whether it is a field trip or an Internet session. The classroom environment should be one that is supportive for exploring reasoning, alternative ideas, or courses of action; this environment is fundamental to all values clarification activities and social studies itself. Teachers should provide ample (i.e., the majority of) time for a discussion of students' beliefs and values in relation to any values clarification activity.

- Rank Order
  Students prioritize a list of alternatives related to using the Internet as an examination of the ways and reasons they (and others) use the Internet.

Elementary-Middle School

Directions.
- Explain to students that they should rank order the following ways they most often use the Internet. Students place a number 1 next to the use of the Internet most important to them, a 2 next to the next most important, and so on. Afterward, students share their rank orders with the rest of the class or a small group of students. Students may also make individual journal entries.

- Conduct searches on search engines (e.g., Yahoo!, Webcrawler, Excite). Download files off the Internet. Send e-mail (including chat rooms).

- Follow interests through newsgroups

UNFINISHED SENTENCES.
This warm-up activity helps students focus on what they value about the Internet.

Elementary-Middle School Directions

If possible, sit the students in a circle and ask them to complete the following sentence stems either in writing or orally. Teachers should lead students in thoughtful consideration about what is shared in a discussion after student responds to a sentence. Usually a sentence a day is adequate for a normal size class.

1. I wish the Internet were more _____ and less _____.
2. I'd rather use the Internet then _____, but I would rather work with _____ then use the Internet.
3. The Internet is _____.
4. The best thing I have found on the Internet is _____.
5. Ten years from now, the Internet will _____.
6. "Hackers" _____.
7. The Internet helps people when _____.
8. One danger of the Internet is _____.

Note: See also the Circle Sessions activity in the empathy section that follows for an alternative way of using these stems.

Middle School-High School Directions

This activity asks students to perceive the Internet in unlikely and insightful ways. As with the above activities, the discussion and deliberation about what is shared is key to the process of clarifying values according to the theory (Simon, Howe, and Kirschenbaum 1972).

Students respond to the following statements. They can physically take one side of the room or the other, write their response, or give it verbally. As with any values clarification activity, the teacher's role is to promote disscussion of the similarities and differences among the reasons for the responses students give.

▌ Which is the Internet more like?: Friend or Foe? Hard or Soft? Threat or Savior? Pleasure or Pain? Puzzle or Solution? Work or Hobby? Tool or Resource? Monster or Messiah?

Values Clarification and the Internet
The adaptability of values clarification strategies to computers in a general sense has been described previously. In that vein, the computer was seen more as data collection and storage device (Braun and Slobodzian 1982). Simply tabulating and providing a convenient format for entering data prompted by modifications to values clarification activities, however, is really a simplistic and an insufficient application of technology. It is the discussion of responses and the perspectives people have regarding values that is central to the values clarification process, and the Internet makes possible extended global conversations among students and teachers regarding positions on values-related issues.

www.classroom.com
This site is a retailer of educational materials related to Internet experiences. Its curriculum uses the Internet and guides students to try and find answers to questions such as, Who has a more interesting life ... the President of the United States or the Queen of England ... an athlete or an astronaut ... a kid living in the United States or Japan? There are other similar

sets of forced-choice responses and Internet-related explorations that will keep elementary and middle school students engaged. Character education and values clarification are not the only approaches to this complex and challenging aspect of affective education known as values education, but probably they are the most widely known. They represent one of the three dimensions of affective education: the normative dimension. The second aim, promoting empathy, is an information processing dimension; and the third aim, promoting cognitive-moral growth, is a developmental dimension.

Empathy: Promoting Social-Emotional Learning

Social-Emotional Learning (SEL) is a growing movement in the field of affective education, and is actually closely related to values clarification in that it aims to help students clarify and cultivate an awareness of self and others (i.e., empathy). In fact, some SEL activities are adapted from values clarification, but they are used for the purpose of promoting empathy. Developing empathy involves perspective-taking and other strategies that lead to social and emotional well-being in our relationship with others.

In short, a rationale for including emotional intelligence as part of social studies instruction centers on the belief that, in the Information Age, students are using a new medium for communication, which is dramatically altering our perceptions of what it means to be human and interact with others. Furthermore, a key aspect of human intelligence—and an explicit social goal of what we teach—resides in the realm of dealing with emotions and learning to get along with others (Goleman 1995). As the venerable John Goodlad (1998, 671) recently pointed out in an article decrying the lack of privileged status for democratic character building as part of the school agenda,

> The losses suffered by the young as a result of the narrowing of school focus extend beyond merely being deprived of learning in the domains of intelligence that are left out of the school environment. First, the several intelligences are part of a functioning whole: the emotional, for example, profoundly affects the academic.

The movement to promote SEL represents well Harmin's idea quoted previously: the best approaches to affective education are comprehensive approaches synthesizing the best of practice. Many of the values clarification activities are included in curriculums designed to teach emotional intelligence (Simon, Howe, and Kirschenbaum 1972). Values clarification activities, however, are not the only source of curriculum. As visits to Internet sites reveal (see below), conflict resolution, listening skills, leadership, stress management, and communication are also sources for activities and learning experiences.

CLASSROOM STRATEGIES

In relation to learning empathy, about the only role computers can play is as a communication device, albeit a far-reaching and relatively inexpensive one. Humans must interact with one another to develop empathy, and the computer serves as a vehicle for promoting certain kinds of interaction. Needless to say, Internet-facilitated communication will not supplant the face-to-face interaction of students in a classroom under the guidance of their teacher as they use activities to promote empathy as a social studies goal. Such interactions for elementary or middle school students can take different formats, such as magic circles of small groups of students (eight to twelve) or classroom meetings in which the entire class is involved (Braun 1992). As with values clarification activities, the specific topics to guide such discussions can be developed by the teacher to fit students' particular needs and the goals of the discussion. Some potential topics for magic circle or classroom meetings are the following:

▮ A way in which I am responsible when using the Internet

▮ Something I learned when using the Internet

▮ A time we worked together when using the Internet

Other strategies appropriate for any age student and consistent with SEL and the goal of promoting empathy are excerpted below from the publication *Computer Learning*, a useful newsletter dedicated to using technology in safe and humane ways and published by the Computer Learning Foundation, PO Box 60007, Palo Alto, CA 94030; 650-327-3347, clf@computerlearning.org, or www.computerlearning.org.

■ Creating posters, slide shows, and multimedia presentations that focus on safe, legal, and moral uses of computers. Post the student creations in classrooms, in the computer lab, or on your school's website.

■ Holding mock trials in which students role play lawyers, prosecutors, defendants, witnesses, judges, etc., in cases dealing with irresponsible use and illegal use of the Internet.

■ Developing a joint teaching project (with teachers in another school) that involves students in safe use of e-mail and chat rooms.

RESOURCES ON THE INTERNET
The following website is a source of curriculum materials and professional development resources that are geared toward SEL.

www.6seconds.org/home.html
> This site provides on-line curriculum ideas for promoting SEL, interviews with leading theorists and curriculum developers, book reviews, and a variety of other information about SEL resources. As the site states, "Six Seconds Materials invite reflection, inspire action, use current research, and reinforce emotional intelligence."

It is important that students find appropriate outlets to meet their interpersonal needs for attention, affection, acceptance, and approval. Newspaper reports and magazine articles abound with examples of young people being taken advantage of by pedophiles and sexual predators who lurk on the Internet, seeking victims. Besides the material about cognitive information that students encounter on the Internet, social studies teachers also can use SEL activities as a way of helping students examine their own purposes and use the powerful communication technologies available on-line. Does the Internet enhance our sense of empathy by creating virtual communities (Rheingold 1993)? Or can it reduce one's ability to feel connected to others, thus generating depression and anxiety? Providing affective education experiences in relation to these questions is the aim of empathy and the use of SEL activities.

Moral Development: Dilemmas Promoting Caring and Justice
Those advocating the work of moral education from a developmental perspective theoretically find their origins in the work of Piaget. Lawerence Kohlberg elaborated on this theory and developed a research base as well as pedagogical models that were widely adapted in schools (Power, Higgins, and Kohlberg 1989). Kohlberg's legal orientation to moral development was challenged because of the anomalies arising in the data from longitudinal studies regarding stage sequence. From these critiques arose two contributions to adjust Kohlberg's theory and accommodate the data. Both of these contributions advanced the theoretical and pedagogical practice of moral development.

CLASSROOM ACTIVITIES
In either case, conducting a moral dilemma discussion is the central teaching strategy for moral development, which is strikingly different from the multiple strategies used in developing values and empathy. To conduct a moral dilemma discussion, the teacher follows a simple five-step teaching process: (1) presenting the dilemma; (2) taking a position; (3) small-group discussion; (4) large-group discussion; and (5) reflection and revision (Braun, Fernlund, and White 1998).

The incorporation of moral dilemmas into computer simulations that promote teacher-led classroom discussions are a hallmark of the Tom Snyder Productions (TSP) software series *Decisions, Decisions* and *Choices, Choices*. Award-winning and noteworthy for its use in one-computer classrooms, TSP sponsors on-line discussions involving multiple classrooms engaged in moral dilemmas based on a *Decisions, Decisions* program and thus takes advantage of the Internet in several ways. Students are exposed to a broader range of thinking, central to the process of promoting moral development, and they are also exposed to regional attitudes that influence that thinking. Moreover, e-mail encourages deeper and more informed discussions as well as promoting better writing skills as students post messages and receive feedback.

Sue Greene, a middle school social studies teacher, took part in such a discussion with classrooms all over the United States, ranging from fourth graders to high school seniors. Her notes and records on the experience provide the following vignette of conducting moral discussions over the Internet. Participation in the project began with the presentation of the dilemma (as described above, the first step in the teaching process). Immigration was the program used to promote the discussion. The dilemma involves students in the role of an incumbent U.S. President facing a key primary election in a state where boatloads of immigrants are arriving on its coastline. The dilemma revolves around what course of action the President should follow: repatriation or assimilation.

After the class reviewed the events of the dilemma, individual students took a position on what courses of action they would recommend and discussed their reasoning (remember, classwide discussion is key to the process). The class came to a consensus and posted its position on the dilemma via e-mail. The class faced a new decision each week as consequences of the final decision produced five additional decision-making points in the dilemma. Because only one decision a week could be posted, Ms. Greene's students had plenty of time to consider a decision and formulate their reasoning. Activities associated with the aims of values and empathy were used to promote thinking and discussion—specifically, sentence stems, mock trial, and classroom meetings.

As students engaged in classroom discussions and formulated what thoughts to post on e-mail, they weighed various perspectives and learned how to work toward consensus. In addition to fostering these interpersonal skills, Ms. Greene provided ample opportunities for students to research the history of immigration in the United States. The weekly timeframe for posting decisions meant students had time and encouragement from Ms. Greene and the media center director, to use multiple resources, including the World Wide Web, to look up information about the topic of immigration and communicate their findings with others via additional e-mail postings. They read and studied about famous immigrants. They interviewed friends and family members. Changes in immigration policy were placed on a time line along with immigration rates for various ethnic groups over the course of U.S. history. Students kept careful records of the data they encountered and used it in formulating their reasons for various decisions during the five weeks. One particular event they uncovered moved them deeply.

A website provided the story of the *S.S. St. Louis*, an ocean liner carrying more than 900 Jewish refugees from Germany in 1939. The ship was turned away from U.S. and Cuban ports, and it was forced to return to Europe where many of its passengers later died in Nazi concentration camps. After seeking verification of this account from other websites and print sources, the students posted this story in their messages to the discussion. This powerful story of the "Voyage of the Damned" caused more careful consideration of the fate of the immigrants they had considered turning away in the simulation. This was a pivotal point in the class's discussions, as the simulation became very real to Ms. Green's students as well as to those in other classrooms.

It was at this point that students realized that this dilemma activity involved more than just a computer simulation conducted over the Internet. The participants apprehended that the kinds of decisions they were rendering might affect real people. This realization and far-reaching exposure to higher levels of moral reasoning, which promotes assimilation and accommodation in any individual's reasoning, were the real benefits of being on-line. Additionally, all of these activities provided a focused context in which students could learn content about the issues and history of immigration, develop both on-line and interpersonal skills for more effective communication, and participate in a discussion of citizenship in an on-line community.

RESOURCES ON THE INTERNET

The following websites are useful to teachers incorporating moral development in their social studies instruction:

> www.wittenberg.edu/ame
> The homepage for the Association of Moral Education offers information for becoming a member. This professional organization is devoted to promoting moral education. It also lists conference dates and links to other moral education sites.

> www.globalethics.org
> This site of a commercial producer of teaching materials includes lesson plans and dilemmas that can promote discussions about moral issues. These dilemmas explicitly address both the caring and justice dimensions of moral reasoning.

This chapter has provided a framework for engaging in what Palmer (1999) has recently described as "evoking the spiritual" in education. By this, Palmer means helping teachers and students confront the big questions of life. The activities that have been described in relation to the Internet and the affective aims of values, empathy, and moral development promote seeking the answers to these questions, "Does my life have meaning and purpose?" "Do I have gifts that the world wants and needs?" "How do I rise above my fears?" How do I deal with suffering—my own and that of my family and friends?"

There is nothing more to the Internet's role in relation to helping students consider these questions than its power as a communicative device—indeed, a very powerful one. The Internet provides an astonishing means for teachers to use in seeking materials, ideas, and conversations with others to help students explore these questions. Additionally, the Internet and all that it represents in the way of access to information and communication are a ripe topic around which questions about our human spirituality and sense of connectedness as a species surface. In meeting the curriculum standards set by NCSS, social studies students should consider these questions as they come to grips with this powerful force of information technology. To fail to provide students with some time to explore these and similar questions in relation to the Internet is like being hopelessly lost and trying to find one's way out of the woods without a compass. There are endless paths one could choose and where one winds up is anyone's guess. Without a moral compass, our students are lost and tend to wander through their social studies education aimlessly.

References

Braun, Joseph. "Social Technology in the Elementary Social Studies Curriculum." *Social Education* 56, no. 7 (1992): 389-92.

Braun, Joseph, Phyllis Fernlund, and Charles S. White. *Technology Tools in the Social Studies Curriculum*. Wilsonville, Ore: Franklin Beedle and Associates, 1998.

Braun, Joseph A., and Kurt Slobodzian. "Can Computers Teach Values?" *Educational Leadership* 39 (April 1982): 508-12.

Goleman, Daniel. *Emotional Literacy: Why It Can Matter More Than IQ*. New York: Bantam Books, 1995.

Goodlad, John. "Schools for All Seasons." *Phi Delta Kappan* 79 (May 1998): 670-71.

Harmin, Merril. "Values Clarification, High Morality: Let's Go for Both." *Educational Leadership* (May 1988): 24-30, volume 45.

Harmin, Merrill. "A Comprehensive Model for Values Education and Moral Education." *Phi Delta Kappan* 73 (June 1992): 771-76.

Huffman, Henry A. "Character Education Without Turmoil." *Educational Leadership* 51 (November 1994): 24-26.

Kohn, Alfie. "How Not to Teach Values: A Critical Look at Character Education." *Phi Delta Kappan* 78 (February 1997): 429-39.

Kohn, Alfie. "Adventures in Ethics Versus Behavior Control: A Reply to My Critics." *Phi Delta Kappan* 79 (February 1998): 455-60.

Lickona, Thomas. "A More Complex Analysis Is Needed." *Phi Delta Kappan* 79 (February 1998): 449-54.

Leming, James. "Research on Social Studies Curriculum and Instruction: Interventions and Outcomes in the Socio-moral Domain." In *Review of Research in Social Studies Education*: 1976-83, edited by W. B. Stanley, 123-213. Washington, D.C.: National Council for the Social Studies, 1985.

Lockwood, Alan. "The Effects of Values Clarification and Moral Development Curricula on School-Age Students: A Critical Review of Recent Research." *Review of Educational Research* 48 (1978): 325-64.

Marshall, Gail, and Harriet Taylor. "Making Friends in the Global Village: Tips on International Collaboration." *Leading and Learning with Technology* (March 1996): 48-51.

Mehlinger, Howard D. "School Reform in the Information Age." *Phi Delta Kappan* 77 (February 1996): 400-407.

Metzger, Devon J. "Viewing Values from Two Perspectives." *The Social Studies* (October 1986): 80-82.

National Council for the Social Studies. *Expectations of Excellence: Curriculum Standards for Social Studies*. Washington, D.C.: NCSS, 1994.

Palmer, Parker J. "Evoking the Spirit in Public Education." *Educational Leadership* 56, no. 4 (1999): 6-11.

Rheingold, Howard. *The Virtual Community: Homesteading on the Information Highway*. Boston, Mass.: Addison-Wesley, 1993.

Scott, Kathyrn. "Achieving Social Studies Affective Aims: Values, Empathy, and Moral Development." In *Handbook of Research on Social Studies Teaching and Learning*, edited by James Shaver. New York: Macmillan, 1991.

Shaver, James P., and W. Strong. *Facing Value Decisions: Rationale Building for Teachers*. New York: Teachers College Press, 1982.

Simon, S. B., Leland W. Howe, and Howard Kirschenbaum. *Values Clarification: A Handbook of Practical Strategies for Teachers and Students*. New York: Hart Publishing Company, 1972.

Turiel, E. *The Development of Social Knowledge: Morality & Convention*. New York: University Press, 1983.

Vinson, Kevin D. "The Problematics of Character Education and Civic Virtue: A Critical Response to the NCSS Position Statement." *Social Education* 62 (1998): 112-15.

CHAPTER 18

SAFE WEB EXPLORATION

Michael J. Berson
University of South Florida
&
Ilene R. Berson
University of South Florida

The Internet is a system of networks that serve a global community, and rapidly growing numbers of children are joining explorers in the territory of cyberspace. By going on-line, students may access up-to-date news, research encyclopedias, and communicate with people around the world. Even young children can benefit from on-line resources as they are exposed to music, explore virtual museums, view art, and join clubs. Touring through cyberspace offers a rewarding experience for students and teachers and provides a wealth of information for all age groups. There exists an immeasurable benefit for children and adolescents who access the research potential of the Internet, and the necessity of evolving this technological literacy will become increasingly salient as young people aspire to function in our globally connected society.

Although the Internet is replete with resources and information that may enhance the educational experience of students, it still harbors the same risks and potential dangers that constitute any expansive environment. This is further exacerbated by the lack of a governing entity that limits or checks the information that people access and maintain in this forum. Although the Internet may have dangers associated with it, the benefits of cyberspace prevail over the potential risks. It is both undesirable and unrealistic to ban students' use of the Internet; however, recognition of its disadvantages is a necessary first step in conceiving creative and commonsense solutions that promote protective and productive learning environments for children.

The Internet is like a new exciting city awaiting exploration. There is a tremendous potential to access information that creates an exceptional learning opportunity for students. But, as with any field trip in the real world, chaperones are necessary to supervise the activity of young people, and explicit directions as to what roads are safe for travel can mean the difference between a unique and educational learning opportunity and an educational mishap. The virtual world cannot be explored without identifying associated risks and establishing rules for on-line protection. This chapter addresses the importance of promoting an awareness of, and attention to, Internet safety in order to empower social studies students for productive on-line learning in the classroom.

Identifying the Risks

Educators generally include among their responsibilities the protection of children from dangers. Yet recognition of this role is undermined by the persistent denial and minimization of the existence of risk. After all, it seems implausible to many individuals that harm may come to a child when engaged in computer activities under the safe shroud of the classroom setting. However, the relative degree of on-line anonymity coupled with the lack of system-imposed restraints creates risk for young people who may be naive regarding the intentions of others. Because children and youth typically are trusting and curious about on-line relationships, they are thus vulnerable to crime and exploitation.

Controversial Information

Without much effort, a student may intentionally or unintentionally be exposed to on-line information that is obscene, pornographic, violent, racist, or otherwise offensive. There should be an ongoing dialogue regarding the kinds of sites that are appropriate and clear identification of areas that are off limits. Teachers should outline explicit rules regarding access to content on the Internet and set out reasonable consequences for violations. Elementary educators should undertake the added precaution of prescreening all on-line material, including e-mail communication, as a preventative measure.

Access Control Software

The existence of hazards that may be harmful to unsuspecting young Internet explorers has resulted in the development of software that controls children's access in cyberspace. The purpose of this software is to create an environment in which children may interact on-line in a safe, educational, and entertaining context. Internet filters are a tool to assist in safeguarding children by enabling parents and/or teachers to block inappropriate sites and to restrict access to certain times of the day. The software often includes lists of researched sites that contain child friendly information. These applications screen sites when a user attempts to gain access, evaluating the location with a predetermined data base of approved and blocked sites. Preestablished lists of blocked areas may be overridden to allow greater access or to further restrict on-line exploration. Some software also provides features that prevent children from divulging personal information, such as name, age, address, phone number, or school name to on-line acquaintances through websites and chat rooms. Popular filtering software includes Cyber Patrol, CyberSitter, Cyber Snoop, KinderGuard, Net Nanny, SurfWatch, and others. Programs typically are inexpensive. Similarly, many Internet providers and on-line services offer site blocking restrictions on incoming e-mail and children's accounts that access specific services. On-line services often offer these controls at no additional cost.

Despite the potential benefits of Internet filtering, there is a rising tide of criticism regarding blocking software. Some opponents complain that it restricts freedom of information and infringes on First Amendment rights on the Internet. Others note that even when safeguards are in place, students' curiosity and evolving computer skills often enable them to circumvent these restrictions. Additionally, objectionable content may slip through the filter (Cate 1998).

Consequently, responsible adults ultimately need to remain accountable for continuous involvement in and supervision of students' on-line activities. Teachers should encourage students to discuss what they enjoy most on-line and provide a forum to address information or messages that make young people feel worried or uncomfortable. Children need an opportunity to make sense of what they see on the Internet. As a result, young users may begin the process of becoming prepared on-line explorers.

Fraud and Privacy Invasion in Cyberspace

The territory of the Internet provides a context that is highly conducive to deception. Cyberspace defrauders find the Internet attractive because it provides a relatively cheap, quick, and anonymous means to scam a large number of unsuspecting consumers. In addition to deceptive on-line advertising practices, the Internet is frequently flooded by hoaxes, including chain letters, pyramid schemes, and fictitious virus announcements (Gelman and McCandlish 1998). The challenge for users is to adequately judge the veracity of information on-line and to take precautions to protect their personal information.

Internet Transactions

Because students make up a large consumer base, they may be easily tempted by the ease of purchasing on-line. Cyberspace creates an absorbing context in which to target children with manipulative marketing techniques. Children are at great risk due to the ease of deceiving them with offers of prizes, games, and products. The Center for Media Education has found that children's privacy is invaded through these marketing and advertising practices, which solicit detailed personal information and track on-line computer use. The development of personal profiles for young people enables marketers to design individualized messages and ads.

Adolescents are an especially big purchaser group, but their sense of invincibility places them at great risk to become a victim of fraud. New products are listed on the web everyday, and the desire to possess the latest and greatest in the here and now may jeopardize safety. Students should be urged to verify information about all sites and businesses when planning a purchase. Even when the business may be a familiar entity, it is recommended that the corporation be contacted directly by phone in order to verify the site. Bank account numbers, credit card numbers, personal information, and financial data should be provided only after careful reflection on who may have access to this information.

Cookies

"Cookies" are files that are automatically saved in the browser's directory or folder, most times transparent to you the user. Cookies are frequently used by websites to store personal profiles on the user. Whenever you visit a site, cookies provide information about who your provider is, where your provider is located, identification of the site you linked from, specification of the software being used by your computer, information on your activities while visiting the site, and additional personal information (e.g., name, e-mail address, home/work address, telephone number, income). There are various ways you can control the use of cookies to protect your privacy, from selecting options in your web browser that prevent cookies from being saved or created, to special utilities designed to help you monitor, edit, delete, and block specified websites from creating cookies. These special software utilities can be downloaded from such sites as www.tucows.com, www.shareware.com, and www.download.com.

Unsolicited E-Mail (SPAM)

Junk mail is as much a problem in cyberspace as it is with regular postal service mail. Unsolicited e-mail, also known as SPAM, includes product offers, money-making opportunities, chain letters, and schemes that may be illegal and fraudulent. E-mail chain letters are illegal money schemes, and no response should ever be made to these requests. Similarly, no reply should be sent to any unsolicited mail without careful reflection about the possible identity and intent of the sender.

Sexual Predators

It is often emphasized that the existence of violence and inappropriate activity in the virtual world mirrors real-world occurrences. In the area of sexual victimization of children, at least 20 percent of American women and 5 to 10 percent of American men have experienced some form of child sexual abuse (Finkelhor 1994). The frequency of abuse cases is of especial concern because child maltreatment experts acknowledge that most crimes against children go unreported (Finkelhor 1984; Wynkoop, Capps, and Priest 1995). The secrecy associated with sexual molestation may be exacerbated when addressing on-line exploitation of children. The sense of betrayal for a young person who has been deceived and/or coerced into a sexual liaison may contribute to misdirected self-blame and subsequent hesitancy to disclose.

Pedophiles know that to gain access to children, they must go where children are. On-line chat rooms have become a very popular activity for children and youth, and there tends to be a paucity of adult supervision in these areas. The technology of chat rooms also enables secret communication through private messaging. Potential perpetrators look for opportunities to interact with children where there is minimal supervision or external controls are easy to circumvent.

Pedophiles gain access to children by overcoming their resistance. They may portray themselves as very helpful, caring, and understanding. They also make the child feel needed and wanted. Often, false identities will be used to make contact with the child. Although initial contact may involve exchanges of personal information, later interaction may include the exchange of sexually explicit mail. Pornography may be sent to the child as a way to desensitize a young person to sexual activity. Pedophiles may provide explicit directions to a child on the downloading of sexually graphic files and setting up separate e-mail accounts for their exchanges. In order to counter these experiences, students must be properly prepared to encounter pedophiles and have opportunities to share bad on-line experiences with supportive adults.

Bullying and Harassment

Students may be both victims and perpetrators of harassment on-line. Some youths engage in on-line attacks against other vulnerable Internet participants, humiliating children to assert their own value. Manipulation of other children on-line may occur, and arguments may result in verbal abuse and electronic harassment. Students may be rude to others, and due to the interface of the computer, depersonalize the interaction with others, thereby ignoring feelings and becoming antisocial.

Teachers and parents have a responsibility to monitor students' on-line behaviors and be watchful for indicators that the individual is being bullied or engaging in offensive behaviors. Netiquette and expectations for polite conduct in and out of cyberspace should be clearly communicated as an expectation. Students also should be engaged in opportunities to learn and practice avoidance techniques, de-escalation skills, and protection strategies.

Internet Gangs

Young people who engage in on-line exploration may be entranced with the variety of virtual relationships in which they can participate. The appeal of cyberspace games and opportunities to create imaginary personas can give a sense of a surreal context. Given this perception, the allure of criminal acts and antisocial behavior on the computer is intensified. Young people may organize themselves on-line for purposes of exchanging information about computer intrusion, and they may be more likely to collaboratively engage in privacy violations or other computer misconduct. Belonging to a peer group on-line can be just as critical as belonging off-line. These participants may share a desire for thrills and intensify their activity until it reaches the threshold of felony computer crimes. To counter this activity, teachers must understand the reality of on-line gangs and the reasons children may participate in harassing and/or illicit activity. Efforts also must be made to provide students with strategies to resist peer group pressures on- and off-line. Close monitoring of student's on-line activity and recognition of suspicious activity may assist students in avoiding the serious consequences of Internet gangs.

Internet Addiction

The benefits of the Internet for students engaged in research and educational exploration are vast; however, these merits can be overshadowed when individuals become preoccupied with on-line use. Students seem to be easily caught by the allure of cyberspace, and may substitute productive activity for chat room relationships and interactive on-line games. Subsequently, excessive Internet use may contribute to a student's failure to complete homework and study for school. Poor grades may be exacerbated by sleep deprivation when time spent on the Internet replaces time in bed. On-line friendships may be used to avoid emotional attachments with family and friends in the community. Other interests may decline as a child becomes further obsessed with computer activities.

When schools introduce students to web exploration, educators have an obligation to openly discuss with children and youth the potential risks of going on-line. Students should immediately be introduced to procedures that restrict the amount of time spent on the computer, and the use of an alarm clock or timer may be advisable if a child tends to lose track of time. Students should be encouraged to explore other modes of communicating with people, accessing information, and engaging in entertainment so that surfing the 'Net does not replace homework, social activities, or other important interests.

Setting Guidelines for Safe, Legal, and Efficient On-line Use

Structuring a safe environment involves a declaration of rules, policies, and procedures that clearly communicate that the school will not support behavior that places children at risk. For example, among the rules designed to minimize the risk to students and promote their emotional and physical well being in the school environment are policies that address the content of videos students may watch in the classroom and how much freedom students have within the school setting. On field trips outside of the classroom, teachers are especially vigilant to reinforce issues of supervision and responsibility. Students are expected to remain with the group and be respectful when interacting with new people. Similarly, students' Internet use requires adherence to rules. Extensive training should address mechanisms for supporting Internet usage while monitoring and supervising these interactions. Adults in the school must be given responsibility to monitor usage and ensure that potential risks are addressed.

Whenever engaged in an interchange with people, students need clear guidelines for relating in a curious and respectful manner. On-line manners, commonly referred to as Netiquette, promote an awareness that computers are merely the mechanism for communicating with people who have feelings, values, and mores. This reality can sometimes be forgotten when typing messages on a keyboard and looking into a screen. Students also must understand the limits on their privacy when using Internet technology. Just as employers have a right to monitor e-mail sent on their systems, schools may have policies to oversee the on-line communication of children using school computers. Teachers may monitor student e-mail, so as a rule, students should be instructed not to send messages with content that would not be appropriate for posting on the class bulletin board.

School policies might include the following guidelines designed to create boundaries and barriers that promote safety:

1. Never give out identifying information (e.g., full name, home address, telephone number, age, race, family income, school name or location, or friends' names) in a public message in a chat room or on bulletin boards. Be sure that you are dealing with someone whom you and your parents/guardian know and trust before giving out any personal information. Also, remember that on-line information is not necessarily private.

2. Never send a picture or video of yourself to another person without the permission of your parent or guardian.

3. When someone offers you gifts, money, or other offers of something for nothing, tell your parent, guardian, or teacher.

4. Tell your parent, guardian, teacher, or other trusted adult if you come across any information that makes you feel uncomfortable or confused. You should be especially cautious if messages imply secrecy or describe mechanisms for hiding information from parents, teachers, or other supervising adults. Do not respond to these messages and end the communication immediately.

5. Never arrange a face-to-face meeting unless your parent or guardian gives his or her permission. If you have parental consent, make sure that you have a parent or guardian with you and arrange to meet in a public place.

6. Remember that people on-line may not be who they say they are. Because you can't see or hear the person, it is easy to pretend to be someone else.

7. Never use rude language or send mean messages. Treat other on-line users with respect.

8. Do not give out credit card information without your parent's/guardian's permission.

9. Never share your password, even with friends. When sites request a password, pick one different from your log-on code.

Empowering Students through Awareness and Support

Students must be engaged in a thorough introduction to and periodic review of acceptable use procedures to promote safety and minimize risk. Moreover, exercises that assist them in using and evaluating information they find on the Internet are critical. No level of safety training can ensure that a student will be prepared to recognize and respond to danger. Even with adult guidance and supervision, children may still encounter problematic situations. If adults are unaware of the perpetual risk that exists, they may not "see" abuse as it occurs, leaving the responsibility to prevent harm on a child's fragile shoulders.

However, it is important to note that creating and following the most stringent policies does not always prevent abuse or liability for abuse. Abuse does occur even without isolation. Grooming activities (creating a relationship with the child to make him or her more susceptible to sexual abuse) and other abusive interactions do take place when parents, teachers, and peers are present. Knowing that the most intense screening and supervision will not be 100 percent successful, it is imperative that the school organization be prepared to encourage and support disclosure if abuse occurs.

Policies of the school should mandate that any suspicion of risk to a student should immediately result in a report and adherence to organizational policy and procedures. Policies should address issues such as how you make a formal report to law enforcement and/or child protection service agency, how to document your response to a report, notification of parents, guidelines about what to say to children, and so forth. In support of the long-term safety of a child, the school's procedures regarding response to disclosure should focus on protecting the child from blame, shame, pressure to recant, and retaliation for telling.

Social Studies Activities: Elementary School

PRIVACY PLAYGROUND: THE FIRST ADVENTURE OF THE THREE LITTLE CYBERPIGS.
Young elementary children should not be given access to the Internet at all except under strictly controlled and highly supervised conditions. Although high standards for child protection may be adhered to in school settings, young children, nonetheless, may have unrestricted access to the Internet in other contexts. In order to promote a high level of vigilance in protecting children, it is imperative as early as feasible to introduce skills for recognizing risky situations and to develop appropriate coping techniques to respond to these situations before children go surfing on their own.

Based on the work of Canada's Media Awareness Network (www.screen.com/mnet/eng/cpigs/cpigs.htm) off-line and on-line activities are used to introduce students to Internet marketing ploys and actual dangers for children in cyberspace. Prior to the lesson, you should download to your class computers the Privacy Playground game found on the Media Awareness Network website.

Provide children with postcards and letters with sealable envelopes. Discuss with students that they will have an opportunity to compose a letter to someone in their family.

Ask the children to describe how letters and postcards are different. If not suggested by the students, it is important to point out that postcards are not private and may be easily read by others.

Ask students, if you wanted to tell something personal about yourself, would you write it on the postcard or in a letter that would be sealed in an envelope?

Ask students to compare e-mail with sealed letters and postcards.

Introduce children to the animated computer game Privacy Playground. This game depicts the three little pigs surfing the Information Highway. As the pigs confront various advertising techniques and invasive questions, the game players assist the pigs in making decisions about whether or not to proceed with an action. The player either receives stars for wise thinking or a gentle warning about the consequences of his or her proposed action. The program stresses the importance of personal privacy in order to promote safety on the Internet.

Following the game, review with students rules for on-line safety, the Cyber-Smarts. This may be done as children recreate the experience of the three pigs through a retelling of the story.

Students may follow up the activity by reading *A Monster in My Mailbox* by Sheila Gordon (1978) or *Nibble, Nibble, Jenny Archer* by Ellen Conford (1993). These children's books address deception in advertising that is targeted toward children.

Other activities and handouts are available in the teacher's guide that can be found on-line.

Social Studies Activities: Middle School

BALLAD OF AN E-MAIL TERRORIST.

This exchange of e-mail messages may be found on a link of the Global SchoolNet Foundation (www.gsn.org/teach/articles/e-mail.ballad.html). This real-life tale of Internet communication provides an opportunity to address responses to obscene mail messages and to emphasize the consequences young people have incurred as a result of sending rude or vulgar messages in cyberspace.

1. Review with students the Netiquette guidelines.

2. Provide students with copies of the exchange of e-mail messages, presenting each item in chronological sequence.

3. Explore students' reactions to each component of the exchange. Students also may engage in problem solving regarding what action might follow each message in order to bring about a positive resolution.

Social Studies Activities: High School

CAVEAT EMPTOR IN CYBERSPACE: PROTECTING YOURSELF AGAINST DECEPTION AND FRAUD ON THE INTERNET.

1. Lead students in a discussion regarding why and how people may be taken advantage of on the Internet. Introduce strategies that advertisers may use to enhance the appeal of their product (e.g., use of misleading "weasel" words, visual effects, cool images).

2. Break students into groups to generate a plan of action for engaging in business transactions via the Internet.

3. Visit the Better Business Bureau (www.bbbon-line.org) and then visit the National Fraud Information Center (www.fraud.org).

4. Compare the group-generated suggestions with what the experts say regarding protection from fraud.

5. Provide students with a copy of *Web of Deception*, an investigation into on-line advertising and marketing practices directed at children, which was published in March 1996 by the Center for Media Education in Washington, D.C. This report is available on-line (tap.epn.org/cme/cmwdecov.html). Discuss the ramifications of advertisers' on-line targeting of children.

6. Using key ideas generated from brainstorming and site exploration, students may devise projects to promote the protective strategies that they learned. They may be instructed to address questions such as, How do you get information to other students regarding Internet safety? How should information be disseminated?

Additional Websites
American Library Association (1997) www.ala.org
    This site includes an ALA resolution on the use of filtering software in libraries. (The resolution opposes filters as violation of the First Amendment.) See www.ala.org/alaorg/oif/filt_res.html
Center for On-Line Addiction (COLA) netaddiction.com
    This site provides resources on on-line addiction and guides to assist parents in determining if a child may be addicted to the Internet.
Child Abuse Prevention Network child.cornell.edu
    This site strives to improve professional and public efforts to understand and address risk factors in the lives of children, youth, families, and communities that lead to violence and neglect.

Child Find Canada www.childfind.ca

Child Find provides information on the benefits of the Information Highway, the risks of on-line activity, suggested guidelines for parents, and kids rules for on-line safety.

Children Accessing Controversial Information (CACI) www.zen.org/~brendan/caci.html

This site is provided for accessing a listserv dedicated to the issues of children's safe on-line usage.

Community Learning Network (Canada) www.etc.bc.ca/tdebhome/spam.html

Links are provided to sites that address Internet abuses and hazards.

CyberAngels Internet Safety Organization www.cyberangels.org

This comprehensive website explores issues associated with maintaining children's safety on-line.

Librarians Information On-line Network www.libertynet.org/lion/lion.html

Information is provided on software products and other technologies to control children's access to objectionable sites on the Internet.

National Center for Missing and Exploited Children (1-800-THE LOST) www.missingkids.com/cybertip

This private, nonprofit organization provides assistance to families of missing children and conducts prevention and awareness programs. A CyberTipline has been created in collaboration with the FBI, U.S. Postal Service, and Office of Juvenile Justice. When you come across child pornography on the web, you should report it by calling or contacting the above site.

National Clearinghouse on Child Abuse and Neglect Information www.calib.com/nccanch/NCCAN

This site provides extensive resources on child maltreatment. Information can be accessed directly from its site.

National Institute for Consumer Education www.emich.edu/public/coe/nice/fraudml.html

The National Institute for Consumer Education has prepared this minilesson plan to help students identify and describe examples of Internet fraud and to list ways to protect yourself from Internet fraud.

Peacefire www.Peacefire.org

This is a teen-run organization that is against censorship of youth on the Internet.

Safe Kids On-line www.safekids.com

This site allows access to the full text of Larry Magid's popular child safety and teen safety brochures.

Safety Tips for Kids on the Internet www.fbi.gov/kids/crimepre/internet/internet.htm

The Federal Bureau of Investigation Educational Web Publication recommends safety tips and relays stories of crimes against children that involved the Internet.

SmartParent.Com www.smartparent.com

This website provides safety tips for children's Internet exploration, a children's pledge to comply with rules for Internet usage, and additional resources for promoting on-line safety.

References

Cate, F. H. *Internet and the First Amendment: Schools and Sexually Explicit Expressions.* Bloomington, Ind.: Phi Delta Kappa, 1998.

Finkelhor, D. *Child Sexual Abuse: New Theory and Research.* New York: Free Press, 1984.

Finkelhor, D. "Current Information on the Scope and Nature of Child Sexual Abuse." *The Future of Children* 31 (1994).

Gelman, R. B., and S. McCandlish, *Protecting Yourself On-Line.* San Franscisco: HarperEdge, 1998.

Wynkoop, T. F., S. C. Capps, and B. J. Priest. "Incidence and Prevalence of Child Sexual Abuse: A Critical Review of Data Collection Procedures." *Journal of Child Sexual Abuse* 4, no. 2 (1995): 49-66.

CHAPTER 19

ASSESSMENT

Pat Nickell
University of Georgia, Athens

Over the past decade, the need to change traditional notions about how to assess student learning in social studies effectively—in particular, what should be assessed and how—has received increased emphasis (Nickell 1992, 1993, 1997). There is much agreement among education theorists that determining what students know is an important first step, but that this information must be accompanied by making certain that young people can make use of what they know in meaningful ways. Thus, measurement theorists in the late 1980s and early 1990s advocated a move from simply testing students' acquisition of information (often forgotten soon after the test) to using more elaborate means of assessing applications of knowledge (Shepard 1989; Wiggins 1989). A number of states (e.g., Massachusetts, Maryland, and Kentucky) have designed fairly complex state assessment systems, which incorporate open-ended questions, performance events, portfolios, and the like, to align with newly developed state standards. Even the "bullies" of the testing world–the ACT, SAT, and other commercially produced standardized tests–have made room for generative item types, or those that call for students to create and write a response to a prompt rather than simply identifying the correct answer from possibilities provided.

At the classroom level, assessment is evolving as well—partially due to pressure to provide practice for new high stakes and standardized formats, and partially due to teachers recognizing the validity of arguments in favor of new test types. Accompanied by increased emphasis on writing skills and higher level thinking skills, new classroom assessments are taking a multitude of forms—from group performances to individual research and reporting and from developing marketing plans to creating solutions for complex social problems. At the very least, more students are writing out responses to exam questions instead of filling in bubbles with a #2 pencil.

Another recent trend along the path toward overhauling schools to better meet the needs of today's students is greater emphasis on contextualizing both learning and assessment and helping students make connections between subjects, and between what they learn in school and the world outside the classroom. In this effort, teachers attempt to provide students with more real-world experiences. Elementary schools are creating microsocieties in which each classroom becomes an institution—a bank, the post office, the court, the mayor's office, one of several industries, and commercial stores (Hoge 1997). Classes learn about the community and the interdependence of its many institutions; competition in the marketplace becomes real for students; and the difficulties and complexities of maintaining order and keeping everyone happy and prosperous are ongoing issues. Middle schools are offering students hands-on experience with social or environmental problems in their communities and encouraging them to seek solutions and become involved as agents for change. High schools, often in answer to School-to-Work initiatives, are sending students into the workplace as "shadows," interns, or even part-time paid employees—not just flipping hamburgers but participating in work environments previously closed to all but those certifiably trained or educated.

Integral to both of these recent trends is the development of engaging students in using complex thinking strategies. In order to perform well on new assessment types, and understand and make use of real-world experiences, students must be able to interpret, analyze, synthesize, evaluate, and apply information. They must be able to gather pertinent data, weigh its validity and authenticity, and make meaning from it for given purposes. Even young children who are developing a marketable product for "sale" to their peers must be taught and then be able to use these skills. Young children must be taught to discriminate between what is good and what is better, what is useful and what is indispensable, what is stated and what is authenticated or justified, and in each case, to choose the latter. It is critical not only that educators teach these skills and dispositions but that the effectiveness of their instruction be assessed.

Enter the Internet

The availability of the Internet opens wide a door of opportunity for teachers to accomplish not only the instructional goal of assisting students in becoming critical thinkers, active participants in learning, and ethical and effective problem solvers and decision makers, but also the goal of evaluating student progress. While other chapters in this book deal with the use of the Internet for instructional purposes, this chapter focuses on the issues and opportunities for using the Internet in student assessment.

Little attention has been given to the use of the Internet in assessing student learning, as this author quickly learned during a fairly thorough search for literature. Braun (1997) made note of this fact, calling assessment "the missing link" in discussions about the possibilities for Internet use in classroom instruction. He correctly pointed out that the nature of the Internet does not lend itself to determining whether users are learning anything. This electronic miracle is engaged in providing information, not evaluating whether that information is leading to academic growth, scholarly achievement, or new insights.

Since the Internet went "public" in 1985, and once personal computers became common, and access to the web became readily available and relatively inexpensive, a world of information (and misinformation) literally found itself at the tips of our fingers. Yet schools lagged far behind other institutions in realizing the potential of the Internet for instruction and shelling out the funds it would take to put appropriate equipment everywhere it needed to be. Just three years ago, my brain was limited to whatever I knew and could recall, plus whatever I had within reach in my home, classroom, or place of work. Only by traveling to a library did I have access to ERIC, for example. Only by telephone, FAX, or snail mail was I certain of other accessible information. Then, in the administrative office where I worked at the time, I was presented with a new computer that had all sorts of extra cables and wires, including a big blue one that went into a mystery hole drilled in my office wall. I was told that we now had access to the Internet. Tentatively, I began to explore, but was quickly overwhelmed and resorted simply to making do with the Internet's pet—that man-eating tiger called e-mail. Only after my sons admonished me with "get with it, Mom!" did I return to the Internet and begin exploring it in earnest. Suddenly the light dawned. My brain, as I sat in front of my computer, had the potential to be part of a huge "world" brain—no bigger or smaller, having no more and no less information available to it than anyone else sitting in front of a computer with Internet access. I was no longer isolated or entombed by my own knowledge or what was physically at hand. While I was writing this chapter, another insight dawned on me. My new "world" brain, limited only by the length, depth, and breadth of the information on the 'Net, might easily become merely a receptacle if not challenged to use all of those thinking skills mentioned earlier. It is this insight that must guide the discussion of using the Internet in assessment. Braun (1997, 152) said it this way:

> While a Web page may have lots of great information readily available, students are not usually asked to do anything with the information. Thus, the teacher must figure out how to determine what, if anything, an individual student has learned from spending time at a site, or engaging in [on-line] discussions.

Assessment and the Internet

Although there has been discussion of the use of technology in assessment, often it has only had to do with students taking a variety of standardized tests using software, complete with computerized scoring. But as Grant Wiggins and Marc Tucker warned (in Bruder 1993), these programs make use of fixed response questions, which do nothing more than earlier pencil-and-paper standardized tests; their only advantage is the reduction of paperwork and time required to obtain results. "We don't need to create a more sophisticated way of measuring the current levels of failure," said Tucker.

Classroom level testing has moved slightly beyond fixed-response testing using technology, taking advantage of packaged software such as computer simulations and CD-ROMs. Such software, while primarily used for instruction or enrichment, does afford students the opportunity to use higher-order thinking skills in a variety of ways for demonstrations of achievement such as creating multimedia presentations, addressing realistic (but not real) problems and issues, and developing electronic portfolios.

Such uses of technology could be improved only by enabling students to access more current information, providing more data to choose from, and offering more choices for methods of presentations or demonstrations of knowledge and skills acquired. Those improvements are the gifts of the Internet.

To summarize, what, then, does the Internet have to offer in relation to new assessment types that incorporate real-life skills and higher levels of thinking? Certainly, if performance of authentic tasks, as called for in the NCSS (1994) and related standards is a goal, then the Internet offers an important resource. Given that the Internet will continue to serve as such a source for the foreseeable future, the skill in using the Internet is "real-world" in itself. And if a central goal of education today is to make students proficient in analyzing, evaluating, synthesizing, and applying information, then the vast options on the Internet open worlds that extend far beyond the covers of any textbook, newspaper, journal, or other media.

But do we know that students learn from using the Internet?

A Bit of Tentative Evidence

While the answer to the previous question must admittedly be "no," Denton and Manus (1995) reported a study in eight elementary and secondary schools in Texas in 1994-95, which enrolled 5,337 students in five school districts. Each of the schools was provided with Internet access, and each took the Texas Assessment of Academic Skills test (TAAS), which measures skills in reading, writing, and math. It should be noted that during the period of the study, teacher training on newly installed equipment to access the Internet and its use in instruction was ongoing, indicating that usage was in its earliest stages. Even so, although not every school yielded positive gains over the previous year, four of the sites did yield higher scores, which, while other factors must be taken into account, provides enough evidence to justify a measure of enthusiasm and certainly further study.

Forging Ahead

So, we know for certain that using the Internet is an important real-life skill to learn in and of itself. We also know that, from it, we can access more current information and, if we take precautions, more accurate information about the world–past and present–for use in authentic tasks. Let's make the leap and assume for now that use of the Internet will probably have a positive effect on developing higher-level thinking skills and higher test scores, so we're going to encourage its use as a tool in classroom assessment. How might it look?

The Internet as Assessment Tool

The following collection of ideas is loosely organized from least to most complex or challenging. The early ideas are easily carried out and could be used in the early grades all the way through high school. As the ideas progress, greater sophistication, both on the part of the student and the teacher, will be required. The reader will note that most of the sample assessment tasks look exactly like activities for instruction. Performance assessment tasks are nothing more than activities. They are distinguished by the fact that they follow necessary instruction, and, although there will be supervision, there is no teacher guidance. The teacher assesses students' ability to demonstrate that they have mastered what has been taught. One final idea that is included regards teacher use of the Internet to locate assessment tools.

Using the Internet to Answer Questions

Students are given a question related to a topic under study and use the Internet to find the answer and present it to the class. Preselected sites may be bookmarked for younger students.

Example: Is "The Ring of Fire" still a useful term? Middle school students plot the five most recent volcanic eruptions and the five most recent earthquakes registering at least a 6 on the Richter Scale on a blank map of the world. They then write a response to the question based on their findings.

A Place to Start: Try Carnegie Mellon's student-made Envirolink site at envirolink.org

Using the Internet to Gather Data or Explore Possibilities

Students are prompted to search for information regarding an assigned or selected topic related to material they recently learned. They may work in groups or individually, depending on teacher preference. At earlier grades, websites are preselected and bookmarked. At higher levels, students are given time limits and are allowed to surf under supervision. The purpose here is to find multiple sources to expand upon information at any given site. For this type of assessment, students should know how to use links.

Example: Upper elementary students are given a hypothetical sum of money to spend on a vacation for four. Prior to Internet use, they must create a list of all items that will cost money on the trip (e.g., transportation, lodging, food, amusement, souvenirs). The teacher can place whatever limits are pertinent to the situation (e.g., we are studying the Northwest, so it must be a place in that region; you must use at least three forms of transportation during your travels; the length of your stay will depend on where you plan to go and how you plan to get there; you are limited to a one-week vacation, so make the most of it). Then using the Internet, students must plan the trip, finding information about the best route, form of transportation, lodging, and so forth, for their individual preferences and needs and write up a complete plan and budget within the given sum.

A Place to Start: You might as well try a commercial site to give your students the added opportunity to discuss the role of advertising on the web. Start with travel.yahoo.com. There are plenty of others, and once students select destinations, questions and answers flow!

Using the Internet to Create Products

Students are each given or allowed to choose a topic based on a unit of study and are asked to explore the web to find data related to the topic. They download the data and use it to develop a product that describes the topic. Students might work in groups of two or three, with each student assigned a role or expected to find additional sites to visit.

Example: Using the Internet, primary students create a photograph exhibit of (one to ten) important monuments in Washington, D.C. In addition, older students should be expected to explain what each monument commemorates and why it was important enough to have a monument created in its honor. (Greater complexity could be added by calling for appropriate background music for each photo displayed, the name of the designer, and so forth.)

A Place to Start: Try one of Washington's tourist sites at www23.pair.com/phil/dcpages/sights.html or another Yahoo! site at dir.yahoo.com/Regional/U_S__States/Washington__D_C_/Entertainment_and_Arts/ Architecture/Buildings_and_Monuments

Using the Internet to Develop a Question or Hypothesis

Students quickly learn that finding an answer often leads to more questions. Likewise, our own experience will tell us that, often, examining one website makes us appreciate links to others. As important a skill as finding good answers is asking good questions and offering reasonable or informed hypotheses. Even young children can do this.

An Early Grades Example: A website is placed on display related to a current geography unit. Children explore what is available to them at the site and then write a question raised by what they read. The younger the children, the more straightforward such questions will be, but it is important for them to demonstrate that they can formulate a good question from a given set of data.

A Place to Start: National Geographic's Amazing Facts site at www.nationalgeographic.com/media/world/amfacts/index.html

A High School Example: Sociology students explore the Internet to find information on one of a set of topics related to material under study. They are to find a website that offers pertinent information and are given freedom to examine links for more information if available. Naturally, they should be prompted to consider sources and attempt to verify their findings. They are to develop a set of questions that are left unanswered, for which they would need to carry out a survey or interview (e.g., regarding attitudes or beliefs about their findings). They create a hypothesis regarding what they would find if they were to carry out the survey through a chat room as opposed to talking to every fifth person who passes them at the mall. Implicitly, they should hypothesize whether they would receive different responses in the two venues, and if so, why.

A Place to Start: For the People and the Press at www.people-press.org

Using the Internet to Examine Information from Varying Sources

By at least the middle grades, students will have most likely spent quite a bit of time surfing the 'Net for information. They should know that much information on the 'Net is actually misinformation. They should also know that perspective plays a very important role in how information is presented. They should be able to demonstrate that they recognize this by locating disparities and either identifying them as cases of misinformation or as deriving from differing perspectives.

Example: As middle or high school students carry out research on the Internet related to any given topic or issue, they may run into examples of misinformation or differing information. Offer simple rewards (e.g., extra credit, deletion of a low quiz grade) for each time they are able to "Nab the Net" or find such instances and correctly identify whether what they found is misinformation or simply another point of view.

A Place to Start: Compare any two sites that purport to cover a given topic (e.g., "Grover Cleveland" or "Islam" or "The European Union"). To compare versions of today's news, try U.S. News and World Report on-line at www.usnews.com/usnews/home.htm and USA Today on-line at www.usatoday.com.

Using the Internet to Connect and Survey or Interview

This is a natural follow-up to using the Internet to develop questions or hypotheses. The challenges here are to teach students how to use on-line services to access groups of people willing to be surveyed or interviewed; develop good survey or interview questions that will give them the information needed; carry out the survey or interviews appropriately; and then make sense of the results and draw reasonable conclusions.

Example: Using an appropriate current events issue that is ongoing, students develop a series of five questions that will elicit opinions about the issue. With assistance, students select and enter an appropriate chat room and ask for individuals willing to respond to a brief survey as part of a school project to send a message to a temporary e-mail address established for this purpose. Once the student has acquired a reasonable number of responses, out goes the survey or interview! The student's report of findings and analysis forms the product for evaluation.

A Place to Start: Netizen (free registration required) at www.netizen.com/netizen/threads or New York Times discussion forums at www.nytimes.com. A discussion site just for kids can be found at Childrens' Express News Service, www.ce.org.

Using the Internet to Find Assessment Items

A final idea about how the Internet can be used as a tool for carrying out assessment is not aimed at students but rather teachers. The Internet can also be a vehicle by which teachers can obtain assessment resources. Of course, traditional test publishers can be readily contacted through the Internet but there are other approaches to assessment that appear on websites. Specifically, approaches, such as rubrics and ideas that promote performance-based assessment of social studies learning, can be accessed. Over time, more and more examples of these alternative assessment strategies as well as student exhibitions of learning are sure to find their way onto the web.

A Place to Start: The State of Illinois has two websites with rubrics and scanned examples of student responses to alternative assessment prompts. One is based on an analytic rubric consisting of six performance levels across three dimensions http:coe.ilstu.edu/jabraun/socialstudies/assess/geo. The other site uses a more holistic rubric of four performance levels http:coe.ilstu.edu/jabraun/socialstudies/assess/socsci.

Naturally, this chapter has raised a number of issues. First, it occurred to the author more than once that, if only one computer is available for students to access the 'Net, many of the examples are too time-consuming to be reasonable. The number of schools having on-line labs is probably fairly low at the time of this writing, but these examples would be most at home there. Second, there always looms the issue of students having open and free access to surf in all the wrong places. Time limits and careful attention on the part of the teacher will take care of that. Third, the teacher must be cognizant that, just as standardized tests in social studies are criticized for testing students' reading ability as much as their knowledge of content, likewise, these assessments will test the student's ability to use the Internet as much as getting the required information and using it accurately. Thus, careful instruction on use of the Internet will be required along with instruction in social studies. Using the Internet during instruction is not enough. The teacher cannot assume that because students watched the teacher access information from the Internet, they paid attention to how it was done. If they were focusing on the electronics of the lesson, your content was probably ignored.

The Internet has great potential in assessment. The currency of information available from the 'Net, the need for students to become proficient in its use, the importance of students learning to be critical users, and the opportunities it affords students to use high levels of cognition all make it an important new tool. Once access issues are sufficiently addressed, there is no doubt that current methods of teaching and testing will undergo significant change.

References

Braun, Joseph A. "Past, Possibilities, and Potholes on the Information Superhighway." *Social Education* 61, no. 3 (1997): 149-53.
Bruder, I. "Alternative Assessment: Putting Technology to the Test." *Electronic Learning* (January 1993).
Hoge, John. "Try Microsociety for Hands-on Citizenship." *Social Education* 61, no. 1 (1997): 18-21.
Nickell, Pat. "Doing the Stuff of Social Studies": A Conversation with Grant Wiggins." *Social Education* 56, no. 2 (1992): 91-94.
Nickell, Pat. "Alternative Assessment: Implications for Social Studies." *ERIC Digest* EDO-SO-93-1 (1993).
Nickell, Pat. "Performance Assessment in Principal and Practice." In *Meeting the Standards: Social Studies Readings for K-6 Educators*, edited by Mary E. Haas and Margaret A. Laughlin, 378-81. Washington, D.C.: National Council for the Social Studies, 1997.
Shepard, L. A. "Why We Need Better Assessments." *Educational Leadership* 46, no. 7 (1989): 4-9.
Wiggins, G. "Teaching to the (Authentic) Test." *Educational Leadership* 46, no. 7 (1989): 41-47.

INDEX

A

B

C

F

G

H

I

J

K

L

M

N

O

P

Q

R

S

T

U

V